BESIDE STILL WATERS

BESIDE STILL WATERS:

Jews, Christians, and the
Way of the Buddha

edited by
Harold Kasimow,
John P. Keenan,
& Linda Klepinger Keenan

 Wisdom Publications • Boston

Wisdom Publications
199 Elm Street
Somerville MA 02144 USA
www.wisdompubs.org

Library of Congress Cataloging-in-Publication Data

Beside still waters : Jews, Christians, and the way of the Buddha /
edited by Harold Kasimow, John P. Keenan & Linda Klepinger Keenan.
    p. cm.
Includes bibliographical reference and index.
    ISBN 0-86171-336-2 (pbk. : alk. paper)
  1. Buddhism—Relations. 2. Judaism—Relations—Buddhism. 3.
Buddhism—Relations—Judaism. 4. Christianity and other
Religions—Buddhism. 5. Buddhism—Relations—Christianity. I. Kasimow,
Harold, 1937– II. Keenan, John P., 1940– III. Keenan, Linda Klepinger, 1942–
    BQ4605.B47 2003
    294.3'372—dc21
                                                        2003001395

07 06 05 04 03
5   4   3   2   1

"Dawn, Lake Louise, Alberta, Canada" from *Landscapes of the Spirit: Photographs by William Neill* (Bulfinch Press/Little, Brown, 1997) Photograph © 1997 William Neill / www.WilliamNeill.com. All rights reserved.

Photograph of Art Green by Ben Harmon.
Photograph of Sallie B. King by Marj Determan.

Wisdom Publications' books are printed on acid-free paper and meet the guidelines for permanence and durability of the Committee on Production Guidelines for Book Longevity of the Council on Library Resources.

Printed in Canada.

CONTENTS

FOREWORD

A NY RELIGIOUS TRADITION that over many centuries has attracted followers of widely differing natural tempera- ment and taken root in cultures with different social mores and even different cuisines and climes will have been required in its passage to grow and adjust like an individual human being who has lived long, traveled far, and developed—under different necessities and provocations—different aspects of his personality. When three such tra- ditions meet, they are like three old, sage, perhaps ever so slightly weary travelers settling in on the same cruise ship to exchange tales.

As the ship leaves port and their conversation begins, each is in turn spellbound by the others. What wonders each has seen! And with what quiet eloquence, or burning passion, or gentle wit, or enviable serenity each shares what each has to share! And yet as each listens, looking out to sea, each suppresses the sentence that will be spoken in due course, at the right moment of pause, perhaps as the sun sets. The sentence, of course, is "That reminds me."

Is it novelty with which each charms the others? Occasionally, yes. Even the oldest, wisest man or woman can still be surprised by a never-guessed human possibility. But it is not usually novelty. Far more often it is a distinctively different and precious experience—that of embers flickering up in a corner of the hearth whence, for many years, no heat has been known to emanate. Or, to stay with the travel metaphor, it is the dim memory of a place visited just once, long ago, and all too briefly. One could have lingered, but one did not. Something else, somebody else seemed so pressing just then. But now, as I sit here listening to you, it all comes back to me. Yes, you bring it all back, and, to tell the truth, I am glad for the reminder.

Though the religious traditions into which we are born are old when we arrive (three hundred years past the French Enlightenment, even Western atheism is an old tradition), we ourselves always begin young within our separate traditions. The language we use to describe the process by which we then grow into maturity (if we do) varies, but rarely is the claim heard that the run of good men and good women begin at their destination. It is all but universally conceded that for everyone there is always some distance to traverse and that the crossing is likely to be arduous.

And what of the resources for this journey? When the cruise is over for the three who meet on board, their separate journeys will continue. In all likelihood, no one of them will depart with much new baggage. Each will seem to travel on with more or less the original baggage. But inside that baggage, or inside that old treasure chest, if you will, there will have been a rearrangement. Old resources in there will be mysteriously available for new purposes, and new resources for old purposes. If I, as a Christian, may offer a special compliment to Buddhism in this foreword, it would be that, again and again, this is what Buddhism has done. The Buddhist presence in the religious world is far larger than a head-count of Buddhists can reveal.

We live in an era in which the experience of fidelity to native tradition often calls for a kind of conversion, an era in which what is conventionally called conversion often feels to the convert like the very opposite of apostasy. But these are the limit experiences. Short of each extreme, there is more commonly the complex, endlessly rewarding, and deeply fascinating process of selective approach and avoidance, anger and embrace, exploration, acceptance and repudiation within the confines—almost always less confining than they first seem—of a given tradition. This is the process that with intellectual acumen, humor, intelligence, and often with great beauty is on display in this book.

I was going to end this little foreword by writing, "In its quiet way, this book will remain a landmark," but that sentence in its ponderous conventionality seemed so unlike the sort of sentence one reads here. "Hey, Miles," I hear one of the contributors object, "have you ever met a noisy landmark?" Take that as a hint, dear reader. Open anywhere. You will not be disappointed.

Jack Miles
The Getty Center
Winter 2003

Acknowledgments

Our deepest gratitude goes to each of the contributors to this volume—for delving deep and for finding the words.

The three editors offer sincere thanks as well to:

Wisdom Publications' editor Josh Bartok, for seeing the importance of this project, for tracking us down, for being such a cheerful presence; Bill Burrows, for encouragement and guidance in the early stages of the work; Lolya Lipchitz, Harold's wife, for patience with the three of us, for reliable feedback, and most of all for companionship along the way.

Harold Kasimow's especial gratitude goes also to:
Sophie and Johanna Kasimow, Angela Winburn, and Helyn Wohlwend.

John and Linda Keenan are grateful to:
Our Hatanaka/Higashi family in Japan, Min and Nora Kiyota, Gwen and Forest Klepinger, Daniel Keenan, Melanie Keenan LeGeros, and Life LeGeros.

INTRODUCTION

Beside Still Waters is a deeply personal book. We have gathered here the voices of fourteen Jews and Christians who describe their profound encounters with Buddhist teachings and practice. Although these writers have been involved with Buddhism at a deep level over a significant period of time, they are firmly anchored in their own traditions of origin. Faithful Jews and Christians, many are authors of articles or books on Buddhism, teachers of Buddhist meditation practice, or participants in dialogue with Buddhism.

Knowing that people who engage publicly in such interreligious activities tend to be religious seekers on the personal level as well, we wanted to hear their stories. We asked them to write candidly about what led them to become open to Buddhism, about how this involvement with two religious traditions has played out in their lives. In the end, we were humbled by the generosity and honesty with which these fourteen people shared their experiences—and we were taken by surprise at the rich resonance between accounts by individuals who on the surface are quite different from one another.

In addition to these fourteen, we have invited prominent representatives of the Jewish, Christian, and Buddhist traditions, as well as a sociologist of religion, to read these accounts and to offer their distinct perspectives on the modern phenomenon of the meeting of Judaism and Christianity with the Way of the Buddha.

The three editors—Harold Kasimow, a committed Jew, and Linda Klepinger Keenan and John Keenan, committed Christians—also have histories with Buddhism. By coincidence, and although they did not know it at the time, in 1968 Harold and John were enrolled in the same class in Temple University's well-known Department of Religion—the first such department to offer courses in the various religious traditions taught in each instance by a follower of that tradition and presented in its own terms and from its own perspective. In taking that course, John and Harold were stretching themselves to learn about and better understand other religions, while both remained very much immersed in their own religious traditions. Harold was engrossed in dialogue and study with his mentor, the well-known Jewish thinker Abraham Joshua Heschel, on whose work he was writing a doctoral dissertation. John was a young Roman Catholic curate in the Archdiocese of Philadelphia, actively struggling with John Cardinal Krol—his mentor and nemesis— over the implementation of Vatican II reforms in the South Philadelphia parish of St. Thomas Aquinas.

After completing his studies at Temple University in 1972, Harold Kasimow went on to teach comparative religion at Grinnell College in Iowa. A Holocaust survivor, he has been active in interreligious dialogue with Christians, Muslims, and Buddhists. Meeting with Buddhists led him to the practice of Zen meditation in the U.S. and Japan. John Keenan left the Roman Catholic priesthood in 1969, and after graduate study in Buddhism at the University of Wisconsin–Madison and two years as a research fellow at the Nanzan Institute for Religion and Culture in Nagoya, Japan, he has taught Asian religions to undergraduates at Middlebury College, served as an Episcopal priest in several Vermont parishes, and applied Mahayana Buddhist philosophy to the writing of Christian theology.

Linda Keenan's first encounter with Buddhism came with a sudden plunge into the life of the Hatanaka family in Kagoshima, Japan, in the summer of 1963. Two years at Grinnell College had already undermined the surety of her Iowa Methodist upbringing. Two months as an exchange student in Japan raised even more questions: "My Buddhist host parents place offerings of food on their home altar and light incense and sound a gong as they bow before it. It looks strange to me, but how could they be any more loving or more wonderful human beings if they were Christian?" and "What is this overpowering sense of the holy that I know with my entire being as I look into the faces of row upon row of bodhisattva images in Kyoto's Sanjusangendo Temple?" Many years of Japanese language and culture study later, Linda has done research on legends about quasi-Buddhist mountain holy man En no Gyoja, been wife and editor to Buddhologist/Christian theologian John Keenan, and participated in a variety of projects, meetings, and practices that overlap the Buddhist-Christian boundary.

The three of us feel very fortunate that our karma (past history) has led us into contact with Buddhism, and with one another, and we are immensely grateful to the many mentors, friends, and teachers in the Buddhist worlds of the United States and Japan who have gifted us with their wisdom and friendship.

Our encounters with such Buddhists and with members of many other religious traditions have convinced us that openness to the teachings and practices of the various traditions enables one to cultivate respect and esteem for persons and groups one might otherwise dismiss as alien. We are convinced that open-hearted, respectful interfaith encounter can contribute to solving some of the major challenges that confront our world. And, as the writers in this volume demonstrate so well, we and our traditions have great riches to gain by opening ourselves to the "other." And one part of that gain is renewed appreciation for the riches of our own traditions of origin.

In the words of Orthodox Rabbi Irving Greenberg:

> The Dalai Lama taught us a lot about Buddhism, even more about *menschlichkeit* [humanness], and most of all about Judaism. As all true dialogue accomplishes, the encounter with the Dalai Lama opened to us the other faith's integrity. Equally valuable, the encounter reminded us of neglected aspects of ourselves, of elements in Judaism that are overlooked until they

are reflected back to us in the mirror of the Other. [1]

In a parallel vein, Oxford professor of divinity Maurice Wiles remarks upon the advantages to Christian theology of learning from other religious traditions:

> What happened in... the history of Christianity's earlier relation with another religious tradition, the philosophico-religious Platonism of the early centuries of the Christian era...was the emergence of Platonic forms of Christian theology, in which the insights of a religious Platonism played a coordinating role in ordering the insights of Christian history and Christian symbolism. We might look forward in a similar way to the emergence of Islamic or Buddhistic forms of Christian theology. These would take insights emerging from the dialogue with the other religions and use them in a similar way to provide a new ordering of Christian resources. They would stand as particular forms of Christian theology alongside others, but would also have implications for those other theologies, sometimes calling for the bringing to the fore of relatively submerged elements within them and at other times calling for the correction of old beliefs now seen to be no longer worthy of assent. [2]

Clearly, there is a wealth of new understanding to be gleaned from deep and serious encounter with other faiths.

We are saddened, then, when we hear some religious leaders not only dispense with the need for interfaith dialogue but actually admonish that any interaction with other religions is dangerous, even harmful to the practice of one's own faith. Without openness and interchange between the traditions, we are each and every one impoverished—our understanding limited by the filters of our particular monocultural faith and insulated from outside influences—while we cling to the nostalgic surety of the familiar.

The accounts in this volume move in an interfaith context to practice an ancient art—religious thinking and reflection on faith. They witness to the depth and beauty of the path of the Awakened Buddha and show how that path can awaken in us a love for and recommitment to the faith of our own ancestors in this present world.

Buddhism has not, as some fearful and worried souls have warned, led these individuals to some New Age jumble or shallow mix of half-baked ideas. Rather, it has deepened their commitment to old and loved traditions. It has enabled them to draw upon paths that are ancient and profound, paths that are able to transform deluded consciousness and lead it quietly and gracefully to abide by the still waters of insight and understanding.

Harold Kasimow, Grinnell, Iowa

John P. Keenan and Linda K. Keenan, Steep Falls, Maine

Spring 2003

PART ONE:

Jewish Voices

IT'S A NO-KARMA EVENT

SYLVIA BOORSTEIN

IT WAS A SUNDAY AFTERNOON IN 1993, at the last session of a five-day conference where seventy or so Western Buddhist teachers had discussed a wide range of topics related to teaching Buddhism and Buddhist meditation in America. The final question we were all asked to respond to—each of us, going around in turn in a circle, in not more than one minute per response—was "What do you, personally, want to say about your own experience as a practitioner? What has your practice done for you?"

I was seated halfway around the circle from where it began, so I had some time to wonder, and maybe even worry, about what I would say, but the man sitting just to my right set me up for a response like a volleyball shot. I couldn't *not* hit it. He said, "I feel so grateful for my meditation practice, and for the Dharma, the Buddha's teachings. I love my work as director of a Buddhist peace organization. I consider myself so lucky. I often think, 'I started out a nice Jewish boy from Brooklyn, and here I am now....'" Then I said, "I also am very grateful for my meditation practice. And for the Dharma. It changed my life. I also consider myself lucky. And I also started out a nice Jewish girl from Brooklyn, and I still am one."

I had imagined my "confession" would be noticed. No one had ever, in all of my practice years, suggested that I would *need* to repudiate Judaism in order to continue serious practice, or even to become a teacher, but I thought I might be challenged about whether I was a "real" enough Buddhist teacher. Perhaps my concern came from so often hearing my Buddhist friends contrasting what they remembered as the unsatisfactory religious education of their childhood to their adult Buddhist meditation practice, saying things like "Dharma makes *sense!*" Perhaps I thought I'd be called upon to prove that being a Jew made sense.

The next day I phoned my friend and teacher Rabbi Zalman Schachter-Shalomi and told him the story of my "coming out." I said, "The surprise was that no one said anything at all. It seemed singularly non-noteworthy." He replied, "That's because you are clear about who you are. That made it a no-karma event. It left no trace."

It's not true that over the years of my teaching there have *never* been any questions about the "two religions" issue. Mostly they are questions from new students. "How can you be both a Jew and a Buddhist?" "Do you pray?" "To whom do you pray?" "In what language?" "Do you believe in God?" "If you recite Buddhist Refuges doesn't that automatically make you a Buddhist?" "Do you bow to images of the Buddha?" Since I am more comfortable now than I was ten years ago about who I am and what I do, the questions seem reasonable—the reflections of normal curiosity and sometimes of concern (Is this syncretism?)—and I don't mind giving direct answers. I will do so, in this chapter, later on. But I'd like to tell my story first, because I think it's more important. It's the story that answers the questions that were asked on that long-ago Sunday afternoon: "What has been your experience with practice? What has it done for you?"

Here is my story: I was born in 1936. I grew up in Brooklyn, New York, in a traditionally observant Jewish three-generation household. My parents—college-educated, politically liberal, passionate Zionists—attended synagogue services only on special holidays but respected the *kashrut* (Jewish dietary laws) of my grandmother, who lived with us and who did the cooking. I was an only child and only grandchild. My parents enrolled me in an everyday-after-school *folkschule*, where I learned to read and write Yiddish (which we spoke interchangeably with English at home) and sang songs in Yiddish and in Hebrew—courageous songs of partisans in the Warsaw ghetto and patriotic songs of Zionist pioneers in Palestine. I also went to a Zionist summer camp. I loved the *folkschule*. I loved the summers at camp. I still remember the words of the songs we sang.

I also went regularly with my parents to the Chinese restaurant in our neighborhood where we all ate Lobster Cantonese. Lobster isn't kosher, but it didn't seem like a big deal. And my mother lit candles every Friday evening. The family Seder (Passover meal) was always at our house. We changed all the dishes for Passover, the whole family helping to wrap the regular dishes in newspaper and unwrap the Pesach plates (special dishes used only for that eight-day period). Then my father rolled the barrel of wrapped plates down the stairs and into the garage. I spent every Saturday morning with my grandmother at the East Third Street Shul (synagogue), and I loved that too. I had, throughout my childhood and adolescence, an intermittent (and secret) prayer life, but I didn't think of it as an expression of my Judaism. It was an expression of me. Being a Jew was something I just was, part of a clan. My parents liked the clan, and I did too.

I grew up. I went to college. I married a man from a nominally more observant, intellectually less liberal family, and we moved together to Kansas, where we joined a synagogue (because joining a new congregation was like getting a new dentist—something you just *did* when you moved to a new town), abandoned (with practically no discussion) our *kashrut* practice, and without a second thought took jobs that required that we work on Saturdays. And we both taught Sunday school in our new congregation every week.

Twenty years later, in 1977, I attended my first mindfulness retreat. By that time, I'd been living in California for fifteen years, and I had four children, a doctorate in psychology, and a full-time psychotherapy practice. I'd been very active in peace organizations during the 1960s, and had anyone asked then about my "spiritual path" I might have described it as social action...*if* I had understood the question. I was a member of the local Reform congregation, but my membership was, again, something I did because I lived in the community. I somehow always remembered when it was Friday, and I always lit Sabbath candles, but religion was not central to my life.

In the 1970s, my friends began to talk about "altered states of consciousness" and "the mind/body connection" and "spirituality." Herbert Benson had written *The Relaxation Response* about Transcendental Meditation (T.M.); the Beatles had become followers of the Maharishi Mahesh Yogi; and Richard Alpert left his teaching position at Harvard, took on the name Baba Ram Dass given to him by his guru in India, and wrote *Be Here Now*, which became a counterculture bestseller. Meditation was *in*.

Benson, in his book, had minimized the religious roots of T.M. and had emphasized the health benefits—such as lowered blood pressure and stress-reduction—of meditation. Ram Dass talked about freedom, liberation, Enlightenment. And there was the promise of special "powers" that came from meditating—E.S.P. (extra-sensory perception), telekinesis (being able to physically move items just by thinking about them), miracle cures. There were conferences—I attended several—at which presenters did amazing things like starting stopped watches, bending spoons by willing it to happen, and sticking pins, even *large* pins, into and sometimes *through* their arms to show that they felt no pain. The conferences were called "The Mind Can Do Anything" conferences. Those were heady times. We were excited about what seemed like an amazing breakthrough in consciousness.

I went on my first mindfulness retreat because my husband, returning from his own first retreat experience, told me, "This is great, Syl. You'll love it." I did not want special powers. My blood pressure was fine. I wasn't looking for a new religion. I *was* anxious, however, experiencing an intensification of my lifelong habit of fear—a condition I imagined was related to my increasing awareness, as my children began to grow into their adult lives, of how fast life moves along and how fragile and tenuous were all of my connections to everything I loved. I was also feeling depressed and more or less resigned to the fact that I would live out my life navigating between bouts of morbid anxiety and my dependence upon wonderful things happening between those bouts to sustain me. I didn't imagine I could be any different.

Little did I know. Two things happened at that first fourteen-day retreat that I think committed me to a life of mindfulness meditation practice. The first was listening to my teachers talk about Dharma, what the Buddha taught. It was a great relief to me to hear, presented as the *main* subject for consideration, the fact that life *is* difficult. By its very nature. That one of the chief difficulties *is* its fragility. That it *is* true— just as I had been thinking, and lamenting—that all of the connections on which my happiness is based are temporal, tenuous, subject to change. And it certainly felt true, as part of my experience, that struggling to have things be different from how they are was the cause of my suffering. I'd known that before, but the idea that I might change my habit of struggling—*that* was new. Here were teachers who said that practicing mindfulness—paying attention, continuously and calmly— could change habits of mind. They promised that mindfulness—*seeing things clearly*, in the moment, without struggle—would establish peace of mind, the end of suffering. Although at the time I didn't understand how the instructions for meditation related to seeing everything clearly, and I had a headache for most of the two weeks I was on that retreat, I felt hopeful.

The second important event of that retreat happened on the last night, after we had ended retreat silence, when I phoned my husband in California to confirm my travel plans for the next day. In the course of the conversation he needed to tell me that my father, then only sixty-five years old and in otherwise fine health, had been diagnosed with an incurable cancer. I loved my father a lot. He lived near us. I spent time with him almost every day. I felt *terribly* sad when I heard the news. But I did not feel *demolished*. I had not thought, prior to that moment, that the two weeks of meditating had "done anything" for me. Mostly I'd been sleepy, or confused, or my body had hurt. I'd hung in from 5:30 in the morning until 10:00 at night, steadfastly moving my body through the alternating rounds of sitting and walking meditation that made up a continuous schedule interrupted only by meals. I'd persevered, encouraged by the message of the teachings, and also because I am by nature diligent at whatever I set about doing. I realized, in the moment of that phone call, that not feeling demolished by alarming news was a new experience for me, and that the thought "I am so sad, but somehow we'll manage" was a new thought. I did not, in that moment, say, "I am beginning, right now, a life of practice." But I did.

————————

Two big changes have happened to me over the years of my mindfulness practice. The first is that my habit of worrying has been very much diminished. It's not altogether gone; I think it is too much a part of my biology to disappear completely. But it's *mostly* gone. *Enough* gone to be a great relief. And, when the habit starts, I recognize it as a habit. I'm less likely to take it seriously. And I'm reasonably compassionate with myself in my suffering. Paying attention, mindfulness, at least *attenuates* habits, and it certainly changes *responses* to habits.

Also, I'm happier. I'm happier in part, I suppose, because I'm less stressed. I'm also happier—and I'm *sure* this is from paying attention—because life itself looks more interesting to me. I notice, quite apart from the idiosyncratic ways in which my particular life unfolds, the ways in which life is continually unfolding, and I keep being amazed.

I think of my own calmer nervous system and happier mood as generic benefits of mindfulness. It happens to most dedicated practitioners. (For those people whose principal hindrance might not be worrying but instead perhaps anger or lust, for example, those habits lessen for them.) The second big change was the arising in me—quite spontaneously and without my wishing it—of an impulse to begin religious practice as a Jew. This happened incrementally, over time.

I noticed, to begin with, that I was saying blessings. It started with blessings of thanksgiving for the experience of a genuinely peaceful mind. Then I discovered that I was saying a blessing of thanksgiving for having awakened again each morning. And blessings of gratitude as I began to eat. They were blessings that I remembered from my childhood but had not said in many, many years. Then I noticed that I was remembering both my parents daily, by saying the Kaddish prayer for each. Had I been following traditional observance at the time, this is something I would have done in the year following each of their deaths. On retreat, I began to recite from memory liturgy that I recalled from my childhood, or perhaps from my inconsistent synagogue attendance as an adult. This reciting pleased me and also settled my mind. I realized that the very saying of prayers, in a dedicated way, was a concentration practice, and the fact that I liked what I was saying made it all the better.

Then, for some period of years, my meditation practice, especially on retreat, was characterized by unusual, and often strong, energy sensations in my body. I'd feel filled with light, as if light were radiating from me, and I would think: And God said, "Let there be light!" Or I would feel my ability to think dissolving, "washed away" in a torrent of energy, and afterward as I remembered the experience, I would think: That was the Flood. As different energy states came and went, and as I realized that my spontaneous way of labeling them was with captions for scripture stories, I began to imagine that I was having the same energetic experiences that serious meditators everywhere have, and that the people who wrote the scripture stories had been people like me, long ago, sitting alone, meditating, and creating a narrative that people could relate to, to communicate their experience. I thought, Taoists who had this experience I am having of being divided down the middle probably imagined the yin/yang interplay of dark and light, form and inverse form. If I were a Taoist, I would be thinking that these experiences I am having are yin/yang images. I am remembering the Adam and Eve story because I am a Jew.

I began, over the next several years, to read scripture, now as an adult. By and by, I synchronized myself with what I knew was the *parshah* (weekly Torah reading), and sometime later I joined a Conservative congregation, the nearest one to my home, where I now attend services regularly. I became, once again, *kashrut* observant. It just all happened. Really, it came from being *mindful*, from paying attention to what I needed to do next, to what felt meaningful.

So, the answers to the questions:

- It isn't, for me, about being a Jew *or* a Buddhist, or a Jew *and* a Buddhist. It's about being a person paying attention to what works for me to keep my mind and heart peaceful, my life meaningful.
- I do pray.
- I generally do not think about a "to whom" when I pray. Prayer, when it is happening, is what my heart feels like doing. And, when I *do* feel that my prayers are directed, it is the connection that feels good to me, and I don't think about "to whom."
- My communal, liturgical life is primarily in Hebrew. I understand what I am saying. I don't speak Hebrew well, though, so English is the language of my spontaneous prayer life. Saying *metta*, prayers for the well-being of all beings, is part of Buddhist practice. I have a practice of saying *metta* prayers. I say them in English.
- I trust that it is a lawful cosmos and that the inherent nature of the human heart is goodness. I think of the noblest capacities of human beings as God-given attributes.
- I think of the formal Refuges ("I take refuge in the Buddha; I take refuge in the Dharma; I take refuge in the Sangha"), which I teach as a Buddhist teacher, as being that tradition's way of reaffirming the ability of human beings to live compassionate, caring, peaceful, happy lives. I am happy to honor that tradition.
- I do not have a bowing practice.

Every year in February, I teach—along with several of my Buddhist teaching colleagues—a month-long mindfulness retreat at Spirit Rock

Meditation Center in Woodacre, California. Each of the teachers takes one day a week away from the center. I leave on Friday afternoon and come back on Sunday morning. Last February, one of the retreat managers tacked a neatly folded note for me on the message board: "Congregation Beth Ami called. They just wanted to be sure you remember you're reading Torah this Saturday. And, do you know which chapters?" I laughed when I read this and thought, "This is a completely no-karma event!"

From JUBU to OJ

NATHAN KATZ

WHEN I THINK BACK on my spiritual peregrinations
from shul to ashram and back, my thoughts turn to
my childhood in Camden, New Jersey, during the
1950s. Perhaps more than I'd care to admit, my spiritual taste and affini-
ties have their roots in the neighborhood and synagogues there.

My family was traditional. We usually attended the large Conservative
synagogue a block from home on Park Boulevard, which was then a relatively fashionable street. As a youngster, I was a regular most Shabbat
mornings at the synagogue's junior congregation, although some of the
time I remember sitting beside my parents in the main sanctuary. I was
enamored of the rabbi, a handsome and eloquent man, and for some years
I wanted to emulate him in the rabbinate. I enjoyed praying and led the
services in the junior congregation. And I was fascinated by the *Aron
Hakodesh*, the Holy Ark where Torah scrolls were kept. I fancied that I saw
light emerging from behind its wooden doors. There were even moments
in the beautiful main sanctuary when the choir and the open Ark seemed
to produce a blaze of light and an elevated feeling. These experiences
were so strong that as I matured I continually sought to recreate them.

My maternal grandparents, who lived behind a storefront on the
commercial street a few blocks away, were Orthodox. My grandfather
was especially influential for me. Sometimes I met him at the Orthodox
shul that was two blocks beyond the Conservative synagogue on Park
Boulevard. I have fond memories of playing under my grandfather's *tallith* (prayer shawl) and of a sense of mystery as I strained for a peek at

my grandmother behind the *mehitzah* (the barrier between men's and women's sections of an Orthodox synagogue). I also remember an occasional family *simha* (joyous celebration) at a small shul on Liberty Street, just a few doors from an uncle's junkyard. If memory serves me, that little shul looked rather like the *shteibl* (small storefront shul) where I *davven* (pray) and learn now.

In those days, there wasn't so much difference between Orthodox and Conservative Judaism. Everyone kept kosher after a fashion, and no one drove on Shabbat. The chief differences were that in Conservative synagogues, families sat together and the clean-shaven rabbi spoke in English. While I admired the Conservative rabbi's eloquence, I was struck by the passion of the Orthodox rabbi's talks in Yiddish, even though I understood only a little. Both synagogues felt cozy, or *hamische* (homey), as we'd say. I especially loved standing in front of the Conservative synagogue after Shabbat services, exchanging greetings both with our fellow congregants and those from the Orthodox shul who strolled by.

The neighborhood was also cozy. My uncle was the kosher butcher, and on the same commercial street was a kosher bakery run by my mother's uncle, another uncle's appliance repair business, and my father's neon sign shop. A couple of blocks beyond was another uncle's propane gas business. There was a neighborhood movie theater, toy store, men's shop, paint store, and so on. We knew all the merchants, who lived in the same neighborhood. So did the postman, my schoolteachers, the florist. It was a self-contained world. After school, I would visit my grandparents, or an aunt, or some of my school pals. My world felt safe with so many familiar adults and friends around. I now realize that the first half of my adult life was an attempt to recover both the spirituality of my childhood shuls and the closeness of my neighborhood. I managed to do so, but that is the end of my story and we're just getting started.

Then came the 1960s, with the breakdown of community and its restraints. My personal teenage rebelliousness coincided with a culture of rebelliousness, just at a moment when the restraints of a traditional community unraveled. As African Americans moved into the Parkside section of Camden, Jews began moving to the suburbs, the infamous "white flight." My family, comfortable in our changing neighborhood and with no special animus toward blacks, resisted the change.

Conservative synagogues anticipated the demographic shift, and in 1950 the movement issued a landmark *teshuvah* (*halakhic* ruling) permitting Conservative Jews to drive to and from synagogue on Shabbat and holy days. Better to remove the prohibition against driving and have people attend synagogue, it was reasoned, than to hold fast to *Halakhah* (Judaic law) and risk near-empty synagogues. Jews who spread out to the suburbs, miles from synagogues, received rabbinical approval. So, while the synagogues may have remained reasonably full, traditional Jewish neighborhoods broke down. Now there was no neighbor to scold a rowdy child or to keep a watchful eye on her. Now it was no longer possible to stroll to the commercial street; instead, one drove to the shopping center where the shopkeepers and shoppers were anonymous. This was the dawning of the age of alienation, a precursor to Aquarius.

My family stayed in Camden until I graduated from high school. When I went off to college, my parents sold the house and bought a condo—a one-bedroom one at that! I was on my own: new friends, new intellectual vistas, no neighbors' watchful eyes. While I embraced my freedom and all the trouble I could find, I was already becoming nostalgic for what was no more. Instead of a hearty "Gut Shabbos" to neighbors clad in fedoras and stoles, now ersatz-community was conjured by a peace sign flashed to fellow long-hairs in paisley shirts and love beads. I sought to recapture that light blazing from the *Aron Hakodesh* with mescaline and LSD.

My mother used to tell this story: When I was five years old, I solemnly announced to the family that I intended to go to India at my first opportunity. I don't recall what prompted this outbreak of *nevu'ah* (prophecy), whether it was something I had read or a travelogue I had seen, but I lived up to it. Between my junior and senior years at Temple University in 1969, I took off for India and Nepal. Perhaps some college courses kindled my interest in Eastern religions, perhaps I wanted to sample inexpensive hashish, or perhaps I was just being adventurous. Probably a bit of each motive was involved, and I spent my twenty-first birthday in Kathmandu. Predictably, I got sick and came home to Philadelphia after a few months—but not before some powerful and eerie experiences made me decide to explore Eastern traditions of meditation, Jungian psychology, and mystical philosophy. After nearly a decade of reading and reflecting, I wrote an academic article that was rooted in these experiences. It's one of the best essays I have ever written, and it has been translated and republished several times.

In those days, gurus and rock bands passed through Philadelphia on a regular basis. Not only did I hear the Grateful Dead, Jefferson Airplane, and Mothers of Invention, I also learned meditation from Kirpal Singh, Yogi Bhajan, Swami Bhaktivedanta, Pir Vilayat Khan, Rabbi Shlomo Carlebach, and Philip Kapleau Roshi. I especially relished learning Zen meditation from a Korean monk who was a visiting professor at Temple. At the same time, I embarked on a Jungian analysis. I learned to cast astrological charts and consult the *I Ching*, I read Gurdjieff, practiced yoga, and embraced Ram Dass. The *Tibetan Book of the Dead* awed me and I vowed to read it in the original someday, which I have done. Writing this in 2001, I look on my 1960s self like a cliché—but I was serious, at least about rediscovering the light that had shone from my childhood Ark.

After I graduated, I set off again for Asia. I booked passage on a Yugoslav freighter for Morocco, where I bought a 1958 VW microbus and made the great overland trek. I was extremely fortunate to land a job with the United States Information Service in Afghanistan, where I spent nearly two years. While working there, I audited Islamic law courses at Kabul University (my Dari was rather good at the time). I also sought out Sufis and learned *dhikr* (an energetic, mantra-like meditation). At the same time, I sporadically attended the synagogue on "Chicken Street," just across from the Saudi embassy.

While living in Kabul in 1972, one Monday morning I received a telephone call with the news that my father had died. I heard myself yelling into the telephone that I would somehow manage to get back by Friday, and that my family should schedule the funeral before Shabbat, as *Halakhah* requires. When I hung up the phone, my grief was mixed with surprise that at this crucial moment, my thoughts were about *Halakhah*. It was the last thing I would have expected.

As a "local-hire" foreigner in Afghanistan, I found myself on the edges of the diplomatic world, a world I didn't like at all. But my love of Asia deepened, so I saved money and spent the next year in India, as an itinerant, unofficial student of Tibetan and Sanskrit. I met many of Tibet's great lamas, including the Dalai Lama, and I began to read texts with some of them. In such traditions, to "read" a text is often to practice it as a *sadhana*. One of the most compelling practices of this type that I learned was "visualization" meditation, wherein an aspect of the enlightened mind is concretely symbolized and mentally drawn in vivid color and detail. Once the meditator is able to concentrate on this mental image, it is put into motion, emitting mantras and blessings. Dissolving the image into *shunyata*, emptiness, completes the visualization. This is said to be a very difficult technique to master, but I took to it and enjoyed the practice immensely.

While working on Sanskrit in Varanasi, India, in 1973, I heard a wonderful story about the late T.R.V. Murti, head of the philosophy department at Benares Hindu University and one of India's greatest twentieth-century philosophers. Professor Murti's seminars on the nondualistic, mystical tradition known as Advaita Vedanta were the stuff legends are made of. To study these gorgeous texts with such a master is to immerse oneself in the purest of mystical systems. Inspired, one of his graduate students, a Canadian Christian, declared his intention to convert to Hinduism. Surprisingly, Professor Murti became angry. "If you think you should convert," he told the amazed and crestfallen student, "then you insult both your religion and Hinduism. You obviously have learned nothing from me." So saying, he dismissed the miserable student and never spoke to him again.

Professor Murti's words haunted me. In traditional Tibet, to study a text is to adopt it, to be initiated, and I had done just that several times. While I thought I had been pursuing noble goals, I began to wonder whether my quest was in some deeper sense an insult. The thought disturbed me, and I could not dismiss it.

I returned to Temple University for graduate school, concentrating on Buddhism but taking seminars in Hinduism, Islam, Judaism, and other traditions as well. One semester I learned the Tanya, the foundational text of Habad Hasidism, from Professor Zalman Schachter, the charismatic Kabbalist. So there I was, reading Nagarjuna in Sanskrit in the morning and Schneur Zalman in Hebrew in the afternoon. Now, *this* was my idea of a good time!

After completing coursework, I won a Fulbright fellowship for dissertation research in Sri Lanka. I was busy studying Pali and reading texts, interspersed with an occasional Vipassana (insight meditation) retreat. When I was confronted with a particularly thorny problem of exegesis, I went to see the island's most erudite monk, the Venerable Nyanaponika Mahathera. He lived near the traditional capital of Kandy in a small, wooded hermitage replete with scores of monkeys. I was struck by how pale skinned the aged monk looked, and I was most surprised to learn he was a German Jew who had come to India in the 1930s to escape Hitler. While incarcerated at Dehra Dun as an "enemy alien" by the British, he and a group of Jewish spiritual-seeking internees had turned their prison into an ashram, studying and debating northern versus southern Buddhism, and Hinduism versus Buddhism. Each of the internees (who will remain anonymous) went on to eminent positions, either within the academic or the Buddhist life. Nyanaponika taught me about Buddhist philosophy, and I admired his spiritual stature. But I also felt pangs.

As my dissertation dealt with images from the Pali, Sanskrit, and Tibetan textual traditions, later that year I spent some months in Dharamsala, seat of the Tibetan government-in-exile and home to the finest Tibetan library in the world. As I was reading texts about the bodhisattva (compassionate enlightenment hero) with a lama, an adjunct to my reading was practicing bodhisattva meditations. I was especially taken with the practice known as "exchanging self for others," where one gives up one's happiness on the out-breath and assumes the sufferings of others on the in-breath. Reflecting on this practice as I strolled along Upper Dharamsala's market street, I passed the offices of the Tibetan Youth Congress. A fresh banner hung over the door: "Next Year in Lhasa." More pangs.

Returning to Philadelphia in 1978, I wrote my dissertation and was offered a position teaching Buddhist Studies at Naropa Institute (now Naropa University), a Buddhist college in Boulder, Colorado. At just that time, I was developing strong attachments in Philadelphia. For one thing, I had just met the woman who was to become my wife and life partner. For another, I was learning with Reb Zalman. So I asked Zalman what I should do, and he told me to go out to Boulder. "It will be good for your meditation," he said.

The founder and president of Naropa was the Venerable Chögyam Trungpa Rinpoche, a controversial lama who many believed was touched by both genius and madness. I jumped at the chance to join Trungpa's circle of students and translators. In a one-on-one interview, he admonished me to observe Shabbat. That should be a meditation practice for me, he counseled. It began to sink in, finally, that this world was not what I had anticipated. Here was my rebbe telling me to do more Buddhist meditation, and here was my lama telling me to keep Shabbat. Who could imagine?

Later that year, I received a job offer from a prestigious New England liberal arts college. It was an offer I couldn't refuse. This was my dream, teaching Buddhism and Hinduism in eighteenth-century buildings nestled in bucolic, maple-tree-covered hills. But early in my first semester, my dream was shaken. "Katz is a Jewish name," my new and intimidating chairman told me. "We'd like you to teach Modern Jewish Thought. Can you handle it?" The words "Of course, sir," were out of my mouth before I had even a moment's reflection. At that point in my life, that would have been my response to anything my chairman asked of me.

(Funny, but now that I am a chair I don't seem to inspire such fear in the assistant professors in my department.)

We agreed that I would teach Modern Jewish Thought during the fall semester of my second year. So while I taught Chandrakirti and Shanka-racharya by day, I read Heschel and Soloveitchik by night, readying myself for the next fall. The irony is that I loved what I was reading. For the first time, I read seriously about the Holocaust and Zionism. The stories of Isaac Bashevis Singer enthralled me. Elie Wiesel inspired me. I loved teaching that course as much as I have loved teaching anything, and I even became something of a role model for alienated, politically active Jewish students at that very WASPish school. The next year, the faculty Hillel advisor went on leave, and I was asked to fill in for him. So there I was, advisor to the Jewish Student Association and at the same time advisor to the Buddhist Meditation Society.

When we decided to marry, my wife-to-be and I concurred that Reb Zalman and only Reb Zalman should do the wedding. We made fitful attempts to make connections at a rundown, sparsely attended syna-gogue in the next town. But the most defining moment during those years came shortly after Israel's 1982 incursion into Lebanon. The cam-pus was in an uproar, and a town meeting was arranged. I was asked to represent an Israeli perspective, simply because there was no one else who would. At the time, I was critical of some of Israel's policies and had misgivings about the Lebanon adventure in particular, but nothing pre-pared me for the venom from my fellow panelists. Outrageous anti-Israel claims were made to cheers from the students. I can honestly say that never in my life have I felt so utterly alone as I did at that moment. I was distraught. When it was my turn to speak, I was compelled to charge my interlocutors with anti-Semitism. What else could account for the packed, hostile auditorium? Why were such vehement protests reserved for Israel? Where I had expected moderation and dialogue, I found nothing short of hatred. A few colleagues privately thanked me for "saying what needed to be said," but none did so in any public way. I knew then that I would not be staying at that college very long.

I had a sabbatical in 1983-84, which my wife and I spent in Sri Lanka
and India. Living near Kandy, I came to know Ayyah Khema, a leading
Buddhist nun, who happened to be of German Jewish background. As
we chatted, laywomen would interrupt to make offerings and seek
counsel. During a lull in the conversation, Ayyah Khema answered my
unasked question: "Of course I am still Jewish. What else could I be?"
And the rest of the afternoon was spent trading Pali-English puns and
exploring Buddhist-Jewish congruencies. As a dear friend, a philosophy professor at Peradeniya University, put it, "With Jewish intelligence and Buddhist patience, there is nothing which cannot be
accomplished."

Later that year, my wife and I visited Drepung Loseling Monastery, a
leading Tibetan college rebuilt in remote, impoverished Mundgod in
South India's Karnataka state. It was the season for the Great Prayer Festival, the Mon-lam Chen-mo, instituted in the fifteenth century by the
great spiritual leader Tsong Khapa. My research kept me in the
monastery's library, and naturally enough, I became friendly with the
librarian, an earnest and unassuming monk. One day we were discussing
how an exiled people could maintain its traditions in alien lands. What
he said amazed me: "We take our cue from the Jews. They lost their
homeland, but despite so much hardship and suffering they maintained
their culture. We must learn from them," he said, entirely unaware that
it was a Jew whom he was addressing.

Some years later, I read and translated a pamphlet by one of exiled
Tibet's most fiery leaders. The essay was published to commemorate a
nationalist day in Tibetan history, and it was entitled "An Outline of the
History of Israel." Page after page lauded Jewish determination, courage,
intelligence, and fidelity to tradition—the precise virtues most needed
by an exiled community—but the highest praises were reserved for the
most militant Zionists, the so-called "Stern Gang." I began to realize that
just as fast as many Jews were running toward Buddhism, many Tibetans
were trying to emulate the Jews. I wondered what the conversation might
be like if and when their paths crossed. I was to find out, years later.

Also during that sabbatical year, my wife and I visited Cochin. I had heard about the ancient South Indian Jewish community, so we planned a week's visit. We quickly became enamored of the people there, proud Indians and proud Jews. It was obvious that the community was on the verge of extinction due to emigration to Israel. To compound the loss, the community would expire without even a book to remember it by. Never in my life have I felt so compelled to undertake an academic project. My wife, a photographer and journalist, shared my enthusiasm. We promised ourselves that we would return as soon as possible for extended fieldwork. We were determined to write the book that otherwise would go unwritten.

Less than two years later we were back, supported by another Fulbright. I was now on leave from the University of South Florida in Tampa. Soon after our arrival, we learned that the community had held a meeting about us. They decided to facilitate our effort and invited us to move in with one of the families on Synagogue Lane in Jew Town. This was an anthropologist's dream, to have such unrestricted access, to be so accepted. While we knew we would be forced to give up most creature comforts, including much-coveted air-conditioning and privacy, it was an offer we couldn't refuse. And so for a year, we ate, prayed, and socialized with this otherwise closed community, becoming, in their words, "*pukkah* Cochinites," which might be freely translated as "members of the tribe."

My wife had her first meaningful "Jewish experience" that Yom Kippur. It is a tradition of the Cochin Jewish women to stand throughout the prayer services, which last all day. By evening, the combination of heat, fasting, and exhaustion from standing for hours converged with Atonement.

Between the holy days, we visited every synagogue in South Asia, meeting community members, praying daily. I came to love the Indian-Sephardic chants and prayers. For the first time in either of our lives, our personal rhythms became synchronized with the Jewish calendar. We were living the life of observant Jews as part of the participant-observation anthropological method.

I was caught unawares by what came next. I didn't anticipate what this year was doing to me internally. Without my conscious knowledge, Judaism had crept into my bones. We left Cochin and, en route to Israel to interview resettled Cochin Jews there, we spent a couple of weeks in Bombay, or Mumbai as it is now called. I was looking forward to the fine restaurants there; in particular, I had been lusting after shrimp, which I had not tasted for a year. We sat down and opened our menus. My eyes leaped to the seafood section. But I just couldn't do it! I couldn't bring myself to order such blatantly non-kosher food. I was thoroughly taken aback. I hadn't known what was happening to me.

Our stay in Israel made a deep impression on both of us. Although it was not our first time there together, our spiritual connections were now of an altogether different order. Before, we had felt like tourists most of the time. Now we felt the connection, the sense of belonging, that many Jewish pilgrims over centuries have described.

Returning to Tampa, one of the challenges facing us was how to maintain the spiritual level we had attained in India and Israel. The other challenge was, of course, writing our book, which took two years. We are proud of our collaborative effort and the requiem we left for the Cochin Jewish community.

We joined a Conservative synagogue and enjoyed it thoroughly. I reverted to my childhood role as prayer leader, at least for the preliminary service, occasionally entertaining the congregants with an Indian melody. Since I am not gifted with a good singing voice, I had to focus myself intently in order to stay in tune. So prior to Saturday morning services, I would retire to the chapel, wrap myself in my *tallith,* and meditate for fifteen or twenty minutes. I found that by practicing mindfulness, I could navigate the liturgy's intricate melodies satisfactorily. After a while, some of the congregants, especially the older ones, asked me what I was doing in the chapel. When I told them I was meditating as a warm-up to praying, they asked if I would teach them. So for the next year or so, I found myself teaching Vipassana for half an hour before leading the prayers.

At the same time, my wife, who had very little Judaic background, was learning Hebrew and catching up on decades of learning. It is remarkable how such motivation can hasten the process.

For a few years, we were pleased with this Jewish life we had created for ourselves. However, we began to feel pangs of dissatisfaction. We no longer felt our Conservative standards of Judaic observance of *kashrut,* ritual purity, Shabbat, and the holy days were high enough. Another nagging factor was our limited Jewish knowledge, which made us feel we were stagnating. When some friends decided to open a small Orthodox shul in our neighborhood, we chipped in, and we increasingly prayed there. Essentially, however, we felt as if we had gone as far as we could in Tampa.

In 1990, I was asked to join a delegation of scholars and rabbis to travel to Dharamsala at the invitation of the Dalai Lama. He wanted to learn the "Jewish secret," as he put it, of how to preserve religion and culture while in exile. The trip was one of the spiritual high points of my life. What are often disparate aspects of myself—my profession as a scholar of Buddhism and Hinduism, and my newly rediscovered commitment to Judaism—for a moment coalesced. I got to greet the Dalai Lama in Tibetan on behalf of the Jewish people. I was able to mediate conceptually the worlds of the rabbis and the lamas, helping the other delegates to formulate Judaic ideas in a Tibetan framework, and helping them to understand Tibetan ideas and spiritual practices.

The Tibetans were so very eager to hear what we had to tell them. We in turn listened to the Dalai Lama speak to a gathering of hundreds of Buddhist leaders from across Asia. He told them about us Jews, how we had successfully coped with so much suffering and hardship, how our "great courage and determination" reached its fulfillment with the reestablishment of Israel in 1948, how lucky they were to have us among them. And this thought struck me: When we see ourselves reflected in the other, we come to shape an image of who we are. In Christian and Muslim cultures, we have seen in those reflections condescension and hostility. We internalized those reflections in feelings of doubt and inferiority—and, paradoxically, in arrogance. Here, we were seeing in the Tibetans reflections of affection, respect, even a bit of awe. How differently one knows oneself through such reflections! It made me utter a prayer at the time that all Jews should be able to generate these feelings of respect, affection, and awe toward ourselves.

And that is my central point. Through various forms of meditation, I learned with some success to recapture the light I saw emitting from the Ark during my childhood. From my reflection in Asian eyes, I learned how to respect and treasure my own tradition. Many times, lamas and gurus explicitly pointed me in this direction. At other times, it was their articulate respect for my *yichus* (lineage) that made me look at it again. After all, if these teachers whom I respected so much saw deep value in Judaism, who was I to dismiss it?

At times, some of these Asian teachers offered a perspective on Judaism that was rooted in their own traditions and experiences and that forced me to see things differently. For example, while meeting with the Dalai Lama, Rabbi Yitz Greenberg told him about our Shabbat. Shabbat, he said, harkens back to the creation of the world at the same time as it envisions the future messianic redemption. He explained how on Shabbat Jews dress in fine clothes, set a beautiful table, and eat the best foods, as a way of anticipating redemption. Drawing on his own tradition of visualization meditation, the Dalai Lama asked, "You mean, Shabbat is your people's visualization exercise?" How perfect. How profound. That is exactly what we do, although we would never see it that way. On Shabbat, we live as though the world were already redeemed, and by so doing, we hasten the cosmic redemption itself. An insight worthy of a Heschel…had Heschel been a Buddhist!

In 1994, I was appointed to the faculty of Florida International University in Miami and assigned to start up a Department of Religious Studies. It would be an understatement to say that this was a once-in-a-lifetime professional opportunity. It is not nearly so common as that. We now have a nationally known department with a graduate program, and in 1999 when the Dalai Lama received an honorary doctorate from

FIU I was able to reciprocate the hospitality he had shown to me in India. A Canadian colleague and I have started up a new academic journal, the *Journal of Indo-Judaic Studies,* which is defining a new academic specialization.

Perhaps more important, my family and I have settled into an Orthodox life in Miami Beach. I am in shul at 6 AM almost every day for *daf yomi* (a way of learning Talmud), followed by morning prayers. I am occasionally invited to teach in synagogues of all varieties. My son attends a Jewish day school, and my wife works at the Miami Jewish Federation. Although my current neighborhood is much more upscale, in important ways it reminds me of the Camden of my youth. I know the shopkeepers and restaurateurs on the nearby commercial street. My son can freely visit many of our neighbors, who keep a watchful eye on him. Our Shabbat table routinely has a dozen guests.

Yet it's not as though I have left Buddhism and Hinduism behind. I remain involved in interfaith groups. We still find time for breaks at a nearby ashram, and to meet visiting lamas. We take regular trips to India. And gurus still help me with my spiritual life. Not long ago, I was in one of those lulls when my daily *davenning* (prayer) felt routine and uninspiring. A beloved Hindu teacher showed me how to recite my prayers in the rhythms not only of out-breath and in-breath, but also the "no-breath." I tried her suggestion and my morning prayers were enlivened and deepened.

I don't believe I would have found my way into an Orthodox Jewish life had it not been via a Buddhist/Hindu route. Buddhist and Hindu teachers urged me to look, and meditation gave me eyes to see the sanctity of Judaic traditions. Coupled with the inspiration of a year in Cochin, I was led where I never expected to go.

BECOMING WHO YOU ALWAYS WERE:
The Story of a Zen Rabbi

ALAN LEW

W HEN I THINK of my spiritual path, the entire narrative seems to flow out of a decision I made in the
waning days of the 1960s. I decided then, or so I like
to think, that I would place the spiritual endeavor at the center of my
life rather than the things one usually finds there, such as earning a living or putting food on the table. Yet the more closely I examine this
decision, the less I see of me in it—the less it seems to be me who was
making the decision—and the less it looks like a decision at all. In fact,
if I am honest, it seems clear that the only decision I myself made back
then was to surrender to the obvious and inevitable spiritual momentum
of my life.

Even the motivation for this so-called decision seems murky or
multi-determined at best. Certainly an early determinant must have
been the exposure to a very intense brand of Eastern European Jewish
spirituality I received from my two grandfathers in the Brooklyn, New
York, of my early childhood. My father's father was an Orthodox rabbi.
He had a storefront *yeshivah* (Jewish religious school) in Boro Park. He
and my father did not get along. There had been a divorce, and my father
had sided with his mother. Still, my grandfather arrived at our doorstep
when I was not yet two years old to fulfill the traditional duty of teaching me the *alef beis*—the letters of the Hebrew alphabet (a duty, he had
every reason to suspect, that my father would not fulfill). He was a small,
pale man in a dark suit, and he was carrying a black leather satchel.

My parents left us alone in the dining room, and when my grandfather left the room for a moment, I sneaked a peek into the satchel. It was full of Hebrew letters printed large on eight-by-eleven cardboard sheets, one letter to a card. It was like peering into a bag full of beautiful snakes. The Hebrew letters were alive. They were writhing and dancing in the satchel, and later, the *alef* my grandfather placed on the dining room table for my examination seemed to be animated, charged, pulsating with life. In fact, this quivering *alef* is the earliest visual image in my memory bank. I now often spend hours a day meditating on the letters of the Hebrew alphabet, often on cards very much like the ones my grandfather first showed me, so the inoculation seems to have taken.

The second image in my visual memory bank is the look of ecstasy on the face of my other grandfather, my mother's father, Zaydie Sam. Zaydie Sam was a mild-mannered floor scraper by day, but evenings and weekends he was the leader of one of the leading synagogue choirs in New York. He sang with all the great cantors—including Moshe Koussevitzky, Yosele Rosenblatt—and he often invited me to stand with him on the *bimah,* or platform, as he sang. Precisely, the second image in my visual memory bank is of holding Zaydie Sam's hand and looking up into his face as he sang, wondering where in the universe he might be. It was perfectly obvious that he wasn't here. When my grandfather sang, he was, in fact, entirely elsewhere. His eyes closed, rapture and abandon filled his face. It was as if he had gone off to a secret place and carefully sealed this world off behind him. Occasionally, Zaydie Sam took me to places where everyone had this look on their faces, like the tiny *shteeble* (small room used as a synagogue) in Coney Island where we went for the *Simchat Torah* holiday every year. There, dozens of older men danced ecstatically with Torahs in their arms and had that same look of rapturous abandon on their faces.

Perhaps an even stronger determinant in the decision I would eventually take was the sudden and utter disappearance of this world. When I was seven years old, my family moved from Brooklyn to a cooperative community in the rural outskirts of Pleasantville, New York, in upper

Westchester County. The streets of Brooklyn had been intensely Jewish, but even more significantly, intensely populated. One could go out on the streets of Brooklyn any time day or night and find dozens of people on the streets—kids to play with, adults to look after you. But when I was seven years old, this world disappeared, closed up after itself, and became a distant dream. In Pleasantville, when one went outside of the house, there was never anyone to talk to except God, and this was the beginning of my conscious spiritual life. From the age of seven onward, I would go out every day into the fields and forests of the immense watershed surrounding my house and feel the presence of God in the marrow of my bones. I would make a circle of stones out in the woods, plop myself down in the middle, and commune with God. Years later, when I read about similar practices in runic magic, I would wonder where I had gotten the idea to do this.

At college, I studied aesthetics—music, art, and especially literature. In a resolutely secular culture (and the world into which I came of age was certainly that) art becomes the repository of spirituality. Thus it was that I locked myself in my room for a week with the "Penelope" chapter of James Joyce's *Ulysses* and emerged with an altered consciousness, the Joycian stream of consciousness having carried me beyond the bounds of conceptual thought and into another kind of consciousness altogether. Years later, I would remember this experience in the midst of a Zen practice that would carry me beyond these same bounds in a much more systematic way. Similarly, while meditating on Beethoven's Ninth Symphony I had visions of swimming in a pool of stars, a vision Beethoven himself had had, I read much later, as he was composing that work.

And so when I was preparing to graduate from the Iowa Writers' Workshop in the late 1960s, it seemed to me that experiences such as these were easily the most compelling I had ever had, and it was a relatively simple step to decide to devote my life to them. Of course, the lack of any reasonable alternative was no small factor in this decision either. People usually came to the Iowa Writers' Workshop to get an M.F.A., a degree which would help them land a job teaching writing at a small college somewhere to support their writing habit. But in the late 1960s, the Ph.D. glut was in full bloom, and the small college jobs that used to go to Iowa M.F.A.'s were now being gobbled up by Ph.D.'s. So I made a virtue out of necessity. Partly out of conviction but largely out of a lack of alternative, I set out to find a spiritual path and to practice that path with all the intensity I could muster for the rest of my life.

Geographically speaking, I set out for California, which—for reasons no one has ever been able to explain—had suddenly become the world capital of the spiritual enterprise. I remember walking through a neighborhood in Berkeley in 1969, and in one house was one of the leading exponents of Tibetan Buddhism in the world, and in another was a world-class Zen teacher, and in another, one of the world's leading Sidha Yoga teachers, and in still another, a fellow who had made up his own religion a few months before. Needless to say, he had more followers than anyone else.

Northern California was a spiritual supermarket, and I was definitely shopping. At first, I settled upon the discipline of Hatha Yoga, which I practiced with some rigor for several years. This choice was largely determined by a remarkable discovery I had made upon my arrival in California, and that was that I was in possession of a body. This had never come up in New York. The fact is, I had been interested in Zen Buddhism for many years on the East Coast, but in that time and place Zen was something people talked about—a philosophy, a psychology, a body of ideas. In all the books of D.T. Suzuki—one of the first great interpreters of Zen for Westerners—and in all the speeches and writings of Alan Watts—another early advocate of Zen—Zen meditation, the basis for all this wonderful psychology and philosophy, was rarely if ever mentioned.

During my first week at the Iowa Writers' Workshop in the mid-1960s, I had had two significant encounters. The first was with Norman Fischer, who happened to sit down next to me the first day of class at Iowa and who has been my closest friend ever since. Norman would go on to become a Zen master and, ultimately, Abbot of the San Francisco Zen Center, one of the most significant Buddhist groups in the Western

U.S. But then he was just a fellow graduate student who had read all the same books about Zen I had read. In fact, this interest was one of the things that drew us to each other.

Later that week, we met a man named Julian Hartzell. Julian had come to Iowa not from the East but from the West Coast, from San Francisco, and he told us the astounding news that in San Francisco people didn't just talk about Zen, they practiced it. They did something called zazen, or Zen meditation, a rigorous physical discipline. We were so astonished to hear this that we made Julian take us right back to his apartment and teach us how to do it on the spot. But we couldn't do it. We were too stiff, too overmuscled, too unfamiliar with the workings of our bodies. Julian kept piling cushions higher and higher in an effort to help me sit in the cross-legged position. When we finally gave up, I was standing next to a pile ten cushions high. So upon my arrival in California, I seemed to understand, at least unconsciously, that I had to work on my relationship to my body and to the physical world in general, before any serious spiritual work would be possible. I practiced Hatha Yoga with a teacher who was a disciple of B.K.S. Iyengar. My body slowly became a softer, more inhabitable place, and eventually I became capable of sitting in the half-lotus without unbearable pain.

Just about then, Norman Fischer—who had come to California at the same time and for the same reasons I had—told me that a famous Japanese Zen master was scheduled to speak at the San Francisco Zen Center that week, and he suggested that we go hear him. I remember the lecture quite vividly. Assuming that his American audience would be entirely Christian, this Japanese Zen master had decided to base his talk on a line from the Gospels: "unless you be like little children, you will never inherit the Kingdom of heaven." I'm sure he had no idea that a great many of the Zen students in attendance that day were Jewish. I think it's entirely possible that he didn't have a very clear idea of what Judaism was in the first place. In any case, his English was not very good. He kept saying, "I mean little, little children. One week old, already too late." Although I remember this lecture quite well, it wasn't the lecture that impressed me the most that morning. Rather, it was the intensity of the practice that surrounded it—the way the Zen students filed into the room for the lecture, the way they took their seats, the quality of their attention, the density of consciousness that filled the room as they sat listening to the lecture. All of this led me to a *"Eureka!"* moment of sorts. This was it, I felt. This was the path, the practice I had come to California to find.

The next week I went to the Berkeley Zendo (meditation hall), to begin what would eventually become ten years of intense and rigorous involvement in the practice of Zen Buddhist meditation. For the next ten years, I would arrive at the zendo every morning at 5 a.m. for two hours of meditation, chanting, and prostrations. At the end of the day, I would return for another hour of meditation. Once a month I would attend an all-day meditation retreat, and four times a year I attended a *sesshin,* a week-long meditation retreat. Here for seven days we would wake up at 3:30 a.m. (when you're meditating all day, you don't need to sleep very much) and sit in meditation until late at night. Later, at the monastery at Tassajara, we would effectively sit in meditation for months at a time. We would do a few hours of menial labor in the morning and a few more in the afternoon, just to make sure that our bodies didn't wither away altogether, but other than that, we sat in meditation all day long, from 3:30 in the morning until ten at night. We ate in meditation. We studied in meditation. The gates to the monastery were locked shut for the winter, and we lived in a state of deep contemplation until spring.

But all this is only to speak of how much we meditated. More significant, of course, is what we were doing when we were meditating. I was a Zen Buddhist for ten years, but the emphasis was on the "Zen" rather than on the "Buddhist" end of the equation. To be sure, we were intimately familiar with such basic Buddhist doctrines as the Four Noble Truths, and we chanted the *Heart Sutra* twice every day until that incredible hymn to the inseparable and paradoxical dance that is always going on between form and emptiness had insinuated itself deep into our psyches. We also studied the works of the Japanese Zen master Dogen and the Chinese Chan (Zen) masters and the original Sanskrit Sutras (scriptures) of Indian Buddhism. But basically we did Zen practice, and Zen described itself as the path to the direct apprehension of the Dharma—the path beyond scripture. Thus, the overwhelming reality of our practice was not the study of theological dogma, but the actual experience of a meditation entirely removed from theological concepts.

I practiced Soto Zen, which—with Rinzai—is one of the two major divisions of Zen Buddhism. The basis of Soto practice is a form of meditation called *shikantaza,* or just sitting, one of the simplest, and therefore one of the most difficult, forms of spiritual activity ever devised. In *shikantaza,* one practices anchoring one's awareness in the two most fundamental elements of our present-tense reality—the body and the breath. Sitting still with balance and awareness for long periods of time is a fairly involved physical skill. It requires one to be conscious of the most minute aspects of our bodily reality—the angle at which we hold the pelvis and hips, the way we hold our spine and our back, the way we set our teeth in our mouth and our eyeballs in their sockets—and this acute consciousness leads to a sense of being deeply rooted in the world.

Focusing on the breath, one begins to feel in tune with the rhythm of the cosmos. Breathing in, we begin to locate ourselves more firmly at the center of our experience, as the in-breath draws the awareness from the many corners of mind—where our consciousness is usually scattered—to the diaphragm, the radiant center of breath. Centered, we begin to feel our world coming into focus. Breathing out, we begin to let go. We let go of tension, emotional and muscular. We let go of regret about things that have already happened and anxiety about things that haven't happened yet. In short, we let go of everything beyond this moment, this body, this breath, and as we do this, as we begin to inhabit the breath and the body more deeply, these things come alive. The more we focus on the breath, the more the breath becomes vibrant, radiant, and in time, this vibrant, radiant sense of things begins to spread from the particular experience of breath meditation to the general experience of life beyond meditation. Soon we find that we are inhabiting a radiant, sacred world, a world suffused with the presence of God. Whenever I read that wonderful ejaculation of Jacob in *Parshah Vayetze*—"Indeed, God was in this place and I didn't know it!"—I think of the feeling I had walking through the world during those early years of Zen practice.

But in time, the experience of meditation begins to yield an even deeper kind of enlightenment, and it is this second stage of practice that eventually led me to the discovery of Jewish spirituality and its own considerable depth. In his landmark work *The Relaxation Response*, Harvard physiologist Herbert Benson endeavors to locate the essential element of meditation practice, the gesture common to all spiritual practices, that moment that sets off the psycho-spiritual effects and the brain wave changes we have come to associate with meditation. All forms of meditation—all forms of spiritual activity—have an object of concentration, something we are trying to focus on. It might be the breath, it might be the body, it might be a mantra or a visualization, or it might be the words in a prayer book (a traditional prayer *minyan* in Cambridge scored surprisingly high on Benson's tests).

Originally, Benson thought, as I would have thought, as you probably would have thought as well, that the essential moment in meditation would be that time that we actually spend focused on the object of our concentration and holding it in our awareness. But in reality, the critical moment was not this one, but another one entirely. If we are trying to concentrate on something, and if we are a human being and still have a working pulse, thoughts will inevitably arise in our minds and carry our focus away. The mind continuously produces thoughts, and eventually one of these thoughts will carry us away. If we have been meditating for many years, this may happen somewhat less frequently, and if we are just beginning, it might happen all the time, but it will always happen. It is not a failure in meditation when this happens, rather it is an inevitable part of the process. In fact it is the essential element in the process, because what Benson found was that the moment common to all forms of meditation—the moment that produces all the psycho-physical changes we associate with meditation—is precisely the moment when we become aware that our consciousness has been carried away and we gently direct our consciousness to return to the object of our concentration.

Now if we are meditating many hours a day for many months at a time, we become intimately familiar with this moment of *teshuvah*—of return. We see it, we become conscious of it dozens of times every day, day after day after day. We continuously witness our mind being carried away, and we come to see precisely what it is that is carrying it away as well. And this is a very significant thing to see. That which carries our awareness away never arises at random and is never insignificant. If it were insignificant, it wouldn't be carrying our awareness away. It carries our awareness away precisely because it is something we need to look at, but will not. This is why it seizes our attention. It needs our attention, but we are withholding it, so it takes our attention by main force. Thus one of the things that happens when we meditate for a long time is that we become intimately familiar with our unconscious material—we are forced to look at that which we ordinarily refuse to look at.

So there I am, sitting in the monastery after ten years of practice, and I am beginning to see that a highly disproportionate amount of my own unconscious material is Jewish. I am suddenly aware, for example, of a kind of Jewish background noise, a Jewish static as it were, constantly whirring around in the background of my life. Every time I come into a room, I now see, a voice in the background is saying, "Well, I'm Jewish; is that guy Jewish? Does he know that I'm Jewish, and if so, what does he think about it?" Jewish static. Jewish background noise. But far more important than this, although far more difficult to speak about, is the fact that now, after ten years of peeling back the layers of my own spirituality and coming closer and closer to the core of it, I am experiencing that core to be irredeemably Jewish—to be directly plugged into that stream of spiritual consciousness from which the Jewish people has been addressing God for the past two or three thousand years.

I went to the Zen master to speak about all this. We were supposed to speak to the Zen master about problems in our practice. I thought it was a pretty safe bet that if you were sitting in the middle of a Zen monastery thinking about Judaism all the time, you had a problem in your practice. He was a very compassionate and helpful man. Keep sitting, he said, and you'll get past this. This sounded like good advice, so I sat for six months, and then I sat for a another year, but the Jewish background noise kept getting louder, and the sense of being Jewish to the core kept getting stronger, and finally, as they say in vaudeville, slowly I turned. I reached the point where I wasn't interested in getting past this business of Judaism anymore. Now, I wanted to turn towards it. One doesn't stop doing something one has done so intensely for ten years in a moment, but for ten years my practice of Zen meditation had been winding up, and now for the first time it began to wind down. Within three years it would be over altogether, and I would already have embarked on the practice of the Jewish spiritual path.

Judaism is a deep and complex path, and I was acutely aware of what a novice I was. For the next fifteen years, I would focus quite single-mindedly on practicing the Jewish spiritual path with the same intensity, authenticity, and discipline that had characterized the Zen practice I had experienced. I wasn't a spiritual consumer at this point. I wasn't dipping my toe into Judaism to see if it would work for me or not. I began my journey along the Jewish spiritual path with the absolute certainty that Judaism was a viable spiritual path, and every step along the way confirmed this sense. My wife and I took up the observance of Shabbat, *kashrut* (Jewish dietary laws), and daily Jewish prayer. I began studying Torah and Talmud, first reading all the English translations and commentaries I could get my hands on, and then going to Israel for immersion studies in the Hebrew and Aramaic languages.

I think the first thing I was aware of taking with me as I moved from Zen to Judaism was a sense of the value of disciplined spiritual practice. In America, spirituality has come to be a kind of leisure activity, something we do on weekends and at retreats, a supplement to life, like exercise or cultural enrichment. But what my ten years as a Zen student had taught me beyond the shadow of a doubt was that if a spiritual practice is to transform us—if it is to have real meaning in our lives—it must be practiced every day, and it must be practiced with discipline. I felt that it would take everything I had to practice Judaism in a serious and disciplined way, and I hadn't the slightest interest in making any kind of synthesis between my Zen past and my Jewish present, my Zen roots and Jewish wings (to put my own twist on that most annoying and insulting rubric of Jewish Buddhists), despite the fact that people were often urging me to do so. I was barely keeping my head above water playing two-dimensional chess. Three-dimensional chess seemed absolutely beyond me.

I think I would have been content to live out this single-minded focus on a disciplined Jewish spiritual practice for the rest of my life, if the following events had not transpired. My first congregation out of rabbinical school was a small congregation in Monroe, New York, a congregation I loved dearly the way one loves the work of one's own hands. This congregation had been a student congregation of some fifty families when I first came to work there. By the time I left, it was a full-time congregation with well over a hundred families. Never mind that we were the beneficiaries of some very powerful demographic currents or that the vast majority of new members had joined the synagogue the month after we paved the parking lot; I took great pride in the growth of this synagogue, and I loved it dearly.

Nevertheless, I woke up one morning after some four years there with the strangest sensation that the experience of being the rabbi of this congregation was over. This was a strange thing to feel indeed. I loved my work there, and things were going quite well, but suddenly I knew it was over. I knew that my useful work at this congregation had run its course. I sat with this feeling for over a year, but it only grew stronger, and presently I knew I had to leave. I went to speak to the president of the congregation, a friend of mine, and told him what was on my mind. He wept, I wept, we hugged each other, and then I left his house and went straight to a convention of Conservative rabbis at a nearby hotel in the Catskill Mountains.

As soon as I walked in the door, a colleague came running up to me. Had I heard that there was an opening for a rabbi at the major Conservative congregation in San Francisco? Hadn't I come from San Francisco? Perhaps I should apply. He hadn't even finished speaking before I knew for a certainty that this was what those strange feelings about my work in Monroe being over had all been about. And, sure enough, exactly one year later I was installed as the rabbi of Congregation Beth Sholom in San Francisco, feeling as I had never felt before that I had been hammered into place by *etzbah ha-shem*—by the finger of God—and having no idea why.

I found out why within a few months of my arrival in San Francisco, when I was "outed" by the local Jewish newspaper. There it was on the front page of the *Jewish Bulletin of Northern California* in second-coming type, big pictures above the front page center fold:

RABBI OF PROMINENT SF CONSERVATIVE SYNAGOGUE WAS BUDDHIST FOR TEN YEARS!!!

I held my breath for a few weeks (thirteen years have passed now, and I think my congregation is still holding its breath), but within a month or two it became quite clear that most of the people in San Francisco thought that this was a very good thing. After all, several of them confided to me, now *we* have someone who can talk to *them,* the *them* in question being the thousands of Northern Californians who had been born Jewish but whose principal religious affiliation was not Judaism, but rather Buddhism or some other form of meditation.

And sure enough, within a few weeks of this article being published, a steady stream of Jewish Buddhists began showing up at my office, most of them with a very similar question. "Rabbi," they would begin, "I've been a Buddhist for the past thirty years. I have no complaint with my Buddhist practice. It's transformed my life for the good. But I still feel haunted by my Jewishness. I expected that this feeling would have gone away long ago, but it won't go away. It's like a stain that won't come off.

And I know enough to realize that if something is so persistent in my life, I probably ought to do something about it....So, rabbi, you were a Buddhist for ten years, perhaps you can tell me what I should do about this." And of course I could not.

A second kind of person began to appear at my doorstep after the *Bulletin* article as well. "Rabbi," this person would begin, "I'm a loyal Jew. I love Judaism, and I love my synagogue, but rabbi, when I go to synagogue services, I can't help thinking that something is missing, something is not happening that ought to be happening there. After all, isn't this supposed to be about God? But where is God in all this? How come I don't feel God when I go to synagogue? Did your ten years as a Zen Buddhist tell you anything about this thing I feel ought to be happening but is not?"

Also coming to speak to me at this time was my old friend Norman Fischer. Norman and I had become one another's path-not-taken by this time. Norman had stayed with Zen practice and had risen through the ranks. He had gone to Japan and received transmission as a Zen master there, and now he was the abbot of the San Francisco Zen Center, the largest Zen group in the West. Also, Norman loved Judaism more than anyone else I have ever known, and of the two of us, he had been a far more likely candidate to become a rabbi. All during our Zen years together, Norman had been my only connection to Judaism. He had frequently dragged me to high holiday services and had instigated a Passover Seder every year as well. Norman had lost both his parents in the past ten years and had said Kaddish for each of them for a full year at the local Conservative synagogue in Marin County. Now his best friend had returned to San Francisco as a rabbi. Norman was encouraged to feel that perhaps this meant that he should begin to explore his own relationship to Judaism a bit more deeply.

One week Norman and I put up few small signs out on Geary Boulevard, the major local thoroughfare, announcing a Jewish-Buddhist dialogue that coming Sunday evening. We set up around fifty chairs in the synagogue social hall for the event, but that night we ran out of chairs at 400. I looked at Norman and Norman looked at me. "We've got a situation here," we said. So later that year, we began to hold a series of workshops—several one-day workshops out at Green Gulch Farm and a weeklong workshop at the monastery at Tassajara in the summer. We called these workshops "Translating Judaism, Translating Buddhism," but they were not exercises in comparative religion. We simply did the two practices that had meant so much to us side by side and then stood back to see what would happen. We did some light yoga and sat zazen for an hour, and then we *davend shacharit* (recited the traditional Jewish morning prayers). We meditated for another hour, and then we studied Torah. We meditated again, and then we studied a sutra. We meditated again, and by now it was time for the afternoon prayers, and so it went.

We found these two practices to be profoundly nourishing to each other. *Shikantaza,* luckily for us, was such a bare-boned mindfulness practice that it had no theological baggage—no visualizations, no mantras, nothing that created the slightest conflict with either Jewish law or Jewish sensibilities. On the other hand, it opened us profoundly to normative Jewish spiritual practice, to prayer, to the study of Torah, and the observance of Shabbat. And these Jewish practices provided a new context and a new language for the spiritual states we were experiencing in meditation as well. People from that first group that had come to see me after the newspaper exposé—the Jewish Buddhists—often had their first positive experience of Jewish spirituality at these retreats. And people from the second group, the loyal synagogue Jews, began to find an opening to that unnameable spiritual sense they felt was missing at synagogue.

Soon I began to integrate meditation into the weekly cycle of spiritual activities at my synagogue. Beth Sholom is a fairly traditional synagogue, at least in terms of its spiritual offerings. We have daily prayer *minyans* twice each day, and the full round of Shabbat and holiday services, all observed in their proper times and with all i's dotted and t's crossed. We began to offer meditation several times a week before daily *minyan,* both early in the morning and before evening *minyan* as well. We began to have meditation before Torah study and before Shabbat services as well. Four years ago, with the help of the Nathan Cummings Foundation and several other donors, we opened Makor Or, a meditation center adjacent to my synagogue. Now we have meditation before every daily prayer service, all Shabbat services, and several weekly Torah classes as well. We have all-day retreats once a month, and the students at Makor Or enter into a formal practice relationship with both me and Norman Fischer, who has become my partner in this venture.

Once, when I was still in rabbinical school at the Jewish Theological Seminary in New York, Norman came to visit me. In those days, the seminary had a pretty hardcore daily *minyan,* a gallery full of zealous rabbinical students and a great black line of ardent European Talmudists up in front. I had always known that Norman had a pretty rigorous Jewish life as a young man, that he had put on *tefillin* (phylacteries) every morning and studied Talmud with his rabbi in the small town in western Pennsylvania where he grew up. Until now, however, I had never actually seen him do any of these things, but suddenly there he was, strapping on *teffilin* as though he had never missed a day in his life and shuckling up and back with a *siddur* (prayer book) in his hands like an absolute crazy person. As we were leaving the synagogue, he was as radiant as I had ever seen him, even after months of meditation at the monastery. He said, "You know, Alan, now that I've done Zen meditation for twenty years, I could do this—I could practice ordinary Judaism—Torah, Shabbat, and Tefillah—and it would be enough. I wouldn't have to do anything else. But if I hadn't meditated for all those years, I wouldn't even know what this was—I wouldn't know how deep it was. I wouldn't know how utterly gratifying it is." These words have become my battle cry for the past ten years or so.

Several times a week, I am sitting in synagogue having a profound experience of Jewish prayer, and some seeker has come to synagogue hoping to have precisely the same experience as I am having, and he is sitting six inches away from me, and he is not having it, and he is furious about this. He is furious at me, he is furious at my synagogue, but most significantly, he is furious at Judaism. He feels betrayed. The religion that is supposed to be nurturing him spiritually is not doing so. Instead, it is shutting him out, or so he feels. Over the past seven or eight years, we have seen meditation help dozens and dozens of such people open to the bottomless richness of their own tradition and gain access to a path they felt was closed to them. Focusing on their breath and their bodies, their consciousness acquires a vibrancy, a radiance, a sense of the sacred. And when they move from meditation to normative Jewish practice and bring this kind of consciousness to an experience as rich and profound as Jewish prayer or Torah study or Shabbat, the Jewish spiritual path comes alive to them. And when they return dozens of times every day, day after day after day, to that moment when their unconscious is illuminated, the core of their being is disclosed, layer by layer, and very deep down in this process they come upon their Jewishness, like an old friend they don't even recognize at first because she is encountered so far out of context.

So it is in this ancient spiritual stream that seems to well up before us of its own accord when we give it half a chance to do so. And so it is in that more intimate stream, the current of our breathing, which replicates the rhythm of the cosmos in our bodies every moment of our lives and which carries us ever deeper into the truth of our lives and the truth beyond them as well.

ENRICHING AWARENESS:

A Jewish Encounter with Buddhism

SANDRA B. LUBARSKY

I GREW UP in a Jewish family that had an intense awareness of the recent tragedy of European Jewry. My mother and father were determined that their children would have a deep Jewish identity, despite the fact that the Jewish population in the suburbs of Southern California was sparse and in the early 1950s synagogues were tributes to the energy of ten families or less. Until our teenage years, we were raised in the Conservative tradition, attending religious school and Hebrew school, separating milk meals from meat meals, and celebrating major Jewish holidays. Our family social life revolved around the local synagogue, where my father served as religious school principal, beloved teacher of the confirmation classes, and congregational president for a number of years. As children, bar and bat mitzvah parties were our singular introduction to late evening social life. We were usually the only Jewish children in our public school classes and the only ones among our classmates who were aware that the world deserved our suspicion, that life—at least for Jews—was more complicated than *Lassie* and *Leave it to Beaver* let on.

It wasn't until I fell in love with a non-Jew that the question "Why be Jewish?" occurred to me. I had never questioned the value and worth of Judaism or my own identity as a Jew. When it seemed like everyone else was following the Beatles on their magical mystery tour toward the East, the bumper sticker on my car read, "Save Soviet Jewry." Rather than introspection, it was ethical engagement that described the Judaism in

which I was involved. This was a form of Judaism shaped by four defining events: the Holocaust, the 1967 Arab-Israeli War, the American civil
rights movement, and the peace movement. There was plenty going on
in Jewish life to absorb my energies. This ethical, activist Judaism was my
form of spirituality, though I didn't use such language then.

Intermarriage is no longer novel or rare, but in 1978 when I married
Marcus, a non-Jew, it was very much a violation of the ethos of the Jewish community, which was still reeling from the Holocaust. At a time
when it was still a transgression of sexual mores for unmarried couples
to live together, friends of my family urged us to do so—hoping that the
relationship would fall apart—rather than transgress the boundaries of
endogamy. We could not find a rabbi who would preside over an intermarriage, and most of my immediate family did not attend our wedding. At one point in the family turmoil, I asked my mother why she felt
it was important to be Jewish. Her response, which I now cherish, was,
"If you don't know, I can't tell you." Partly, I think, this was an answer
piqued by frustration and bewilderment. I now also think it was an
answer that belied the depth of my mother's embodied understanding of
Judaism. But at the time, I was hoping for a logical, persuasive response
that would clarify religious attachment.

I don't know how often marriage influences people's intellectual path
as well as their emotional path, but this was so in my case. I set out to
answer the question I had put to my mother. Included in that inquiry was
also a desire to untangle the problem of evil, which had concerned me
long before my marriage and which I came to understand as part and
parcel of the whole question of religious adequacy for many people,
Jews and non-Jews alike.

———————

I didn't study Eastern traditions in graduate school, though the opportunity was there. I wanted to learn about belief systems, especially the
philosophy and theology that informed them, and I particularly wanted
to learn about modern Jewish thought. I took courses at Hebrew Union

College in Los Angeles, which complemented my doctoral studies in philosophy of religion at Claremont Graduate School. I think we are lucky if our life interests intersect with our formal studies so that personal passion stirs our inquiry. Because of my relationship with my husband, and my new status in the Jewish community, I decided to write my dissertation on the concept of chosenness in Jewish thought.

I had been taught that Jews have a special role to play in the cosmos, and as a child this teaching had provided me with an unspoken confidence in my status as a member of a religious minority. (It was also of a piece with my mother's explanation for why she had given birth to a severely handicapped child. As a very young girl, I was completely satisfied, even smitten, with her explanation that God chose us because God knew that we would care for this child.) For years, I understood chosenness as tied up with the Holocaust and the founding of the State of Israel, and as having a heroic gloss. It wasn't until I began to read Jewish and Christian theology that I recognized the difficulties with the concept.

In studying the concept of chosenness, I was led to the wider conversation of religious pluralism. I came to the position that the idea of chosenness as either a divine designation or a sociological strategy is without merit, in Judaism or any other tradition. This is not to say that a personal God, acting in the world, does not make decisions about individual lives or even the collective lives of a people. God's declaration, "You shall be my people and I shall be your God" can be celebrated for its intimacy without asserting an exclusive relationship. We have been in error when we have sought a symmetry between monotheism and chosenness—the existence of one unique God in relationship with one unique people. Monotheism entails the opposite of exclusivity, asserting the supreme relativity of the divine nature. Chosenness does damage to divine relativity and divine justice. It also leaves us vulnerable to damaging human conceits, particularly a blindness to our own limitations.

It is possible to hold on to the concept of chosenness and enter the arena of religious pluralism, seeing each tradition as embodying a special relationship with God and thus chosen for a particular task. A stronger case can be made for what I came to term "veridical pluralism," the position that there is a multiplicity of traditions that "speak truth," that are legitimate forms of truth-bearing ways. While the traditional Jewish attitude toward people of other faiths was remarkably tolerant for its time, it nevertheless did not affirm the validity of other religions as either truth-bearing or salvation-granting. Instead, based on the Noachide Laws it maintained that a place in "the world to come," i.e., eternal life, was available to any person *regardless* of their religion, if they abided by seven basic principles of morality (to refrain from idolatry, murder, blasphemy, incest, theft, the eating of a limb from a living animal, and the one positive commandment, to establish courts of law). This is a form of salvific inclusivism—acknowledging that salvation is available to all, while at the same time disparaging the power of other traditions as themselves paths to salvation. An individual can gain salvation but only apart from, and not as a consequence of, their own tradition.

Veridical pluralism begins with the premise that religious traditions reflect the metaphysical, historical, physical, and psychological limitations that characterize all nondivine life. I am quite amazed that our conditionedness is a relatively recent concession in the conversation between religions. The realization that there are limits to our understanding leads to the recognition that no tradition can be absolute and then to the insight that dialogue between traditions might lead to a fuller and more accurate understanding of reality. When we admit that God, truth, beauty, or love might exceed our personal experiences of them, other traditions become theologically relevant.

In seeking to construct a nonexclusivist attitude toward other religions, I relied heavily on the theological insights of process theologians and on the model of transformative dialogue developed by my teacher, John B. Cobb, Jr. In his ground-breaking book, *Beyond Dialogue,* he asked, "How can one better serve the universal revealing and saving presence of God than by submitting all that one believes to radical questioning and opening oneself critically to alien ideas?" And he also asserted, "It is the most radical differences that stimulate the most fundamental reconsideration."

I have learned many important things from John Cobb, not just about interfaith dialogue. One of the most important things I have learned is not to be afraid when it comes to seeking understanding. "Opening oneself critically to alien ideas" is a powerful, liberatory action for those of us who remain committed to religious traditions in the modern era. By applying the method of modernity to tradition, we subvert the usual disintegrating effect of modernity on tradition, allowing criticism and radical difference to temper our traditions. Embracing conditionedness and the concomitant knowledge that all traditions have been and are mutable, while opening up to the possible truths in other ways, seems the best way to be loyal to truth-seeking, meaning-making traditions.

The picture of the world given in process philosophy offers additional reasons for exposing one's own worldview to another's worldview. Above all, I have found the idea absolutely convincing that relationality is at the heart of all life. For process thinkers, the world arises out of relationships, and all beings are constituted by their relationships with other beings. Connectedness is not accidental but is fundamental to the structure of existence. Process thinkers also maintain a nonsubstantialist view of reality, including the human self; at every instance, we become a newly constituted self in relationship with other lives. Whitehead used the language of "perpetual perishing" to describe this ongoing process of change and new life.

Moreover, the universe as conceived by process thinkers is infused with creativity. At every moment, new events arise, wedded to the past but responding to it in new ways. The response is shaped in reply to the past and to divine encouragement, determined by neither but in relation to both. This ongoing creative activity is found at both micro and macro levels of life. At the macro level of human life and culture, religious traditions are part of this dynamic movement. There is, then, no unchanging essence of a tradition. There are, as Cobb has pointed out, shared histories, stories, and memories, "but which features...are emphasized, how they are interpreted, what implications are drawn from them—all changes." This is, on the one hand, a tremendously destabilizing tenet. On the other hand, it is remarkably honest regarding the history of traditions and the creative process that is at work in living religious systems.

Transformative dialogue is the kind of dialogue that grows out of this worldview. It takes seriously the idea that we are *internally* related, that we become who we are in relationship with others. It is thus a more rigorous undertaking than is dialogue that is merely for the sake of tolerance or appreciation. It is dialogue undertaken with the assumption that there may be something of merit to learn from other traditions that is not now present in one's own tradition. If something of value is found outside of one's tradition, it is incumbent upon us to consider the meaning of this finding *for ourselves* and our traditions. The distance between traditions is narrowed, and language of "crossing over" is used to describe the intimacy of the encounter. Because of the mutability of traditions, the encounter with other ways does not necessarily lead to either conversion or rejection but may result rather in a reshaping of our own tradition. In returning to our home tradition after venturing out, we may bring new ideas and practices to it. Not every encounter will lead to transformation, but when we are exposed to a significant truth or to great beauty, it seems to me that we desire to participate in it.

———

Along with a significant number of American Jews, I recognize Buddhism and other Eastern traditions as embodying striking truths and great beauty. By the time I encountered Buddhism, the ground was well-prepared for a thoughtful engagement. But even then my approach was superficial, and my understanding remains inadequate. Deep understanding of great ways requires, at least for me, conversations and encounters over a long period of time. I haven't yet had this kind of history with Buddhism.

I turned to Buddhism when, in the course of finishing a project on Jewish responses to religious pluralism, I was asked to illustrate how transformative dialogue might look. Because of the very difficult history between Judaism and Christianity, I undertook a thought experiment, imagining an encounter between liberal Judaism and Buddhism. Here were two traditions with very little common history. What might they have to say to each other? Because I did not have a living teacher to instruct me on Buddhism, the dialogue was asymmetrical. I spoke for Judaism *and* I determined the framing of Buddhism. Clearly, there is a richer way to proceed! Nonetheless, the lessons for me were significant and continue to be important in my efforts to reformulate aspects of liberal Jewish thought.

Buddhism's teachings on suffering have been especially attractive to Jews of my generation. Between modern science and the Holocaust, liberal Judaism has been in theological disarray for much of the last half of the twentieth century. At a time when the ability to talk about God and divine healing in the world was most needed, liberal Judaism offered little spiritual solace. Theological language emphasized a transcendent God, community action emphasized temple-building programs, and religious school classes spoke about values clarification. The Jewish community as a whole was like so many individual Holocaust survivors who, fifty years after their ordeal, have only begun to speak about their suffering. Throughout my childhood and adolescence, the Holocaust was the dark edge around conversations, marking the boundaries between good and evil, us and them. Nonetheless, the questions "How can we end suffering?" and "How can we speak of redemption?" went largely unaddressed. Buddhism's straightforward declaration that "life is suffering" spoke what was already known to post-Holocaust Jews, but its path for ending suffering presented a new way of understanding reality and held out hope for healing the self and the world. It offered many Jews a spiritual way that was consonant with their rejection of God and yet nourished their need for moral guidance, interconnectedness, and self-transcendence.

By the time I began to study Buddhism, I had been persuaded by process philosophy of the nonsubstantialist nature of reality and the internal relations that bind each to all. Buddhism added an emphasis on compassionate living that gave ethical grounding to this worldview. It offered a method for disciplining action that I had not found in liberal Judaism. And in fostering right concentration and mindfulness, it clarified my understanding of the Jewish idea of holiness-in-dailyness. Above all, I began to see that the question "How can we end suffering?" was a legitimate one for religions to ask and to seek to answer. I began to search for the answers that might lie within Judaism, though I had not learned them.

Although I found much within Buddhism that was compelling and instructive, I did not consider exchanging Judaism for Buddhism. Like my mother, I find that part of the reason cannot be easily or adequately articulated, lying in memory and deeply marking my personality. Mostly, I have been blessed with a lived experience of Judaism that is exceedingly satisfying both for what it has been and for what I believe it can become. I know that the well of Judaism extends deeper than I have reached, remaining a source of renewal and creativity. But I know this even better because of my encounter with Buddhism, which has led me to ask new questions of Judaism—questions that seek complementarity with some Buddhist insights, ways to reimagine some aspects of Judaism, and clarifying alternatives to Buddhism.

Partly because of my marriage to a non-Jew and partly because I have lived most of my adult life in small communities that lack a well-established Jewish presence, I have had much latitude to develop a personal form of Judaism that is responsive to my intellectual and emotional needs. In Flagstaff, Arizona, our little Jewish community of forty families consists mainly of intermarried couples who are struggling to shape a form of Judaism that grants legitimate status to non-Jewish partners who, though they have chosen to affiliate with a Jewish congregation, have not chosen to convert. Many of our members, both Jewish and non-Jewish, are drawn to Eastern and New Age forms of spirituality.

Many find spiritual fullness in a relationship with the natural world. Because of my exposure to Buddhism, I am more sensitive to this prodigious variety of needs and desires and more open to finding creative ways to respond. Judaism, like all religious traditions, is "in the making," renewing itself in conversation with other ways of negotiating life. This in-the-making is not an interim phase, but the reality of our situation for all times. A non-essentialist understanding of Jewish identity and its long history of transformative change, coupled with the belief that Buddhism is a religion of great wisdom, has led me to an openness to the possibilities that characterize this period in American liberal Judaism.

One of the consequences of dialogue is that the change that happens in one relationship is carried forward into our encounters with other traditions. My encounter with Buddhism has helped me to develop a more discerning understanding of the history of Christianity and a more sympathetic relationship with those who continue to identify as Christians. Having crossed East, I have found a way into Jewish-Christian dialogue that is more compassionate than it would otherwise have been. In Buddhist-Jewish dialogue, I learned to listen closely to thinkers and practitioners whose spiritual lives differ from mine but whose tradition carried no legacy of anti-Semitism. I became more aware of the complexities and subtleties of traditions and of the very personal nature of interpretation.

Perhaps most importantly, I learned that the generosity of understanding that I want for Judaism must be granted to other traditions. In coming to Christianity through Buddhism, I am better able to regard Christianity as a tradition with insights that may be of value to Jews. Christianity's emphasis on incarnation, for example, is a powerful testament to divine immanence and may be of use to Jews who are engaged in creating an intentionally ecological Jewish theology. Indeed, it seems to me that the encounter with Eastern traditions may have quite momentous consequences for the relationship between Western traditions, ones that we are only beginning to glimpse.

What kinds of Judaism will grow from this listening to other traditions cannot be predicted. My hope is that Judaism will continue to be a tradition that teaches its followers how to be alive to the great beauty and goodness in the world and deeply connected to it. I am convinced that Jewish renewal is tied to the creative transformation that follows from encounter with other traditions. Of particular importance is our participation in conversations with those whose insights have not been formative for Judaism but could enrich it.

THE GARDEN IN THE MIDDLE

RICHARD G. MARKS

Thailand, 1980. Near the Samsen Railroad Station in Bangkok, Ratri and Nung lived in a house with a small garden. The neighborhood's narrow lanes, mango trees, and flowering bushes hushed the harsh roar of ten-wheeler trucks and motorcycle taxis in the busy avenues all around. Ratri was an instructor at Mahidol University, where I was teaching; I had arrived only a few months earlier and had come close several times to giving up and going home. She stepped in to teach me useful Thai behavior—which peppers to avoid, when to pay for meals when dining with Thai colleagues, and how to express an opinion without directly stating it. But mostly she just gathered her "gang," as she called it in English—her husband Nung, her older brother, friends, and mother-in-law—to travel with me on weekends to weddings or ordinations of her friends, to homes of her relatives, or to beautiful old temples. The shorter trips might end in her garden, among the potted plants and the birds in large wooden cages, under the trees, away from the traffic.

Her advice for my problems was always the same, and characteristically Thai in content: *Yah khit mak*—"Don't think too much!"—which seemed impossible to heed. But there in her garden one afternoon, beside the birdcages, under the mango trees, having gone nowhere in particular and being in no hurry to move on, worries retreated like the traffic noise to the dim edges of my mind, leaving me to think about…nothing in particular. I had no more lessons to prepare, no Thai colleagues to please, no foreign culture to penetrate, no career to pursue in America, no broken ego to protect. Time had stopped, and I had stopped, and there was only the twittering bird garden, the clouds passing overhead, the gentle smiles of friends.

It could have happened anywhere. There is nothing essentially Buddhist about it. I was suddenly at peace in a noisy world, like the eternal Now that mystics speak of. It was around that time I stopped fighting against Thailand and began to enjoy living there. Thai classical music, which had at first affected me with almost a nausea as it slid around and between the tonal scales of the Bach and Brahms I loved, began at last to take on a heart-aching beauty of its own. The frustrating opaqueness of Thai behavior became a gentle, dignified flow of intricate expression. I began to realize and admire the age and sophistication of Thai culture.

But I do think there was a Buddhist dimension to that afternoon in Ratri's bird garden. A phrase similar to her advice, *tam jai hai wang*—"make your mind empty"—is heard frequently among Thai people, and also from monks in their sermons. *Yah khit mak,* when it comes out of acceptance and not just escape, reflects Buddhist wisdom, related to the goal of gaining detachment from our desire to control and possess. And I was traveling and talking, eating and drinking, with one of the most cheerful and gentle "gangs" I had known. Sure, they quarreled and got upset, but conflicts could pass away in an instant, and the sweetness, sensitivity to others, and good cheer emerged again, and who could be angry for long? They were skilled at giving up grievances and adjusting private paths, navigating a middle.

In which our Author wonders over the unlikely Road
that led him to Siam—

As a teenager in my synagogue youth group, I would write verbose "closing prayers," which I read in a grave voice while puzzled teenagers fidgeted in "friendship circles" at the end of our meetings. I had deep intentions, meant every florid word. I also contributed my prayers to "creative services," made no enemies, was elected president of Temple

Emanuel Youth Group in Dallas. I liked the Friday evening worship services in our large, strikingly designed sanctuary, formal and friendly, where we listened to rabbi and choir and voiced our parts on cue. My friends and I were drawn to the prophetic and moral sentiments in the Reform prayer book. Sermons echoed with the liberal politics of Bertrand Russell and Walter Lippmann. Nuclear disarmament and civil rights were big items.

My parents, children of immigrants, were struggling to join the American middle class. My father worried every night over his small business, splendidly named "Marks the Seat Cover King." My mother stayed home and worried over the children and house (later going to school to earn an R.N. certificate). Impressed by socialist speeches he had heard in Chicago, my father had little use for religion; alienated by her father's "fanatical" Hasidism, my mother thought Judaism was really about having a good heart, not following ritual. They gave their first two children proper Anglo-Saxon names—a Richard and a Kenneth. Their Richard, however, acquired a baffling insecurity and escaped into books, wrote poetry, and turned his passion to satellites and astronomy, and then to the JPS Bible, and to "closing prayers." Eventually he found in *Look Homeward, Angel* a mirror of both his drive to leave home and his romantic sense of loss.

In college I entered a rigorous intellectual world of Western classics, science, and social theories, with heavy doses of existentialism and contemporary poetry. Then I spent nine months studying in Israel; decided to settle there; decided not to; observed Orthodox law under the direction of my Orthodox roommate; and gave it up before I left. After a year in VISTA on a Seneca reservation in New York, I enrolled in a rabbinic seminary in California as a graduate student. This was the early 1970s—days of Vietnam, ethnic roots, social turmoil. I found escape, I see now, in the mysterious sounds of the Hebrew language and the grand mythology of rabbinic literature. I discovered an orderly cosmos centered in a family God and a community called Israel, and learned the sweet secrets of holy action and the melodies of prayer. I undertook the exalted task of studying the revealed Torah, became an actor in the drama of exilic punishment and yearning for messianic return. Abraham was still being tempted by Satan, Rabbi Akiva was defying Roman decrees, Jacob and Esau (Israel and Rome) were still in mortal conflict. But this Judaism was private and poetic, more in my head than in my actions.

I did not plan on Thailand. Yes, when I studied History of Religions at UCLA with Professor Kees Bolle, the rabbinic story shrank to just one among a crowd of profound stories from sophisticated cultures beyond Europe and the U.S. There were suddenly many orientations, not just one, and I felt myself adrift without compass points in an ocean of possibilities. And yes, Alan Watts had intrigued me with the peaceful tone of his Zen, and I took a class in *tai qi* (tai chi). I studied some Indian religious classics with Kees, while Professor Amos Funkenstein tried to teach me to read Jewish historical documents creatively and modern historians critically, and to find the flaws in any explanation. So perhaps I was at that time the only doctoral student in Jewish studies with enough interest in Asian religions to accept Mahidol University's invitation. I agreed, with little concern for consequences and vast ignorance about Thailand, to teach Judaism there in a comparative religion program.

In which, with a little Help from his Friends, our Author goes Native—

It was harder than I expected. Ratri and other Thai professors took pity on me. Ratri's garden happened in many forms and places, over and over. I rode to work on stuffy, crowded buses, ate with Thais what they ate (minus a few peppers), taught Thais, drank beer with Thais, haggled (poorly) with street vendors, took orders from, was hurt by and nurtured by, Thais. I admired their temples and learned to sit respectfully before monks and Buddha images like my friends, feet pointing behind me, palms pressed together in a gesture called a *wai*. In this society of the shy and gentle, I felt supported and accepted. In classrooms of gentle students, who greeted me with a smiling *wai* when I approached, I began to teach better, with more assurance and more attention to students, than I had taught in Los Angeles. Certainly there were things I didn't like—well-mannered cruelty, the outrageous wealth of the few, abuse of power. I never succeeded in learning the language well or bearing the heat, and my income gave me a freedom few Thai professors had. But I felt elated when a new Thai acquaintance exclaimed, "You don't act like an American, you're so Thai."

I learned their Buddhism. Unlike the usual American image of Buddhism as a solitary discipline with an airy philosophy, this was an everyday Buddhism for ordinary people. I think, for example, of the constant stream of fruit, curries, bottles, currency, and cloth passing as gifts from one Thai person to another, more gifts given more often than I had seen before. My Thai friends explained it as *than* (*dana* in Pali), "giving," the main way they practice the Buddhist teaching of non-attachment, and I found myself drawn into this act of buying things only to pass them on. I think also of one of my favorite scenes of Thailand: At dawn, before the trees and canals take on a clear form and color, a line of monks walks silently on bare feet past the neighborhood houses, appearing almost to float, expressionless, with eyes to the ground; parents and children spoon steaming rice into their bowls, offer fruit and bags of curry, then bow or kneel as the monks bless the household before continuing on their way. The day begins with this first act of giving and offers a large realm for the practice of *dana*. Merit arises, and one's karma improves, through every act in which parents care for their children and children thank and honor their parents, in which elders guide younger people and are in turn honored and served by them, and in which teachers bestow concern and knowledge upon pupils, who show respect and gratitude toward teachers. This web of interdependence extends beyond death to ancestors, to whom the living transfer the good karma they've acquired and from whom they expect protection, and also to household spirits and guardian spirits of the rice field or the village. This ritualized *dana* merges into social acts of giving—caring for sick neighbors, sending used clothes to a poor family in the village, or offering guests only the best of one's food, always freshly cooked. To be *jai kwang*, "broad-hearted," is a central Thai virtue.

I also heard the word *karuna*, "compassion," mentioned often. My friends apply it to their many acts of visiting the sick, attending funerals, helping and comforting families with sick members or in mourning, bringing orphans into their families, giving coins to beggars, inviting foreigners like myself into their homes, feeding stray dogs, and freeing caged birds. A related word, *metta*, "loving-kindness," is the subject of a beautiful scriptural passage recited by Thai school children every morning: "May all beings be happy, may they live in safety and joy.... As a mother watches over her child, willing to risk her life to protect her only child, so with a boundless heart should one cherish all living beings, suffusing the whole world with unobstructed *metta*."

As an aspect of giving way to others, of living in community, my friends would explain their behavior as *thang sai klang*, "the middle path," a phrase used often by monks in their sermons. *Mai mak, mai noi* goes the Thai proverb, meaning "not too much, not too little," in matters like eating, sleeping, working, and saving money, but also as a model for balance—we can compromise, live with limits.

A Jew has to admire these ideals and how often they are put into practice. Despite the obvious differences, a Jew would see reflections of *rahamim* (compassion), *nedivut* (generosity), and *gemilut hasadim* (loving-kindness), a *halakhah* (religious law, literally a walking or way) of required acts of discipline, in a communal interdependence of giving and receiving. "The middle path" reminds a Jew of Maimonides' *middah beinonit*, the (Aristotelian) mean between extremes.

I myself began to observe more Jewish ritual (with certain big adaptations) and even to think of God in a rather biblical way. So much in my life was uncertain from day to day: People got sick, were injured, died too easily. The newspaper told recurrent stories of ten-wheeler trucks colliding with buses, the truck driver fleeing the scene to escape arrest. Unpredictability, horror, the luck of the draw. Beggars on the streets, the shacks of migrant workers. The tropical odor of decaying plants and fetid ponds, the heavy moisture of the air.

I savored the slow, tense buildup of monsoon storms and exulted in their explosion into curtains of rain, fierce lightning, sudden cracking thunder, and then the wild croaking of frogs when the rain stopped. Bangkok seemed to me a city of brief pleasures followed by loss and decay, like the wreaths of flower buds sold by tired women sitting on the street—sweet fragrant jasmine turned brown in a day, covered with ants. My friends repeatedly invoked the word *anicca*, "impermanent," in their reflections. It explained their disappointments and the suffering around them. I began reading books by the contemporary Thai monk Buddhadasa. The traditional Buddhist characterization of the world as *anicca, dukkha,* "dissatisfying," and *anatta,* "non-self," fit my growing sense of the decay, poverty, and illness surrounding me, and my surrender of individual wants and habits one by one. I learned meditation and experienced it also as a giving up, a letting go, of cherished desires, of identity, ambitions, and control. In Thailand I felt I was experiencing the truth of Buddhist emptiness (an *anatta* world) and the lay discipline of making merit through repeated giving away. All this, while I was somehow working with the traditional Jewish prayers, stretching them for symbolic relevance, and observing Shabbat at home with ritual and rest.

In which our Author defends Judaism,
and then becomes one of the Family—

Meanwhile I was teaching courses on Judaism. My students—about thirty of them during my four years of teaching, most of them Buddhist and in their mid-twenties—had joined the graduate program in Comparative Religious Studies knowing they would study religions other than their own. A few of them had special Buddhist training at a university or monastery, but all espoused a form of Buddhism they had learned in public school, which, I later learned, the anthropologist Charles Keyes calls "Reformed Buddhist Worldview." Influenced by Western science and emphasizing ethics and spirituality, this form of Theravada Buddhism discards the traditional Indian cosmos of multiple gods and higher and

lower worlds and rejects the popular veneration of gods and local spirits. For my part, I was fascinated with my students' ideas as Thai Buddhists and with what Judaism looked like to them. I regularly asked them
what they thought about the Jewish concepts and rituals I was present-
ing, and they replied to my questions with goodwill and honesty. The
result was a dialogue of sorts, one particular Buddhist response to the
traditional Jewish worldview I presented, which was based on the
Orthodox prayer book.[1]

I learned from my students that classical Judaism could look like
magic and like blind faith. One student, Sriphen, wrote, "The goal of living with God is to gain the sudden advantage. Isn't this a characteristic
of magic, not religion?" She was thinking of the petitionary prayers in the
prayer book and the Jewish hope for messianic redemption. Why pray to
God if not to gain something one can't gain by one's own powers? Likewise, students thought that Jewish theology (like Christian and Muslim)
was so irrational that Jews could believe it only through blind faith,
whereas the teachings of the Buddha, based on human wisdom about
the nature of this world, can be verified through experience and daily
practice. I heard often from students and acquaintances that Buddhism
can be "proved," implying that the Western theisms could not. Students
associated Judaism with the eerie realm of the *saksit* in Thai culture. This
word refers to "sacred" things or people that exhibit an extraordinary
power—such things as amulets, spirit houses, statues inhabited by the
spirits of strong gods, and monks who bring rain and heal the sick. Good
"Reform Buddhists" look down on such practices. My students said
repeatedly that we must work out our own happiness by understanding
the nature of things (*dhamma*) instead of relying on a spirit or a God to
make us happy. They said much more (including their distaste for the
idea of chosenness), but they found much the same flaws in other non-
Buddhist religions as in Judaism. On the one hand, they had been taught
in school to think tolerantly of other religions and would say that all are
good because they teach morality. On the other hand, though no one said
so explicitly, my students and other Thais with whom I discussed religion

thought that only Buddhism reached deeper than morality, only it taught
the basic truths about the world. Only Buddhism was not a superstition.

My reaction was to defend Judaism by finding ways to remove it from
the category of *saksit* beliefs and to relate it to the category of "Reform
Buddhism," but my students' responses also impelled me to recognize
the frequency with which the Jewish prayer book associates holiness
with power—which is indeed part of the rabbinic worldview. I discovered that Reform Buddhism was not so different from Reform Judaism,
in that both (born in the late nineteenth century and embraced by the
middle class) sought to remove "magic" and opaque rituals from religious life, to harmonize doctrine with the Western scientific cosmos.

The only people I knew there who were not Thai I had met at the
Bangkok synagogue—Americans, Israelis, Lebanese—and a kind, humble missionary couple from the U.S., who cared for me after I was hos-
pitalized with hepatitis. I lived in Thai neighborhoods, ate and drank
with Thais, worked with them, and eventually married a Thai woman
named Walapa. We lived for two years in her townhouse near a tree-
lined canal on the outskirts of the city, where I was the only *farang*
(American or European foreigner) for miles. Now I became part of her
large Thai family, with its varied stories and intimate dramas, moods, and
conflicts. Walapa was a midlevel official of the Royal Thai Ministry of
Education, having earned two master's degrees, one from the University
of Iowa. The first Friday after our Buddhist wedding we held Shabbat in
her house.

Our first child (named Daniel, the foreign Jew, and Ari, a name with
both Pali and Hebrew meanings) was born at a time of autumn flooding
in Bangkok, and we adopted Walapa's niece, who had been abandoned
by her parents. When I returned to Mahidol years later to teach through
the Fulbright program, we adopted the son of Walapa's brother who
died unexpectedly that year. Our daughter Ariya (a name with both a Pali
and a coined Hebrew meaning) was born in the U.S., and when we all
assemble, I'm the one whose looks don't quite fit.

Many years pass as our Author and his Family survive the Shock of Trans-
plantation to a small College Town in rural Virginia. They thrive among
its friendly Citizens. One day our Author is queried by three wise Editors
as to the Effect of his earlier Experiences on his present religious Life.
First he exclaims, "Oy v' oy," and then . . .

Well *(he says),* to begin with, you'd see me doing pretty ordinary
(Reform) Jewish things. I pay dues to a synagogue thirty-five miles away
where Danny's Bar Mitzvah ceremony was held. I have driven him and
Ariya on Sundays for nine years to a Jewish religious school another
twenty miles up the road, where I've recently begun teaching Hebrew
and religious topics. We attend High Holy Day services and occasional
Shabbat services, and we celebrate Sukkot, Hanukah, and Passover at
home. Ariya kisses the *mezuzah* as she enters her bedroom. Most Friday
evenings find us saying the Shabbat blessings and eating dinner together,
and on Friday nights I read Torah interpretations sent to me by e-mail.
I read Jewish stories to my children. When I teach Judaism courses at my
college, I feel a personal excitement about the Jewish texts. I advise the
Jewish student organization on campus, and lead my town's Neilah service ending Yom Kippur. I listen to Debbie Friedman and Craig Taubman
tapes and read Israeli novels and some modern Jewish thought. I worry
about Israel and about God.

At the same time, however, you would see the most important person in my life, Walapa, a Buddhist. She has the more interesting story.
Now it's she who is the foreigner, faced with a culture that alternately
perplexes and welcomes, outrages and attracts her. She has read biog-
raphies of the American Founding Fathers and Abraham Lincoln and
Franklin Roosevelt, pores over the *Washington Post,* and expresses sharp
opinions on Washington politics. Proud of her Thai culture and upbringing, she views American excesses and individualism with a prophet's
scorn. Walapa works to inculcate Thai social values in her children and
continues to live out her Buddhism in her own nonritualized way. She
objects to Jewish theology for the same reasons that my Thai students

stated, but she finds value in Judaism as a folk culture, and she cooks for
and participates in our family ceremonies. She bakes, I'd guess, some of
the best challah bread in the state—which she gives to neighbors in acts
of Buddhist *dana!* She did all the cooking for Danny's Bar Mitzvah, from
the cheese blintzes to the tofu springrolls (he gave a sermon on the veg-
etarian implications of his Torah selection, Genesis 1). Warm, charming,
thoughtful, and capable, she makes friends easily and has endeared herself to many.

You would see, too, my adopted children (now college graduates),
who are also Buddhist. You'd see statues of the Buddha in our living room
and Thai and Burmese art hanging on our walls. We remove our shoes
when entering the house and eat lots of rice. We visit Thai relatives in
Louisiana and Texas and have gone for month-long visits to my wife's
home in Thailand. There we offer food to monks, visit temples and pay
respect to Buddha images, and honor our elders. I've read the Indian
epic *Ramayana* to my children, as well as the Buddhist *Jataka* tales, and
in discussions with Danny I sometimes offer a Buddhist interpretation of
the subject. He has learned to meditate. I teach Theravada Buddhism as
a unit in my Introduction to Religion course and occasionally suggest a
Buddhist reading of a Jewish or Muslim text being studied in class. I
chose to teach in Thailand for my first sabbatical. My family traveled in
Burma under the guidance of Burmese friends and was privileged to
meet three of the great *sayadaw* monks of the country, as well as many
good and generous families. I listen to tapes of Thai music, even the *luk
tun* (country) variety disdained by my city friends. I attended a ten-day
meditation retreat at the Insight Meditation Society (IMS) and I meditate a few times a week.

The Jewish and Buddhist adjectives seem to coexist, to maintain a
functional relationship with one other. At Ariya's Jewish naming ceremony, Walapa read the *metta* prayer quoted earlier, and my Buddhist
daughter read verses from the *Dhammapada*. Walapa read the same prayer
at Danny's Bar Mitzvah. In my speech on that day, citing a traditional
Hebrew blessing to be said when encountering non-Jewish sages, I said

I hoped he would grow to be a thoughtful and knowledgeable Jew who could appreciate the wisdom of the Thai people, Buddhists, other religions, and secularists, and still be a Jew and think for himself. I hope the same for Ariya.

I have been privileged to learn from two profound religious traditions in some of their varied cultural forms.

———————

Yet there are adjectival conflicts on various levels, and I sometimes worry about them. Pieces from different puzzles appear intermittently to fit or to collide, to leave empty spots or to overlap.

Walapa will notice and point out various doctrinal and practical inconsistencies in the religious lives of myself and other Jews and Christians and will remind me, through argument and example, of the possibility of morality and spirituality without God and prayer. Sometimes, moreover, I think about Jewish prayers from her viewpoint and notice, for example, how the *Aleinu* prayer isn't as tolerant as I grew up thinking it was: In envisioning a future humanity united in the worship of the one God, it belittles or excludes Theravada Buddhists, who don't need to bend their knees or call upon God's name in order to live good, pious lives. Nor do they need to be coworkers with God in order to build hospitals and feed the hungry. On the other hand, I doubt they expect to find any unconverted Jews or Muslims in the perfected world of Maitreya, the future Buddha.

To think about these puzzle pieces, I've turned in my research to the topic of interreligious dialogue, trying to follow contemporary events in Buddhist-Jewish discussions while working to reconstruct a history of medieval and early-modern Jewish perceptions of Indian religions. (These European and Mid-Eastern Jews knew and lived a fuller Jewish life than I, but none gained an intimate knowledge of a Hindu or Buddhist society in Asia, whereas the Jewish merchants who did live in India and Southeast Asia left us nothing in writing about their neighbors' religions.) I began studying the modern Jewish thinker Abraham Joshua

Heschel and the contemporary Thai monk Buddhadasa, with the idea of comparing themes of transcendence in their works. Soon, however, I felt overwhelmed by the cultural chasms of language, concept, history, audience, and intention, and their resistance to generalizing.

Meditating at an IMS retreat was emotionally powerful for me, far more so than any Jewish experience that I've had recently, but it felt like therapy. I can see the Theravada Buddhist description of the world (*anicca*, *dukkha*, *anatta*) as circular reasoning. The claim is either obvious by definition or makes a metaphysical leap that cannot be demonstrated. The concept of non-self is counterintuitive; it can be "experienced" only after engaging in a required set of thoughts (much like faith). Is eliminating *dukkha* the main thing? But Jewish philosophies are equally problematic. I keep looking for a new Jewish philosophy that makes sense of secular thought and the sciences and takes seriously the world's diverse religious and secular myths. I haven't read widely enough, but what I have read—by Buber, Heschel, Wiesel, Waskow, Lerner, Hartman, and L. Kushner—fails to sustain me for long. I have found in novels not an answer but a more subtle mirror of my feelings, of this modern perplexity and yearning for wholeness—for example, in the wounded characters of Amos Oz, in the cosmos of pain and indifference in his *A Perfect Peace,* and in Anne Tyler's gently humorous stories of broken people seeking small reconciliations in a baffling world. Perhaps Heschel, with various adjustments, comes closest, especially in his sense of humanity's suffering and the world's grandeur calling us to respond.

In my private rituals, I've turned to a loose cycle of meditative intentions that I practice late at night. The cycle varies with the moment's needs, perhaps beginning with a Buddhist concentration practice, then with Jewish bedtime prayers, sometimes personal prayer consisting mainly of questions to a hoped-for Other, and ending with as long an insight practice (Vipassana) as I can maintain that evening. I'm still experimenting. Sometimes I would rather read a novel.

But my research and meditation function on the borders of my personal life. In the middle are scenes of home: Sitting with my daughter at night as she does her homework. Washing dishes, sweeping the floor, mowing the grass. Greeting Walapa as she arrives home exhausted from her work in the hospital. Driving a child to baseball practice or the swimming pool. Arguments with children over curfew, parties, computer games, messy rooms, pets, chores. Playing catch, sitting together on the porch watching a summer sky flash with lightning, making up silly songs. Reading to children at bedtime, hugging my daughter before she leaves for school. Discussions with my wife about the children, our house, spending money; hurt feelings, sweet intimacies. Conversations with my daughter about mean classmates, God, death, and cats; discussions of films and English papers with my son. Satisfactions and disappointed expectations, inappropriate anger. Trying to learn, to compromise, to listen, and to influence. This is the work to be done and also the fruits.

I still feel the urge to travel—to meditate for a year at IMS, to study Kabbalah with teachers in distant cities, to live in Jerusalem, or just to drive to my office to prepare better lessons or do research. My wife sometimes thinks of nunhood at a Thai temple. But we resist. We tend the garden.

Often Buddhism and Judaism seem irrelevant, in outer space. Sometimes all I hear is a traffic noise of dissonant voices. But it seems here, at home, in this imperfect wrestle with children, spouse, job, and religious traditions, full of blendings and compromises, pieces from different puzzles, many-toned voices, I am navigating—as Ratri once showed me— a path of middles and betweens. It is a *halakhah* of duties, a weave of *dana*. The Buddha taught rules of family and communal responsibility to his lay followers, the rabbis composed homilies about and legislated for the troubles of everyday life. That was the locale of *dana* and *karuna*, the locale of holiness. It's hard to see up close, when siblings argue or Shabbat candles light only distracted faces. But occasionally I catch sight, and time stops, and it's fine.

Interview, April 25, 2001

Rabbi Zalman Schachter-Shalomi

T his project was conceived as a response to the concerns of some religious people that studying Buddhism will somehow warp a person. So we are asking you and several others—Jews and Christians—to tell us about your own encounters with Buddhism.

You know, in the late 1960s Dom J. M. Déchanet published a book called *Christian Yoga,* and there was another one called *Zen Catholicism* by Dom Aelred Graham. So you see that they didn't feel that way about it [then]. Since Vatican II and Pope John XXIII, Cardinal Ratzinger and his crew have backtracked.

That's exactly what leads us to do this project. It was hearing Cardina Ratzinger describe Buddhism as a threat, and thinking, "Wow, this is not our experience at all!"

Well, you know, he doesn't know what Buddhism aims for from *inside.* This is a real problem, when people are bound by their dogma and aren't able to breathe in and trust in the spirit.

When and where did you first become interested in Buddhism?

Well, let me go back. It wasn't Buddhism first, it was Hinduism. My Dad, rest his soul, once told me about Rabindranath Tagore, the Nobel-Prize-winning Indian poet. He told me that here was a *Zaddik*—a holy man—

although he was not a Jew! That was already the beginning of my down-fall. And later on, whenever I came across some writings of the Bud-dhists—especially when it got to the stories, the Zen stories—I felt such a closeness. So when *Zen Flesh, Zen Bones* came out, I read it with great joy. In my library, I have a book in Yiddish called *Die Reyd funim Buddha,* which means "The Words of the Buddha"—the *Dhammapada* in Yiddish.

So if you go back, it was a slow infiltration, one that sneaks up on you. Then the question was always: Where is my tradition with that? So, Deuteronomy would decree like Ratzinger. But Ecclesiastes, let's say, would go with the *Dao De Jing (Tao Te Ching)* and with the Buddha. So Buddhism didn't create that heavy a problem for me. Alan Watts once said about himself that he had "graduated" from the Anglican Church. He didn't want to say that he repudiated the Church. And I feel the same way—that I graduated from Habad Lubavitch Hasidism. That's not to say that the Lubavitchers are a bad "school." They are a great school, but some people get fixated in first grade all the time.

So the dance with Buddhism continues over time. If I had to mention a particular year, it would be 1946. I'm in New Haven, Connecticut, and I pick up Ballou's little *World Bible,* along with a book by a Trappist monk, Father Eugene Boylan, which was *Difficulties in Mental Prayer*. And I was amazed that the goyim knew about such things! And then at Boston Uni-versity, I had as one of my mentors Howard Thurman, God rest his soul, a very special human being. He was the Dean of the Chapel at B.U. So more and more I was looking over the fence and seeing what our neigh-bors were doing and sometimes getting inspiration that would wake me up from what Buber called *"Der Aussatz der Gewohnheit,"* the leprosy of habit.

What was it that drew you to take a closer look at Buddhism?

Gradually, my interest moved away from the philosophical-theological-creedal word modes to the experiential heart and soul modes. Once you get into experiential stuff, you are interested in *upaya*—What are

the skillful means for awakening? I was looking in various places, checking out skillful means of hot-housing the spirit. It wasn't solely in Buddhism. Reading about Ignatius' method of prayer was also important.
And Saint Francis de Sales. The Anglican Caroline Divines were very
important to me as well, because of things like Jeremy Taylor's *Holy Living* and *Holy Dying*—"*ars moriendi*"—these kinds of things interested me,
and so wherever I could find some spiritual direction literature, I was
interested in that.

So you were reading widely all the time.

Yes. Someone once introduced me by saying, "He's very wildly-read!"

*How has Buddhism impacted your Judaism? Has Buddhism caused you to
question or doubt any facets of your own tradition?*

You know, let me launch into what I want to say, really, because it may not
answer exactly this, but it's close to it. What I found was that Buddhism
is a great method. It isn't a "good religion." It becomes a good religion
when it's embedded in Japanese Shinto, in Tibetan Bon, or in Chinese
Taoism.

Embedded in some specific context, do you mean?

Yes, it has to have something ethnic, something chthonic, that picks it up
from the soil, that lives with the seasons. And the Sangha [the religious
community] and the Dharma [the Buddha's teaching] and the Buddha
didn't quite take us into those seasons and into chthonic things. So,
wherever it was a vital religion, it picked those things up from the life,
the culture, the indigenous beliefs of that place.

For instance, I had the opportunity to be in a Shin Buddhist church in
Winnipeg, Manitoba, and there I saw how Protestant the Shin Pure Land
people were in their Buddhism. For instance, they had a calendar that

showed a picture of Gautama Buddha sitting surrounded by little children, and the legend was almost the same as "Suffer the little children to come unto me." Shin Buddhism, in contrast to Zen and other more monastic forms of Buddhism, is more of a householder's religion. But it's this generational stuff that is missing in export Buddhism. The kind of Buddhism that most Westerners adopt is not a householder's religion and, from my point of view, wherever there aren't any householders, a religion can't live. It needs to have a matrix in which it is embedded. That matrix is related to Buddhism like the ground to the figure. The ground becomes invisible to people.

To many Christians, the ground of Judaism is invisible, and yet Christianity arises out of that ground. Lots of stuff in the Gospels wouldn't make sense otherwise. In fact, I keep pointing out to people the ordination of Peter, where he is told "whatsoever you will bind" and so forth. If you re-translate that into rabbinic Hebrew, it makes immediate sense, because it's the same formula that we use for *Semikhah,* for ordination, to say "whatever you will bind (meaning 'make forbidden') will be forbidden, and what you will permit will be permitted." That gives each bishop in his see the power to declare what is kosher and what is not kosher there.

In the same way, for Buddhism in India, the matrix was Hinduism, from which it arose. When you go a little bit later in history, then you see that the mother matrix generally swallows back up the new message, unless that new gospel is lifted out and put into another matrix, like Christianity into Greek and Roman religion and like Buddhism into Japan, Korea, China, and Thailand. Why did Bodhidharma come to China? is one of the Zen-Chan koans.

Now, having said that, I come back to the issue of Judaism. A person who wants to be able to practice mindfulness—and I love Thich Nhat Hanh's book, in which he says, "Why don't you do a day of mindfulness? For instance, it's Saturday," and then he goes on to describe what looks like a perfect Shabbat—which itself calls for letting go of being driven and spending the day in sacred mindfulness.

For a Jew, the problem begins when you get to the iconic element in Buddhism, that is not for export—the statues of the Buddha. (I don't like what the Taliban did in Afghanistan, destroying the Buddhist images, but I can understand where they came from, because the Muslims still have the story of young Abraham—Ibrahim—iconoclastically going around and breaking up idols. I think that it is unenlightened and shows how narrow their own faith is, and that they don't have elastic space in their heart, but that's another story.)

But you think there is too much focus on icons?

Icons are needed at times—especially where there are people to be instructed who cannot read. These *Lehrtafeln,* or teaching aids, are very useful. In Bombay I saw a shrine that had illustrations by which the *pandit* [learned teacher] could teach the *chelas* who could not master the Sanskrit. While it is true that we Jews have an aversion to icons that want to invite adoration, I don't believe that this touches Jews who are involved in Buddhism too much. The "Ju-Bus," people who do mostly Zen or Vipassana meditation, are not into the icons. I don't see too many Jews going to the *go-honzon* [the main object of veneration] and chanting *"Namu myoho renge kyo"* ("Hail to the Lotus Sutra").

The other thing is that most of the Buddhism that comes to America is Buddhism for export. It has been stripped of the chthonic and ethnic things from Asia. So the people who do Theravada Buddhism here do it very much American-style.

I'll tell you a story: I've been teaching at Naropa University, and one of the students came up to me and told me about how "dry" things were for him in Buddhism. I asked him, "Do you make music?" And he said, "Yes." So I said, "Why don't you write a couple of ballads, because there isn't any hymnody around. Take a look at 'Davy Crocket.' You know: 'Born in a palace in India-land,' or something like that. And tell the story that way!"

And I've shared with the Buddhists in Dharamsala, and others, the idea of making a Buddhist Seder in which the order of the Seder would be the same, with the four stations (which is very much like the Mass). And when it comes to where the tale is told, where the ministry of the word is, they could tell the story, the Haggadah, of the life of the Buddha. Or, if you wanted, you could bring it to Avalokitesvara [the Bodhisattva of Compassion], or to [the great Tibetan sages] Tilopa or Naropa. Tell these things, and set up on the table the various things that would make you remember. So, for instance, put *tsampa* and yak butter on the table and say, "This is the food our forefathers ate in the land of Tibet," you know?

This came out of wanting to help the Tibetans to have continuity in a place where they are no longer on their own land with lamaseries and lamas around, and they need to do things for themselves as a family. And I suggested to them that they should have *pujaris*, or worship leaders, appointed from among the laity.

Has Buddhism deepened your practice of the Jewish faith, and if so how?

The answer is yes. Imagine how many times you do things by rote with a formula. And to be here and present and now in doing it, that of course deepens it. At the same time, what is so wonderful is that once you do it that way and you go back to your own literature, you see that it's there in the faith of the religion of origin. It's been there all along! But it's almost as if the scales fell off the eyes because we went next door.

Does Buddhist meditation help you to understand Jewish texts more deeply?

The answer, of course, is yes. However, I have a sort of complaint. My complaint goes like this: Most of the people who bring in Buddhism for export are talking about "empty" in a way that does not deal with pleromatic emptiness—the emptiness of fullness. Now, the problem is that we live bombarded by stimuli in the cities. If we lived in a rural place and didn't have so much input, emptying would go more easily.

Furthermore, we don't have that much time. Most of the sits, the *sesshin,* require that you spend extended time on the cushion. Now, for the average person today, twenty minutes in the morning and twenty minutes in the evening is all they can handle. So, we are looking for *upaya* that are not vacuum-packed, but pressure-packed. For instance, when Ignatius is told that his Jesuits are going to be dismantled by the next Pope, he says, "Give me fifteen minutes in the oratory; it's all the same to me." He can do this because he has a method in which he fills rather than empties. And my sense is that there is not only Jewish meditation like this, but there is also Buddhist meditation like this, which doesn't get talked about.

I learned something gorgeous when I was in Dharamsala and I saw the Kalachakra mandala three-dimensionally. Inside the second floor, as it were, sat a figure that looked like one of the cherubim, but it had arms, not wings. It was the Bodhisattva of Compassion sitting in that center place, the "u" of the "aum." It would correspond as the seat of infinite compassion to what a Jew would see in the Tetragrammaton *[YHVH,* the four Hebrew consonants of the unpronounceable name of God], or a Catholic in the Sacred Heart of Jesus. So the *yantras* [mandalic aids to meditation], the *tankas* [holy pictures] all are to say, "Fill yourself with that." You look at the green Tara [Buddha-goddess of compassion], and you want to let her walk into your heart. Finding the image you see before you in your *chakras* [centers within your body], in your *kabbalistic sefirot* [mystical emanations], is somehow different than adoring the image on the outside. The Tibetans, for instance, have this practice, but the Buddhism for export that comes to us is not *bhakti* enough, not devotional enough.

I saw the way the Buddhists in Dharamsala turned to their prayer wheels, for instance, with a devout humility. There was a Buddhist nun who was supposed to be our attendant reciting in the morning in front of our residence. You could see how heartful she was in her prayers.

It looks to me as though the Buddhism for export isn't heartful, despite the fact that there is *metta* [loving-kindness] and *tonglen,* a compassionate way to relieve others from darkness and pain. What it amounts to is that all this *karuna,* this compassion, doesn't have a warm place. That's why Joe Goldstein and Jack Kornfield, both Insight Meditation teachers, have been writing about applying the sitting to engaged Buddhism.

Another young man came to me for spiritual guidance, and I asked him, "What is your practice?" He said that now he is involved in doing prostrations. So I said, "Show me a prostration." Whup-whup-whup-whup, he did it. I said to him, "Would you just show me what it is that you are doing internally? Do it slowly, and talk to me while you are doing it." And he did it slowly, and all of a sudden there was heart in it. Then I said to him, "I tell you what, I'm not a Buddhist and I can't make it kosher for you, but if you listen to me, one of the slow ones is worth at least ten fast ones!"

Why do you think so many Jews are attracted to Buddhism?

Well, first, if Buddhism were to come with all its baggage, they wouldn't be! It comes stripped, so it doesn't seem to come with all its moral and ethical demands. Take a look at the precepts that a Buddhist monk has to keep. They're just like the 613 that we have! So the likelihood is they wouldn't go for that either, you know?

The second thing is that in Judaism you really need to know—to have some way of dealing with—Hebrew. Now let's say this Ph.D. suddenly "got it"—that there is a God, or that there is spirit, and that his soul is waking up—and he comes back to Judaism. Then he gets infantilized, because he can't even read *alef beis,* the first two letters of the Hebrew alphabet. So Buddhism is a much easier thing to reach for.

Because they are not enculturated within Hebrew?

That's right, and so they are sent back to square one. Imagine somebody who suddenly decides he wants to come to Mass. He embraces Christ, then says, "I want to become a Roman Catholic." If he were to walk into a pre-1935 Mass—back when the catechism still said "Don't go to the YMCA; it is a mortal sin"—he wouldn't know how to make the sign of the cross or how to deal with holy water or when to kneel, or what responses to make, so he would feel stupid. And in Judaism, Orthodoxy is the one that attracts people, because it feels genuine, and it has practices that you can actually do. But at the same time it repels, because it demands so much know-how. So one of the attractions of Buddhism is that it isn't so demanding in that way.

Another thing is that Buddhism here gets practiced solo most of the time—which is actually a problem, because if you don't have the Sangha [the religious community] to be answerable to, everybody can have his own private Buddhism. In Judaism, it is necessary that other Jews should say you're a Jew, and for Christians the same way.

Do you think the Shoah has been a factor somehow in Jews' being attracted to Buddhism?

Yes, and partly because, you see, the Deuteronomic God made promises that He didn't keep in Auschwitz. And of course those people who haven't encountered Job—"Yea, though he slay me I still trust in him"—can't get to that place.

But let me tell you the wonderful way in which my friend Shlomo Carlebach of blessed memory used to talk about it. He was a singer, troubadour, guru, traveling person—he was my buddy. Once we had a meeting on "Torah and Dharma" in San Francisco. He couldn't make it to the meeting, and so I asked him, "Would you tape something for us?" He did, and on the tape he asked, "How come so many of our people go to the Eastern religions?" Then he answered, "It is written that a priest must not defile himself unto the dead. And why is that? One of the Hasidic masters explains, 'Because when you see a corpse, you feel angry at God.'"

And Shlomo Carlebach says, "Look—six million corpses can make you mighty angry at God. So we couldn't learn from our own people. But God is merciful, so he sent us teachers from the Far East, to whom we could listen."

I think there is a deep truth in there.

Do you think, then, that the way Buddhism treats suffering has a particular resonance with Jews?

Not quite. We want to know whether we are suffering for God's sake. We want to say, "I accept the suffering as part of divine will. I submit to that."

You know, taking on the cross isn't just from the outside. It is something that we also have been saying, and we call it *Yissurin shel ahavah,* the pangs of love that you take on. And it's weeping for the *Shekhinah,* for the divine presence. And there is a feeling that suffering has a redemptive quality, that it is a sacrificial thing. That doesn't show in Buddhism.

So if I had to say something about the Far East, I would say that they are on the schizoid side, and we are on the paranoid side. The schizoid says everything is *maya,* illusion. And the paranoid says, "Surely goodness and mercy shall persecute me all my life." The word here is "shall follow me," but the verb root means to "chase" or "hound" me. It has the sense that everything is happening because I did or did not honor God and his commandments. That's the difference, that we have a different way in which we sit in the cosmos.

Has Buddhism affected your approach to the construction of your religious identity?

Well, again I need to go to another issue first. When we saw Earth from outer space for the first time, reflected to us, that became the most obligating icon that there is. More than a cross, than a star of David, a Torah, anything. This is Earth. And when you see Earth that way, without boundaries, you get into a post-triumphalist mode, because you see that

Gaia is alive, and you are part of that life of Gaia. And every religion is a vital organ of the planet. So the heart cannot claim superiority over the liver or over the lungs or the kidneys. Even if you have a low opinion of the colon, for instance, if you don't have it you're in trouble.

So you recognize that we are all tied together organically, that each religion is offering something really vital to the planet. So, for instance, the question "Is something kosher?" is very important to all of us—especially today with the genetic stuff being done, the "Franken-foods." And so we each make our contribution. And the fact that in Judaism we have the Sabbath is a fantastic contribution in an age when commodity time is speeding up so crazily and hardly anybody takes off for enough organic time, to rest. So each religion is doing an important job.

Then when I go back and ask, "What has Buddhism shown me in this situation?" first of all, I want to say, "Look at the Axial Age." There was Plato, Aristotle, Socrates, and at the same time you had Isaiah, Jeremiah, Ezekiel, Zarathustra, the Buddha, Mahavira, Laozi (Lao-tzu), and Confucius. So I ask myself, "What happened?" There was a blip on the radar of the global brain that people who were receptive with their heart and their soul were able to catch, and each one brought down to their constituency something that took them out of their encapsulation into a wider place. Judaism after Isaiah is different because of the vision that he had. And that vision in India shows itself in Mahavira's *ahimsa* (nonviolence). And in the Buddha's knowing about those Noble Truths. And then the trickster Laozi says, "You talk about it, you ain't got it!"

Who embodied Buddhism for you?

His Holiness the Dalai Lama most of all, but Geshe Wangyal was the first one. He was a "geshe," a doctor of theology, whom I met in 1963 in New Jersey. Still earlier than that, when His Holiness the Dalai Lama made his way out of Tibet into India, I sent a telegram asking Ben Gurion to offer him sanctuary. He didn't, and it's a pity. But I had the sense that that would have been really important.

So, when in 1963 I went to that lamasery in New Jersey and I met Geshe Wangyal and sat with him and talked, I suggested to him then that we might have something to share with the Tibetans on surviving in the diaspora. It took about thirty years before that became a program, and that was important because they needed first to handle their own simple survival. But now this dialogue is happening on surviving outside the homeland in many places, and they have learned from us about summer camps and so on and so forth. Of course, on our side, we have learned from them some important things about meditation.

Has Buddhism had any influence upon your ideas about mentoring?
I saw you on television discussing your work in mentoring, and I thought this was wonderful.

Hmmm. I'm smiling, you know. I tell you, if I had a flower to hand to you right now, I would do that. Yes, you see, it is this element of space in mentoring—the recognition that no one is really ahead. And the exchange is a two-way street in every moment.

I wish more stories would circulate about the Buddha. The ones that we have are, how would I say, teaching stories that so rush to make a point that they don't want to tarry around the heart. But there are some wonderful stories around, especially in the Zen places. Stories like "Nan-chuan Kills the Cat":

> The priest Nan-chuan found monks of the eastern and western halls arguing about a cat. He held up the cat and said, "Everyone! If you can say something, I will spare this cat. If you can't say anything, I will cut off its head." No one could say a word, so Nan-chuan cut the cat into two.
>
> That evening, Chao-chou returned from outside and Nan-chuan told him what happened. Chao-chou removed a sandal from his foot, put it on his head, and walked out.

Nan-chuan said, "If you had been there, the cat would have been spared."[1]

In Hillel and Shammai [influential Rabbis of the first century C.E.], too, going back to the Mishnah time, the same kind of stories exist. How about I put it this way? The martial art of mentoring deserves to be written up as a book. Just as in *aikido,* you take a person's question seriously, and the energy in that question already has the answer.

THE IMPACT OF BUDDHISM

SHEILA PELTZ WEINBERG

BETWEEN THE AGES of nine and seventeen, I was a very pious Jew. I don't think I have ever again succeeded in having the certainty I then possessed about God's presence in my life or the ability to connect with God through prayer and the observance of commandments. I wasn't raised as an Orthodox Jew. In fact, while my parents did attend a Conservative synagogue and keep a kosher home, they were not Sabbath observant. In those years of religious fervor, I would go to synagogue on the Sabbath by myself while my parents were in their respective retail carpet and linoleum stores in the Bronx. Saturday was a big day for business in those days when everything was still closed on Sunday.

Unbeknownst to me, the kids in the neighborhood used to refer to me as the "little rabbi." This was long before women could even imagine thinking about wanting to become rabbis. My greatest religious inspiration and motivation came from Camp Ramah. I attended this Jewish educational and Hebrew-speaking camp every summer from the time I was nine until I graduated from high school. I met the most extraordinary teachers at Ramah. They inspired me to be passionate about Hebrew language, Bible, and everything connected to the history of the Jewish people. I was taught to grieve the loss of the Jews in the Holocaust as my personal tragedy and to experience the newly independent state of Israel as my personal triumph. My own life in the Bronx—living as an only child (my sister was much older than I and married very young) in a landscape of six-story brick apartment houses as far as the eye could see, with two parents working six days a week in the floor covering business—was easily subsumed in the dramatic, colorful, heroic life of the Jewish people I learned about at Ramah. I fervently believed that God wanted me to be righteous and to lead my people to a life of purity and goodness. I believed that God called us to a life of justice and compassion, healing the sick and freeing the bound.

The fact that Camp Ramah was in the country was very important. (Connecticut was indeed the beginning of the wilderness.) It was the only time I got to see hills covered with grass, shady, leafy trees—and our very own lake. I got to swim, dance, and canoe in wondrous ways that made me feel good to be alive in my young, energetic body. I associated all this fun, goodness, and delight with Judaism and with God. Somehow it was all of one piece—at least in camp. There were the friendships and the summer romances, the study with brilliant teachers, the moral demands, the identification with the land in all its dimensions—body, earth, the Zionist dream. I was willing to do whatever was necessary to find my place in that vision of wholeness.

I start a story of my connection to Buddhism as a practicing Jew with these memories because my life has been in some ways a series of moments when this vision of wholeness comes into focus. It is then that I am young again. I am connected in body, heart, mind, and spirit. I understand what is being asked of me. The teachings shine. I am part of something great, holy, and luminous. The moments don't last, but they move me on and sustain my hope and courage to live this life.

Many things shattered the wholeness of Camp Ramah. When I went to Israel in 1962, I realized there was no one practicing anything like what I understood as Judaism. People were either totally secular, ridiculing ritual and practice, or extremely orthodox, making me wear long sleeves and long stockings on the hot Jerusalem summer days. Meanwhile, it was the middle sixties in America. The Vietnam War and the Civil Rights movement called for moral audacity, and there were very few religious Jewish leaders who were marching and shouting. (Abraham Joshua Heschel was a solitary voice in those days.) Feminism had yet to break through to the Jewish world. I didn't yet have the questions, but I felt something was not right. The boys in my cohort from camp and school were going to be groomed to be rabbis. Meanwhile, my teachers told me I could marry a rabbi or become a Hebrew schoolteacher.

My first encounter with Buddhism actually came right before the sources of internal and external stability started to unravel. I read *Siddhartha* by Herman Hesse. All I remember is that I felt sure it was the most important book I would ever read in my life. When I went on my first date with the boy I would eventually marry, I loaned him that book. I knew that this would bind us together eternally. Soon after, when I was a sophomore at the University of Chicago (I transferred there from City College to get away from New York, my parents, the stifling quality of my life), I chose to study Indian Civilization as a year-long course. I read Buddhist and Hindu texts in their primary sources. I was intrigued, but it was purely intellectual and had no manifestation in community or practice.

Things in my life changed radically. One summer I tutored disadvantaged kids in New York City instead of going to Camp Ramah. I stopped being an observant Jew. I was lured by broader horizons. I got arrested at Columbia in 1968. I got married and we joined the Peace Corps. I lived in Israel as a secular Jew. God, religion, and spirituality had little place in my life for a decade. The search for a sense of wholeness can lead us in varied directions. We can imagine that one passion, person, place, or project is the whole. We can give ourselves over to these powers and mistake our relationship with them for a connection with life. It is a subtle skill to disentangle what motivates our choices. Are we seeking escape from pain or are we seeking serenity and peace? Are we foolish thrill seekers or are we people of courage and commitment? Are we pleasing others in the spirit of kindness and love or in the search for approval and fear of rejection? In retrospect, I was an unmoored Jew looking for a safe harbor. I was also a pretty confused young woman in a lot of emotional pain.

During this period I was introduced to a group run by an extraordinary philosophy teacher, David Brahinsky. David and his wife Naomi
were friends of ours. We had children the same age. He knew that I was
searching. First he encouraged me to read a book by Ouspensky called
In Search of the Miraculous, in which he writes about his teacher Gurdjieff.
I was blown away. The book awakened the part of my being that was
hungry for meaning and connection with the infinite. The meetings I
attended, led by David, were even more remarkable. I sat in an old barn
with twenty strangers and felt a presence of something hard to describe.
David taught about the difference between essence and personality and
the possibility that reality or truth was much more layered, dynamic, and
profound than the external levels of our lives. My experience of being
in the group was vastly different than reading a book. I actually felt that
I had an essence that was pure of personality, unconfused, and free of
fear, turmoil, and sadness. In many ways David was my first Dharma
teacher. His very being transmitted the teaching. The group also did spiritual practices together, consisting mostly of meditative movement and
dance. David spoke a lot about waking up from our sleep of unaware-
ness, about not identifying with every feeling, thought, and role. He
taught liberation.

Although I was in a very dark period of my life, I felt certain that I had
found my own purpose. I wanted to embody these teachings and teach
others. I was prepared to devote time and energy to this work. Then I
realized I had to do it as a Jew. Suddenly shock waves ran through my
body. I could become a rabbi and teach about waking up in the language
of my own ancestors. I knew in my heart that these teachings could be
found in Judaism despite the fact that the local synagogue felt utterly
devoid of spirit to me. One Yom Kippur eve, in fact, I walked out in the
middle of services and drove to David's group to be in an environment
of true longing for transformation, of working on oneself, as we called
the process of liberation.

I started reading voraciously. I read Holocaust literature mostly to
know the mind of the victim, the perpetrator, the bystander, and the

survivor as they each manifest in my own mind and life. I read Abraham
Joshua Heschel and Martin Buber and Mordecai Kaplan. I was quite sure
they understood about waking up. I also learned that the more liberal
rabbinical seminaries were now admitting women and ordaining them
as rabbis. I decided to apply.

When I arrived in Philadelphia in 1977, I was a single parent with a
seven-year-old and a two-and-a-half-year-old. I ended up deferring for
five years my admission to the Reconstructionist Rabbinical College.
During those years I worked on various campuses in Philadelphia, organ-
izing Jewish students and arranging programs for them. I found some
wonderful treasures in Philadelphia in those days. I joined the Weaver's
Way Food Co-op and the Germantown Minyan at the same time. They
are both incredible institutions. One feeds the body and the other feeds
the soul. The Food Co-op is, of course, owned by its members, who
each volunteer a certain number of hours a year to keep it going.

The *minyan* was a group of Jews that had no rabbi. The members took
turns leading services and preparing teachings. They happened to be
very learned and creative teachers for the most part—so it worked. It
was there that I saw a woman wear a *tallith* and read from the Torah for
the first time. It was there that I saw people talking Torah from their
hearts each Shabbat. People shared very personal stories and then related
them to the process of spiritual discovery that they understood to be
unfolding in the reading for that particular day. The energy was alive.
People took risks to tell the truth to each other and themselves. Not
surprisingly, many of the founders of similar groups known as *havurot*
were "graduates" of Camp Ramah, finding their way back to wholeness.
I was home.

My first week on the job at Temple University, I saw a poster that
advertised "Spiritually-Oriented High Holy Days" at a place called Fellowship Farm with Rabbi Zalman Schachter and B'Nai Or. I had only the
vaguest idea of who this rabbi was. The idea of spending my first Rosh
Hashanah and Yom Kippur in my new life on a farm sounded good to me.
Fellowship Farm sounded good. Spiritual sounded good. I went with

my young children. It was an amazing experience. Zalman was the embodiment of my understanding of Judaism as a way to work on one-self. I found myself crying, laughing, dancing, and singing from my heart. Earth and trees surrounded me. I don't remember any specific teachings, but I do remember feeling filled with life. I fantasized about introduc-ing David to Zalman. I glanced through a window into a reconciled mind, body, heart, and spirit. I glimpsed a religious life that could mat-ter deeply and that could help shape the scattered fragments of my life into a unity.

The other thing that was so amazing about Zalman, who then showed up as a regular at the Germantown Minyan, was his willingness to draw upon any spiritual tradition, as well as his seemingly bottomless knowl-edge of Judaism and all world religions. The point was getting closer to spirit, liberation, and loving. Zalman used to say we need to take the freeze-dried crystals of Judaism and mix them with the pure water of our intention, our creativity, our very lives, so that we can be nurtured and nourish others. I saw and heard things in liturgy and text that I had never imagined were there. My thirsty soul drank deeply.

During those years I began to meet rabbinical students, students of Mordecai Kaplan, who were also engaged in translating God language into the spiritual currency of our times. How do we live in two civi-lizations? It was wondrous to be honest for the first time about what we really thought, not only about God, Torah, and the chosen people, but also about subjects previously only whispered in Jewish circles, like homosexuality and the rights of the Palestinians.

It was in Philadelphia, over twenty years ago, that I first put together these three words: spirituality, feminism, and Judaism. I signed up for a workshop with that title, offered by Judith Plaskow. All my friends made me promise that I would tell them what happened there. So after I got home, rather than having thirty separate lunches, we all gathered in a large living room to talk and to plan to talk some more. We, Jewish women, were filling in the silences in the tradition. We were emerging from the white spaces in the Torah. My heart was bursting from recognizing my own story in the singing and sobbing voices of my new sisters. We were daring to say that our lives were central to our tradition, to our people. We were moving from the margins to the center, holding one another as we took each scary new step. Coming in our wake would be many others from the margins of our culture—gays and lesbians, bisexual and transgendered Jews, Jews by choice, differently-abled Jews, non-white, non-Ashkenazi Jews, young Jews, old Jews, poor Jews.

I was fortunate to be one of the founders of a remarkable group of women called B'not Esh. We pledged ourselves to a yearly five-day gathering where we would share our lives and our search for spiritual meaning as Jews and as feminists. We grappled with the thorniest issues— sexuality, class, work, power, relationships, and identity. We pushed each other to go deeper and deeper. We also sang and celebrated together in ways we had never envisioned. We encouraged each other to tell the truth, even if it was not so pleasant or comfortable or complete. It was hard and beautiful, and we all changed in ways we could not have predicted.

The willingness to risk honesty and openness marked the culture in Jewish feminist circles, as well as in experimental *minyanim,* and in the various efforts at greater diversity and inclusivity. We were doing a lot of personal stretching to encompass and enlarge our definitions of self, other, and community. We confronted new models of family—single parent, lesbian, blended—and we looked to new models of religious authority and interpretation within structures that were totally lay-led and democratic. Sometimes it felt like the stretching would rip us open. How could we keep expanding the container? How could we grow our own hearts in patience, tolerance, and compassion for self and other? How could we balance truth telling and loving acceptance in one life, one group or institution?

All that I have written is a prelude to my first encounter with Buddhist meditation. Still, it would not be complete without writing about something else enormously important and extremely sensitive. My search for wholeness had taken many side excursions since Camp

Ramah. One was my tendency to fall in love with a man that I would then enthrone as my god to be worshipped and served. I mistook merger with the human beloved as a route to merger with the Divine. Relationship was often an escape from being alone with myself—a way of being okay, proving my worthiness, meeting the expectations of my mother and her society, and stilling the anxiety that hounded my days and nights.

While still in my teens, I found a reliable and trustworthy relationship of a different kind, one that deepened and grew as I got older. It was always there—through my marriage, through other romantic connections, through the early years in Philadelphia, and ultimately even through rabbinical school. It was also part of my search for wholeness. It filled a desire for release, relief, pacification—a ceasefire in the mind and heart. I am referring to my love affair with alcohol and marijuana. To ignore this topic would leave a gaping hole in the story of the impact of Buddhism on Judaism in my life.

Both my drinking and pot smoking began in great innocence. They induced sociability, made me less afraid of people. They were entertainment and amusement. As time went by they became my best friends. I was a daily drinker and frequent pot smoker for many years. I tried to keep these habits hidden and explained them to myself as a healthy way of coping with a difficult life as a single mom, or as a way of gaining spiritual insights, or as a way of mellowing out the rough edges of my slightly hysterical temperament. Despite the fact that I was engaging in circles of truth telling, I kept this secret from others—and its gravity from myself.

I continued drinking and smoking pot even after I gave up cigarettes in my first year of rabbinical school. The school met in a new building that was a nonsmoking zone, and we smokers had to stand outside during breaks to indulge our habits. I was overwhelmed with shame. "How could I be a rabbi and exert so little control over myself?" I would ask myself. I did stop, thanks to a program sponsored by the Seventh Day Adventists that instilled terror at the consequences of smoking and relied on frequent prayer. My drinking and pot smoking, however, continued for another four and a half years.

I don't know whether I could have stopped if alcohol and drugs hadn't betrayed me first. They stopped working. I was as paranoid and anxious "under the influence" as not. I was always worried about hiding my habit, especially from my kids. I hated myself for so many things—for my lack of control, the shame of my habit, my falseness, my dependency, my fear of stopping. I couldn't find respite from the shame.

During that period, I spent a year of rabbinical school in Israel with my kids. My best friend while there was another single mom with three kids close in age to mine. She was also an American, an artist and a hippie of sorts. I was still drinking and smoking pot. She meditated, and would go off for ten-day silent retreats, which I thought was astonishing. It stayed in my mind. Once, I contacted her and asked if I could attend a retreat with her. After years of study, reading, verbiage, I welcomed the idea of silence. I also figured that I wouldn't be able to drink or drug during the retreat and that that could be the beginning of a sober me. However, on the way there, I stopped to visit a man I had a crush on. He encouraged me to spend the ten days with him rather than put myself through what definitely sounded like an ordeal. I smoked a joint to ponder the options. It wasn't too hard to make a decision.

It was another year before I got sober and another four years until I made it to a meditation retreat. Overcoming this powerful physical, mental, and emotional addiction turned out to be another crucial turning point in my life—the most important one of all. I can't even imagine my life today if I were not sober. There would be no hook upon which to hang spiritual practice and meditation. They would be mere abstractions. The resources that helped in my recovery continue to sustain me. They include fearless truth telling, spiritual community, an ongoing moral inventory, prayer and meditation, taking responsibility for my thoughts, feelings, and actions, and an ongoing practice of amends making, forgiveness, and returning to my intention. Ironically, the misguided search for wholeness that fueled my drinking and drugging eventually led me to a more wholesome way of life suffused with a practice based upon telling the truth in order to become more awake, conscious, and free.

My life in Philadelphia was good in many ways. I served a suburban congregation as the rabbi. At noon I would leave my office and drive to the nearby church for spiritual succor with a group of recovering drunks. It was great to be with people from varied traditions, classes, and backgrounds and to share such a profound common language and experience. We just listened to each other. It wasn't so different from my women's group or from the *minyan*—the deep listening, the honesty, the willingness to risk closeness, the openness to transformation, the silences in between that formed a container, a resting place to hold all that was hard, unknown, difficult, painful, and beautiful.

The first year that I was sober I reconnected with a man I had dated in high school. He had been divorced; he was a professor and the father of two boys. We felt like home together. It was miraculous. Soon after we reconnected, he was diagnosed with kidney cancer. He told me I didn't need to stay with him now because that was not what we had bargained for. I thought the opposite. Why had I come back into his life except to give him the love and hope he needed to fight the illness and triumph? We read Bernie Siegel's *Love, Medicine and Miracles*. We were sure he would be an extraordinary patient. He was. And he died. I was completely overwhelmed with grief. He died two days after the first anniversary of my sobriety. I was held through the pain by friends and strangers and my own ability to pray, to know it would change, to be with what was there. I also went on healing retreats at Kripalu with the yogis and at the Abode of the Message with the Sufis. There was no comparable Jewish place in those days. Or maybe I just wanted to do the healing away from the Jewish places where I would be known and recognized as a rabbi—someone who helped others but didn't need help herself.

Months later I received a note from two friends from B'not Esh urging me to consider applying for the job as rabbi of the Jewish Community of Amherst. The only thing I knew about Western Massachusetts

was the Berkshires, and Kripalu. I loved the idea of being near the beautiful mountains. I was open to moving away from the place of my mourning. I was ready to consider moving on. My daughter was in college and
my son was ready to begin high school. It was the moment for a change.

My son Ezra and I came to Amherst for an interview. I loved it. It
was quaint New England in snowy December. The head of the search
committee was an intensely spirited man named Ted Slovin. Aside from
being a founder of the synagogue he was also a board member at Insight
Meditation Society in Barre, Massachusetts. "You realize, Rabbi," Ted
told me, "that we are down the road from one of the premier Buddhist
meditation centers in the country. What an opportunity for you to have
this resource for your own spiritual renewal! Amherst, you understand,"
Ted said in a dramatic way, "is midway between Kripalu and IMS." I
recalled my missed opportunity several years earlier. I was now even
more curious about meditation, as it was always mentioned as a com-
ponent of one's recovery.

I arrived in Amherst in the summer of 1989. The following summer
I registered for a ten-day retreat at IMS. The teacher was Christopher
Titmuss. I had a roommate who was not particularly respectful of the
vow of silence; I also had a friend who arrived on retreat in the middle
and invited me for two long walks. Otherwise, I was alone with my own
mind. Sitting, walking, sitting, walking, eating, doing my yogi job—pot
washing—sitting, walking, sitting, walking and then finally the evening,
when Christopher would speak, and there would be some relief from my
own mind. Then sleep and dreams and getting up early and beginning
again. The sitting was painful. I had pain in my back, in my neck, and in
my shoulders most of the time. I was sleepy a lot. I was distracted most
of the time. I couldn't pay attention to the directions. I felt hopeless, useless, inferior, a fraud as a spiritual person. I was certain I was a failure,
an imposter.

Despite all of this, the teachings were incredible. I felt as if the teachers had been in my mind throughout the day. Their words created a sense
of spaciousness. The process of returning again and again to the simple

object of attention—the breath, the step, the pot I was scrubbing—was expanding the dimensions of my mind. All the painful thoughts, the judgments, the fears, the endless desires for this or that to be different were loosening their grip.

I understood that the teachers were teaching Buddhism. The stories they told and the texts they cited were from the Buddhist tradition. At IMS, however, it was always very clear that no one was interested in your becoming a Buddhist. This was critical for me. As the days unfolded, I started to translate the teachings into a Jewish spiritual language. I understood the reference to suffering, craving, and the conditioned "I" that is always wanting attention and amusement as equivalent to the false gods and idolatry of Judaism. How indeed do we recognize and weed out idol worship from our own hearts? How do we end suffering? How do we heal the wounds that force the walls of separation to be erected that keep us from ourselves, others, life itself, or God? How do we see the transient and the fleeting and distinguish that from the eternal and enduring? How do we deal with our own destructive habits without destroying each other or ourselves? How do we recognize what is fantasy and what is truth? What are the stories that rule our lives? These are Buddhist questions, Jewish questions, recovery questions, human questions.

I was moved by the practice of mindfulness. My entire being was engaged. I saw how the stories in my mind proliferate. I saw that when I allow my attention to rest on sensation in the body, I see dynamism, change, and instability. Things become loose. I am less a victim. I open myself to the infinite power of pure awareness, the light of presence. I open to the nameless energy of life that just is. I open to compassion. In Jewish language, I open to God's love, the power that heals, forgives, comforts, and—through the pure act of presence—ultimately transforms. I see infinite references to this process of liberation in Jewish prayer, in the texts of Torah, and in the practices of a Jewish life. I experience how hatred and contention lock in an experience and deepen suffering. I understand through attentive patience and self honesty that the more open I am to what is arising in this moment, the more balanced and clear my mind is and the more able I am to make wise and compassionate choices. The more *shalom* (wholeness or peace) is created, the more *tikkun* (mending the shattered and divisive nature of reality) is achieved.

The teachings that I heard at this first retreat have been reinforced at many other retreats with many other brilliant teachers over the last thirteen years, as well as through my own regular sitting practice. The teachings and the practice of mindfulness have entered my life to inspire, sustain, and strengthen me. I now teach mindfulness to Jews, using the language of Jewish story and symbol. The key factor is that people are given a chance to see for themselves the nature of their minds, to know impermanence personally, to see the insubstantiality of the separate self, to experience the interconnection of all beings, and to know viscerally both the causes of suffering and the end of suffering. Mindfulness practice contains the same principles that so moved me in David's circle, in the women's group, in recovery, and in Judaism. The principles are easy to articulate and difficult to practice. We ask ourselves to tell the truth; to be engaged with a community of seekers and practitioners; to keep returning to our intention; to develop tolerance for the other, the different, the unknown, the unpleasant, the frightening; to develop curiosity and a keen desire and ability to listen. Listen! Listen! *Shma Yisrael*—"Listen up, Israel"—is the passionate Jewish affirmation of unity and interconnection.

The impact of Buddhism on my life as a Jew has been to give me a new lens with which to interpret and understand the sacred teachings of my people and more deeply apply those teachings to my life. To what end? To live with more awareness, more compassion, more wisdom, and more love. I have discovered that we cultivate wholeness when we learn to pay awakened attention without pushing away, grabbing, or fleeing. This leads us to a contentment that transcends the vagaries of changing phenomena, the contentedness of the psalmist who wrote, "Ashrei Yoshvei Vaytecha"— "Happy are those who dwell in Your House." The house of this body-mind and the house of life in this complex human reality and the house of this struggling planet can all be embraced when we sit down and partake of the infinite clarity of awareness.

I would like to close with a poem I wrote during a month-long silent retreat at the Gaia House in England. It is based on a Jewish teaching about the two sets of tablets Moses received. Upon descending from Sinai and seeing the Israelites worshipping the golden calf, Moses smashed the first set. Later he was given a second set, and both sets are placed in the Holy Ark together. The poem was my way of expressing the insight I received and keep receiving.

They all dwell together in the Holy Ark
The whole tablets and the broken pieces
The fear, the greed, the envy,
The judgment, the hunger,
The rage.
All these jagged slabs
All of this, too—
The wanting, the bragging, the dreaming,
The impatience, the intolerance.
It is all here.
In a human package.
Along with the courage, the love, the generosity, the energy, the joy, the wisdom,
*   the tenderness.*
All there. All mixed together.
A human being
Separate and unique.
Related and the same as you and me.
But the broken bits have no enduring substance.
They soon turn to dust.
And the whole tablets are the ark,
Contained in and containing all.

Part Two:

Christian Voices

———————————

CONTACTS WITH BUDDHISM:
A Christian Confession
JOHN B. COBB, JR.

I GREW UP in Japan as the son of Christian missionaries. No doubt that shaped my largely unconscious views of both Christianity and Buddhism. I remember no hostile or pejorative comments about Buddhism on the part of my parents or other missionaries. It was little discussed. What was important was Japanese culture, which everyone knew was influenced by Buddhism. But sorting out the various influences was viewed as an academic exercise.

To me, Buddhism suggested serene temples surrounded by large trees. It also suggested superstitious clapping of hands and ringing of bells to get the attention of some god, and the tying of paper prayer slips to the branches of trees. And then there were the Buddha statues of all sorts, along with fearsome demonic figures in some temple gates. I had little knowledge of what all that meant, and chiefly viewed those things as a tourist would. I was vaguely aware of Buddhism as an influence in the arts that we all appreciated and admired, but to which I paid little attention as a boy. I was aware of Buddhist holidays with their special celebrations. In the most interesting of these, the spirits of the ancestors were invited back and then sent away again in little paper boats. In short, I had no contact with Buddhism as a sophisticated religious practice.

Of course, I knew Japanese who were Buddhists. Usually, I did not know that they were Buddhists, and it was not particularly important to them either. They were Shinto and Confucian as well. Only occasionally was I aware of Buddhism in a more significant way.

Since both of my parents were expected to teach and engage in other missional activities on a full-time basis, we had a live-in cook. She was much loved by all of us as a part of the family. I remember my father once talking about her faith. She had become very attracted to Christianity, he reported, but her husband had died a Buddhist. She was afraid that if she converted, she would end up in a different heaven from his. Of course, my father did not believe in separate heavens for Buddhists and Christians, but he reported her decision with respect and without condescension. Nevertheless, I suspect that the story strengthened my sense that Buddhism was a somewhat superstitious cultural inheritance toward which one should be appreciative but which could not be taken seriously as an option for contemporary Japan.

I remember another incident. Japanese residential areas are usually very quiet. But once a week there was an extended period of noise from a nearby house. I asked my father about it. He told me that it was a Buddhist religious group. What were they doing? I asked. My father thought they were chanting. Today I can imagine retrospectively that this was a fine group of people with admirable religious purposes. But at the time I was not impressed. If that was Buddhism, I was not interested.

Christianity, on the other hand, was serious business. Obviously my parents took it seriously, and so did the other missionaries who constituted a good portion of our adult acquaintances. Many of the Japanese I knew were strongly committed converts to Christianity. Becoming a Christian was a major decision that affected the way one lived in quite apparent ways. Sometimes it was costly in relation to one's family. Most of the other Japanese I knew may have been vaguely Buddhist, but insofar as they considered religious commitment seriously, it was Christianity about which they thought.

In retrospect, having since met so many serious Japanese Buddhists, I have sometimes wondered how it was possible to live in Japan in the years between the two world wars and be so oblivious to Buddhism. The answer, I think, is that many Japanese were almost as oblivious. In the process of urbanization, many Japanese had left their village Buddhism behind. The system of family-owned temples made it difficult for temples to follow shifts in population. If we had lived in a rural area, we would no doubt have been more aware of the social importance of the local temple. But even then we might not have sensed that Buddhism was a body of wisdom that challenged Christianity and could evoke the deepest loyalty and devotion. Few Japanese thought in those terms. Even today the great majority of Japanese students in colleges and universities do not identify themselves as Buddhists, even if they know that their families have an ancestral tie to a Buddhist temple.

Since World War II, religious life and organizations have been far more visible in Japan. But this is chiefly because of the new religions. Some of them are explicitly Buddhist, and most are predominantly so. Christian missionaries in this period would be likely to recognize these as competitors in the quest for attention and members. In terms of membership, many of them have been far more successful than Christianity. Some of these groups existed in the prewar period, but they were far less visible then.

Japanese nationalism was an important factor leading up to World War II. As foreigners in Japan, we were aware of it and critical of it. It had a religious character, which Christians opposed. But we named it Shinto rather than Buddhism. Buddhism seemed irrelevant to the political life that eventually forced us to leave Japan.

I am writing of this at some length, because people sometimes assume that my interest in Buddhism is connected with my growing up in Japan. There may be some connection. I may have sought out Japanese conversation partners more than I would otherwise have done. But beyond that, I cannot discern that childhood in Japan contributed positively to my appreciation of Buddhism.

I had no further occasion to respond to Buddhism until I was a student at Chicago in the years after World War II. I still had no contact with serious Buddhists. But I was drawn to Charles Hartshorne as my teacher. Hartshorne had come to his philosophical ideas quite independently of Buddhism, but he had realized the remarkable similarity between them, especially in the understanding of the self. He called his own doctrine "Buddhisto-Christian." Still, this did not lead me far toward a serious encounter with Buddhist thought for myself, especially since the spiritual-existential conclusions Hartshorne drew from the doctrine were answers to questions as formulated in the Western philosophical tradition rather than Buddhist ones.

Both Hartshorne and my theology teachers introduced me to Alfred North Whitehead. Whitehead had also come to his Buddhist-like doctrines without special influence from Buddhism, and his religious vision and attitudes were quite different from Buddhism. Indeed, he occasionally spoke of Buddhism somewhat harshly. His knowledge of it was quite indirect. Nevertheless, he recognized its importance. In *Religion in the Making,* he made the telling observation that there are three great spiritual forces in the contemporary world: science, Christianity, and Buddhism. The reversal of spiritual decay would not occur, he thought, until these three mutually informed one another and developed a more adequate religious vision.

That comment stayed with me and began to reshape the attitudes toward Buddhism formed in childhood. I was already engaged in an effort to integrate my Christian faith with a worldview informed by the natural sciences. Now I realized that there was a major additional source of needed wisdom. That awareness opened me to new possibilities, although I did not immediately pursue them seriously. I was too preoccupied with relating my own faith to the intellectual culture of modernity.

Another influence at Chicago was a fellow student, Tom Altizer. Tom's theological and spiritual world was quite remote from the Chicago theology in which I was immersed. But it was clear to me, then as now, that Altizer must be taken seriously. He thought about his Christian faith in the context of the intellectual and religious history of the world, and for him Buddhism was the most profound and challenging "other" to Christianity.

For those who know Altizer, I need hardly say that what "Buddhism" meant to him had little to do with what it had meant to me as a child, or with what it meant to Hartshorne or Whitehead. It was above all Buddhist negation of the world that fascinated Altizer as he struggled with his own deep alienation. I experienced Altizer even then as—quite unlike myself—a true *Homo religiosus,* and I was convinced that he was attuned to a deep level of the meaning of religious ideas and images, even if scholars might point out "errors" in his interpretations. My interest in Buddhism was heightened through him, first at Chicago, and later when we were colleagues at Emory University.

I spent my first sabbatical (after ten years of teaching) at Drew University. That year there was a lecture series on psychotherapy in its relation to religious thought. A series of psychiatrists spoke, and I was startled to find that almost all of them turned to Zen for insight and support. Clearly, Buddhism was alive and well in that field! Again and again in later years I have found some of the most interesting thinkers in a variety of fields to be influenced by Buddhism.

Claremont at last offered me the opportunity to engage seriously with living Buddhists. This was especially because of the presence there of the Blaisdell Institute. An earlier, farsighted president of Pomona College had looked toward the day when the Pacific Rim would become the center of world events, and he wanted to prepare for it. The institute that bore his name was the chief expression of that vision. It brought to Claremont for extended stays both faculty and students from across the Pacific, chiefly from Japan. Many of them were committed Buddhists. The two with whom I became best acquainted were Masao Abe and Ryusei Takeda. My serious education in Buddhism had begun.

In 1973, it became possible to establish in Claremont a Center for Process Studies. My hope was to explore a variety of fields and topics from a Whiteheadian point of view. It made sense, in view of what I had learned from Whitehead years earlier, that the first two conferences were on the natural sciences (evolutionary biology) and Buddhism (primarily Japanese Zen forms). The question in the first conference was whether a Whiteheadian approach to the place of subjectivity in nature could fit with the evidence from biology and help to bridge the gap

between the natural sciences and understanding of the human. The purpose of the second conference was to ask whether Whitehead could help
Westerners to understand and appropriate the insights of Buddhism.

There were a number of fine Buddhist scholars at this second conference, but the one whose formulations most intrigued me was Masao
Abe. I could understand much of his critique of Western ways of thinking from my Whiteheadian perspective, but there were features of his
more positive formulations that were both fascinating and frustrating.

In one sense, I was not sure that he wanted to be understood conceptually. The point of Zen is, in part, to frustrate such a goal. But one
should at least be able to understand the purpose of such frustrating and
to gain some clue as to where that frustrating was to lead. At that conference I had a number of "aha!" experiences and a breakthrough into
such understanding as I have attained. I have attended numerous conferences dealing with Buddhism since then, but this was for me the most
pivotal.

For the most part, I concluded that the basic concepts with which
Abe worked could be translated into Whiteheadian terms, and that at
that level I could understand them. On the other hand, Abe revealed
meanings and implications of the acceptance of those concepts, or rather
of *living into* them, that had never occurred to me, nor, I think, to my
Western process teachers. These were, of course, for Abe, far more
important than the concepts themselves, attachment to which could
block the realization for whose sake they were developed. In my apprehension of Buddhism I felt so near and yet so far! Largely, I have
remained there.

Abe saw, I think, that my failure to move into the deeper spiritual-
existential dimensions of Buddhism stemmed from the fact that my
understanding and acceptance of his central concept of *pratitya samutpada,* often translated "dependent origination," did not lead me to give
up belief in God. I affirmed that God is also an instance of dependent
origination. My spiritual orientation was to that instance. That orientation is, of course, Christian and not Buddhist, at least not in the Zen

form. Abe tried to persuade me that this integration of Buddhist and Christian emphases was intellectually unacceptable. It showed, to him, that I had not really understood *pratitya samutpada*. In the sense in which to "understand" is to appropriate and realize its spiritual existential meanings, he was no doubt correct, at least insofar as those meanings are the ones drawn from the doctrine by Zen Buddhists.

Conceptually, the only error he could point out was my refusal to acknowledge that, from the deepest point of view, relations to the past and to the future are the same. I could see nothing in the reasoning in favor of the acceptance of the doctrine of dependent origination that led to that conclusion. Insofar as Zen spirituality is geared in this way to the ultimate unreality of time, I was not eager to assimilate it. It seemed to me to undercut the commitment to history that is central to my own, biblical, piety. I could appreciate the complementary contribution of Buddhism as I had come to understand it through Abe, but I knew that my contribution would be from the Christian side, supplemented by the use of process conceptuality as a bridge to conceptual understanding.

Subsequently, I have come to realize that, just as there are many Christianities, so also there are many Buddhisms. The Zen depiction of Zen as the purest distillation of the Buddhist tradition is just that, the Zen depiction. That realization was both a relief and a disappointment. It meant that I could not rest in my partial acceptance and partial rejection of the Buddhism that I had encountered. I needed to become aware of some of its other forms. Of these, the first I met in any depth was Japanese Pure Land.

Ryusei Takeda spent several years as a student and as a scholarly visitor in Claremont. Whereas in my relations with Abe, I was always the student, even if an argumentative one, in my relations with Takeda, I was initially the teacher but soon also the student. He wanted to understand process philosophy and Christianity. I wanted to understand Pure Land Buddhism. He was excellent in both roles.

I became aware that I was not the only one who tended to think of Zen as the purest form of Buddhism. Some contemporary leaders of the

Pure Land movement minimized its differences from Zen. But Takeda was interested in those differences and in affirming them. This led to a significant contrast with Abe, who grew up in Pure Land and was dramatically, even painfully, converted to Zen by Shin'ichi Hisamatsu. Sometimes Takeda, Abe, and I had rich three-way conversations.

For Pure Land Buddhism, the notions of grace and faith—so central to my Christian piety—are important. The participant looks to the "Other" to bring her or him to the ultimate goal of realization. This Other—Amida, or Amida's Primal Vow to save all sentient beings—is imaged quasi-theistically. Although many Pure Land Buddhists continue to demythologize in such a way as to bring their tradition closer to Zen, it is also possible to relate the object of faith and source of grace very closely to the Primordial Nature of God in Whitehead, which, like the Primal Vow, is both transcendent and immanent as the working of saving grace. The reality of Pure Land Buddhism suggests that Abe's view of the utter incompatibility of the Buddhist vision with any kind of theism is exaggerated. When the theism in question makes much of grace, this Christian is reassured that the basic Buddhist vision, although very different from the traditional Christian one, is not in contradiction to a reformulated Christianity. Buddhism and Christianity may be complementary rather than contradictory, in which case Whitehead's vision of the joint contributions of science, Christianity, and Buddhism to the spiritual life of the world may not be impossible.

My experience with these Japanese Buddhists had left me with the concern that in both Zen and Pure Land, though especially in Zen, there was a detachment from the real issues of history and thus little place for social ethics. For me, these issues were even more important than the interior and private ones, which seemed to preoccupy Buddhism. I realized also that some contemporary representatives of the two traditions, including both Abe and Takeda, shared my concern. It was my great privilege to supervise one disciple of each of these men in dissertations on this subject. It turned out that one can develop a social ethic from each of these traditions, that the ways of doing so are quite distinct, and that the whole process in both traditions differs dramatically from the Christian one. The limited development of social ethics in these forms of Japanese Buddhism does not imply that central commitments preclude it, only that the necessary work is just now being done. My consciousness was also raised with respect to the dangers and limitations of the traditional Christian approach and the possibility of learning better thinking and practice from Buddhists.

My education in Buddhist social ethics has gone furthest by contacts in the Theravada tradition. I was prepared to appreciate this by my own conversion in 1969 to the recognition that our whole Western, and now global, history is on a trajectory that leads to destruction. I did not come to that realization through my Buddhist friends, but it liberated me from any Western notion of progress and opened my eyes to the extremely ambiguous results of the Christian understanding of history. I turned against the whole scheme of growth-oriented economic development. I tried to renew the traditional Christian critique of greed, but this is not easy when the whole structure of global society is based on greed as a desideratum.

Looking around the world for positive models, I found some promise in Sri Lanka. This primarily Buddhist country had opted not to take part in the dominant model of development. It emphasized meeting basic human needs instead of economic growth. The result was that, while it ranked very low in terms of per capita income, it ranked quite high on the Physical Quality of Life Index, which is intended to measure human well-being. Surely this is more important!

The effort to organize its social and economic life apart from the global trade and development system finally collapsed. The leaders knew that to stay out of the international system they must keep out the advertisements of international goods. They did not allow television in the country. When, later, they accepted the gift of a complete system from Japan, the handwriting was on the wall. One problem was that Sri Lanka provided free education through the university without changing from a Western educational system to a Buddhist one. The result was hundreds of thousands of persons educated away from Sri Lankan Buddhist villages and for life in a westernized country. More and more of the elite could not appreciate or accept the Buddhist reasons for refusing economic growth as a goal.

I had the opportunity to visit Sri Lanka briefly with Dr. Senanayeka as my host. He was a leader in a Buddhist political movement that wanted to restore Sri Lanka to the condition that British colonialism had destroyed. The people then had lived in self-sufficient villages, each with its irrigation pond and with water buffalo providing power, while the Buddhist temples had offered moral and cultural support for the peoples' life. It was hard to tell how much of this was nostalgia and how much could guide actual political and economic practice. But compared with the destructiveness of growth-oriented development, it was a moving vision.

I learned of the work of Sri Ariyaratne, the Buddhist Gandhi, who was implementing a program of bottom-up development but working outside of the political process. His movement paid a great deal of attention to the spiritual condition of its workers, having them spend much time in meditation. The goal was to still the ego so that their work in the villages would be done for the sake of the villagers.

I met Dr. Ariyaratne at a small international meeting in Rome, which was intended to bring religious perspectives to bear on development issues. The meeting was held under the auspices of an organization of former heads of state, chaired by Helmut Schmidt. Schmidt and all the others took the dominant development paradigm for granted. Only Ariyaratne spoke up in favor of the alternative, bottom-up approach, oriented not to growth but to the well-being of communities. I judged that my only useful role in the conference was to urge the former heads of state to listen to what Ariyaratne had to say. I am afraid they could not hear it. In any case, I was then, and am now, impressed that a Buddhist culture, despite its participation in the modern world, can give rise to so many sustained efforts to build a society on sufficiency rather than with the orientation toward endless growth that greed promotes.

The Tamil revolt has set back all such programs in Sri Lanka. Ariyaratne has made heroic efforts to express his Buddhist compassion by mediating that dispute, but to no avail. The Sri Lanka story is not a happy one, but it has shown me that Buddhist culture can produce and support a realistic vision of a Buddhist society that is quite different from the Western model.

I say "Western" rather than Christian, because the economic ideals that drive the Western world are not derivable from traditional Christian sources. Still, Christians have offered little resistance. Christian social ethics has not provided nearly as fundamental a critique of contemporary development practices as have Buddhists in Sri Lanka. No movement for an alternative society in the Christian world has had the staying power and effectiveness of Ariyaratne's Sarvodaya movement.

I do not think it is only Christian defensiveness that causes me to ask: Is the possibility of sustained popular resistance in Sri Lanka based on the influence of the Buddhist critique of craving, or is it due more to the fact that more of traditional society is intact? Of course, these two contributors may go together. Traditional society in Sri Lanka is deeply informed by Buddhist values, and these may have helped such a society to survive. But Buddhist teaching has not stemmed the tide altogether, and I am not sure there are instances of it turning the clock back. In urbanized Sri Lanka society, it is hard to generate support among Buddhists for a return to traditional society. My underlying question is whether Buddhists can contribute to reflection and action in the context of a nontraditional world.

For an answer to that question, I turn to Sulak Sivaraksa in Siam. I think I met him first at the Berkeley meeting of the International Buddhist-Christian theological encounter. Since then our paths have crossed frequently.

Sivaraksa is unwilling to call his nation Thailand, since it is the land not only of Thais, but of other people as well. He is a Buddhist thinker and activist who thinks and acts on the basis of Buddhist values in a largely post-traditional context. He has brought into being the worldwide movement of socially-engaged Buddhism. In Siam, he has certainly not stemmed the tide of growth and greed, but he has won some significant battles. He is a master of social analysis and of developing strategies responsive to social reality. It would be hard to find any spiritual leader in the Western world who has been equally successful in comparable struggles.

Sivaraksa identifies consumerism as the diametrical opposite to Buddhism. Consumerism cultivates desires for goods. It provides many goods but opposes any idea of sufficiency. Buddhism calls for the quieting of all craving and satisfaction in what is available. Sivaraksa hopes, through spiritual renewal and education, to slow and stop the growing dominance of consumerism as the religion of his people and of the world. Insofar as there is a mass following of Sivaraksa, it seems to depend on the presence in Siam of remnants of traditional society. Although he has many programs and institutions that are not part of that society, and these are doing great work, it is not clear that working against craving is very effective in the more modernized segments of society, even among serious Buddhists there.

If the direct application of Buddhist values to society depends on the survival of traditional society, then there are few places where this can work even now, and there are likely to be still fewer in the future. The most promising place is Bhutan, where the ruler has suggested making happiness rather than wealth the national goal. The question is whether even there the lure of possessions can be countered unless the awareness of these goods is blocked out by public policy. On the whole, it seems that in order to prevent or implement social change, there must be a combination of public policy and popular support.

There has been one other large ingredient in my encounter with Buddhists. This has been with intellectually sophisticated Euro-American converts to Buddhism. They are playing a growing role in American universities and in the wider culture. Many of them are involved in the movement of socially engaged Buddhism. In many instances they combine the best of Eastern and Western wisdom and spirituality. They combine analyses of power and how to organize and act with the egolessness that frees both analysis and action from distortion. If I were to name any one group whose analyses and actions I would most trust in this country today it would be these Western converts to Buddhism.

A disproportionate number of these intellectual converts, so far as my experience has gone, have become Tibetan Buddhists. Apparently the Tibetan teachers are unashamedly interested in the life of the mind as well as that of the spirit. They have cultivated rich traditions in Tibet for many centuries and, having been driven from their country, they are sharing their knowledge and wisdom widely. Their converts are a remarkable group. And I have been honored to know some of them.

I raise, nevertheless, a question about Tibetan history. Tibet seems to have been a country in which power was often in the hands of highly trained and highly committed Buddhists. It was largely isolated from the rest of the world, so that these people were free to implement their ideals. There are few other examples in history of such an opportunity. My question is, "What happened?" This is an honest question. If we universalize the values of the Western enlightenment, then our answer will be largely critical. The ruling monastic class exploited the peasants and treated them inhumanely. Buddhist teaching was used to justify this exploitation.

But does the account read better when we set aside the values of democracy and human rights and ask that Tibet be viewed in terms of traditional Buddhist values alone? Was the relation of the monastics to the peasants compassionate? Did the dominant religious class practice the overcoming of desire so as to make minimal demands on those who provided its necessities? Or were arrogance and cruelty justified in the name of the superiority of the intellectual and spiritual life? I assume that the answers are mixed. But unless they are somewhat positive, the implications for the possible transformation of our society, or any society, through Buddhist teaching and practice are not encouraging.

These reflections express what I take to be a Christian point of view. Jesus taught that the Sabbath is made for human beings, not human beings for the Sabbath. That can and should be generalized. Religious practices exist for human beings, not human beings for religious practices. This is true for both Buddhism and Christianity. It is true also for science.

The future of humanity and other creatures is threatened today by human actions. What can Buddhists, Christians, and scientists contribute to stemming and reversing the tide of destruction? My encounters with Buddhists have shaped and reshaped my answer to that question. I have at present more hope for Buddhist than for Christian contributions, although on another occasion I could discuss the latter. But I am still looking for an analysis of what is happening in the world that provides guidance for profound change and galvanizes the energy to effect it. I see some promise of such wisdom coming from Buddhists, but I am not really optimistic. It may be that we can find our way forward only when there is a real collaboration of scientists, Christians, and Buddhists to find that way. Perhaps Buddhists will lead in bringing that kind of collaboration into being.

CLOSE ENCOUNTERS OF A
CERTAIN KIND

RUBEN L.F. HABITO

I N HIS CELEBRATED WORK *I and Thou,* Martin Buber comments that "all real living is meeting." The word translated as "meeting" here is *Begegnung* in German, also translated as "encounter." In Japanese, this term is rendered by the compound word *deai*, which literally means "going out of oneself, and becoming one with an entirely new reality."

As I reflect on the significant turning points in my own life, among the innumerable encounters that have made me what I am today are four distinct and outstanding instances of "deai." I continue to look back to these in wonder and awe and gratitude. I take them by no means as "chance encounters," but rather as visits of grace in my life, for—come to think of it—they are all totally gratuitous and utterly independent of my own merit, or better, lack of it.

The first of these four encounters, which underlies all the others, I would call "the encounter with Mystery," which led me to enter the Society of Jesus in my late teens to pursue religious life as a Jesuit. The second is my encounter with Buddhism, notably with Zen, after having been sent to Japan in my early twenties as a seminarian preparing for priestly ordination. The third is the encounter, during trips to various Asian countries, with victims of the structural and other kinds of violence that characterize our fragmented and wounded world today. The fourth is my encounter with the Feminine, mediated by the pivotal encounter with Maria Reis, the woman who is now my spouse and the mother of our two children, but also confirmed in encounters with many other women and men.

What I am today is but the continual unfolding of these close encounters of a certain kind, drawing me out to an ever new reality with each new day.

The Exit of the Grandfather God

Raised Roman Catholic by devout parents in the Philippines, from early childhood I was used to saying prayers with the family every morning and evening, not eating meat on Fridays, going to confession on Saturdays and Mass on Sundays, and whatever it took to be a good Catholic child in the fifties. All this was held together by a belief in a "God up there," benevolent and all-powerful, who would reward us when we did good and punish us if we did wrong. I even imagined "Him" up there, from the pictures in the Sunday catechism, as a white-robed, white-bearded grandfatherly figure, looking down upon His creation with concern and listening to prayers to see which ones He would answer in which way.

At the age of fifteen, in my senior year of high school, as I was sitting in a classroom half-listening to what the teacher was saying on some aspect of Renaissance poetry, my gaze slowly shifted to the clear blue sky visible through the open classroom window. I still remember quite clearly how the flash of insight came to me at that moment. I can only describe it in a roundabout way, by first noting that since grade school I had been fascinated by the movements of the stars and had wanted to become an astronomer. I was then led to books that explained how the universe "worked," governed by the laws of physics, and was thus drawn to marvel at the intricacies of Einstein's relativity theory, the Uncertainty Principle, and related notions.

In one of my readings of these books about the warp and woof of the universe, a notion that struck me in particular was that the universe is understood to be "finite, yet unbounded." The example presented to explain this idea, as I recall, was that, if one sends a beam of light from one point of the universe in the same direction—"straight on," as it were (although it was also explained that there is no such thing as "straight on," as the universe manifests the nature of a curve)—if that beam travels long enough, it will come back to the point from where it is being sent. In other words, the universe as we know it has no outer limits as such, but it is also a closed and integrated structure, all parts interrelated to one another.

All this was at the back of my mind as I was sitting in that classroom, half-bored with what was going on, when, as I gazed outside the window at the clear blue sky, I realized in an instant that there was no need to posit a "God out there," that is, beyond this universe, to make it work as it does. In short, what came to me was that there was no need to imagine another layer of reality over and above that which we called the universe. This was it! I was convinced of this in a flash.

It was a complicated feeling, on the one hand, of exhilaration, of liberation, that is, of being freed from the need to imagine a being out there called "God," who made the universe separate from himself, who checks on human actions, looking at us over our shoulders, as it were, to reward the good and punish the evil, and so on. It was as if in one fell swoop, my childhood beliefs and ideas about the world taught to me by my Roman Catholic heritage up to that point gave in, and the flash of insight described above ushered in a new scenario of "the way things are." Our understanding of the way things are can only be expanded and deepened by continuing investigations in cutting-edge physical sciences, as I thought at the time. It was also at this point that my resolve to become an astrophysicist, if not a nuclear physicist, was set in place.

On the other hand, there was also an undeniable feeling of loss, of dislocation, of heightened insecurity, having my up-till-then all-too-secure "God-given" worldview collapsing out from under me. Soon after that, I turned to reading Dostoevsky, Camus, Sartre, and the like, and was able to identify with what one of the Karamazov brothers proclaimed—to the effect that "if God doesn't exist, everything is permissible." But this thought left me hanging in midair, bereft of a foothold, of a foundation for my life. So those big questions that human beings inevitably ask at some point in this earthly existence came thundering into my life at this time. What is the meaning of it all? Who am I? How may I live my life in a way that is authentic and worthy of what I am?

It was during this period of my life that the first of the four visits of grace I would like to relate here came about. The annual Fiesta—that is, the feast of the patron saint of our town—was just around the corner, and there was a big formal dance to be held in the open air at the plaza in front of the town hall. I was of age to be able to participate in that dance for the first time. So I was excitedly counting the days till the dance. What heightened the expectation was the fact that I had learned that the girl next door, M., whom I had a big crush on, was also intending to go. She was a year older and was already attending a university in Manila, the Big City two hours away, while I was in my last year of high school in my hometown of Cabuyao. But she was coming home for the Fiesta and dance, and I could hardly wait for the moment to ask her to dance with me. For weeks in advance, I imagined the scenario as I tried on the new jacket I would wear, tested out various colognes to use, checked which way of combing my hair would look best—all the crazy things teenagers smitten with a crush will do.

The day finally came, and that evening, I was walking with a group of friends to the plaza where the dance was to be held. I happened to be walking at the same pace shoulder to shoulder with a new acquaintance, let us call him Al, then a first-year medical student from the Big City, who came at the invitation of one of my cousins. In the midst of the small talk among the group, he turned to me in a rather casual way and said, "You know, this past week in anatomy class we dissected a cadaver."

"Ugh," I thought, "why does he have to bring up such a morbid topic at this time?" My heart was already thumping in expectation, as we could now hear the music of the band from the dance arena not more than a couple of blocks away.

But he went on: "And, you know, looking at all the internal organs, the heart, the lungs, the liver, the blood vessels, the nerves and all, and marveling at how all this came together with all the other parts to make up a human organism, it came to me very very strongly."

"What was that?" I was only half-listening. My heart and mind were already at the plaza a few minutes ahead, where I knew M., in her formal dress, must be waiting for the dance to begin.

"You know, it came to me quite strongly. It's unthinkable that all this could be out of mere chance."

"Unthinkable...out of mere chance..." Hmmm. His words began to strike a chord in me at that point. My mind began to imagine the scenario of the anatomy class he was describing, and to have a new and uncanny awareness of my own body, right then, heart thumping, excited about the dance and M. waiting there for it to begin. I could feel the blood flowing through my arteries and veins, my muscles moving my feet as my pace began to slow down a bit, my lungs taking in and sorting out the air I was breathing, my whole body "at work."

"It is unthinkable, that all this could be out of mere chance."

Let me unpack this a bit, to fill in what came to me in those moments. One can imagine, for example, a television set, the work of human ingenuity and labor, but also a contraption that runs based on the laws of the physical universe: electricity, wave transmission, and so on. As human intelligence came to a point of being able to figure out all the mechanics of how things work (put in a rather coarse way), people put their heads together and worked out a system whereby events and scenarios at a given location could be transmitted and shown on electrically connected little boxes called television sets. In other words, a television set is not just something that dropped from the sky, and lo, there it is, a wondrous little box showing pictures. Human intelligence—putting together all those elements and ideas about how things work in a painstaking way—is behind this thingamajig that shows us these moving pictures and broadcasts sounds from afar. It is unthinkable that a television set would just get assembled and get to work in the way it does "out of mere chance," that is, without all the effort and planning and intellectual work and experimenting that went into its assembly.

This was something I understood quite well, all in an instant. And somehow, becoming more intensely aware of this wondrous organism called a human being that I was, that my new acquaintance from the medical school was, that M. who caused my heart to thump faster was, that all these other people were as well—the single thought overpowered me: *"It is unthinkable* (indeed!), *that all this could be out of mere chance."*

Understand, this was not just an assent to what is known as the cosmological argument, or else the teleological argument for the existence of God. For me in those moments, it was not so much an intellectual conclusion that I arrived at, looking at evidence and proceeding toward a logically ordered conclusion. Rather, those words, *"It is unthinkable, that all this could be out of mere chance"* triggered in me the sense of being enveloped in a mysterious yet intelligent, immediate, and most of all, loving kind of Presence, that made it possible for my heart to beat, my feet to walk, my eyes to see the stars above. It was a Presence also manifesting itself in and through those stars, as it was manifesting itself in my own bodiliness, in and through each breath and each heartbeat, each step.

That night took on for me a significance that went way beyond the thrill and excitement of the dance itself. Needless to say, I enjoyed every minute of it, dancing with M. as often as I could, swaying with the rhythm of the music, mesmerized by the sweet perfume of the young ladies, simply having great fun with everyone else. But the barrage of pleasurable sensations brought on by the music and the perfume and the dance that lasted until the wee hours of the morning also left me with an empty feeling afterward, knowing that I would have to wait another year before something like this would take place again. Yet, amid this empty feeling, the sense of Presence that I felt at the start of the dance, triggered by Al's words, stayed with me, and led me to a new stage in my search for "the meaning of it all."

It was not that my belief in the Grandfather God of my childhood religion had been reinstated. That figure had already exited from my horizon with the previous experience of the clear blue sky. It simply opened my heart and mind and being to a new appreciation of the Mystery that is this universe, that underlies every heartbeat, every breath, every tree, rock, and star.

Upon graduation from high school, I began university studies toward a degree in physics, supported by a scholarship from the Philippine government. But instead of doing my homework in mathematics and science, I was spending hours in the library reading book after book on philosophy and religion, in a search for answers to those big questions that came with that experience of the clear blue sky. I realized I had to give my life to the pursuit of this Mystery, which I had been acutely aware of ever since that night of the dance at the annual Fiesta. To make a long story short, after a year of work at the university, I found myself drawn to enter the Jesuit novitiate, training for a religious life and service to people as an ordained Catholic priest.

Zen and the Big Bang

The Jesuit novitiate initiated me into the Spiritual Exercises of St. Ignatius, a month-long rigorous program of meditative and contemplative practice that culminates in what is known as the *Contemplatio ad Amorem*. This is a particular mode of contemplation whereby one simply basks in the Presence of that Divine Love that undergirds each and every element in this universe. This contemplative practice brings the practitioner to the very core of the mystical experience of Ignatius of Loyola, founder of the Society of Jesus. Each Jesuit undergoes these Exercises soon after entry into the Order to orient the entire course of one's life toward a yielding of self to the beckoning call of this Love. The Jesuit then takes vows of poverty, celibate chastity, and obedience to his superiors, offering himself to the service of his fellow beings on this Earth through the Church.

Under this vow of obedience, though also at my own request, in 1970 I was sent to Japan on mission, to take part in the Jesuit educational enterprise in that country. The Second Vatican Council, held from 1962 to 1965, had just begun to make its impact felt, and new directions were being taken on various levels in the work and witness of the Catholic Church throughout the world. In this vein, the assignment I was given was to study Japanese religions, notably Buddhism, to be able to serve the Church in the task of dialogue with other religious traditions, as encouraged by the spirit of the Second Vatican Council to "open our windows to the world."

It was this spirit of openness that gave me the confidence to heed the advice of my spiritual director, Father Thomas Hand, S.J., to take up the practice of Zen, when he introduced me to Yamada Koun Roshi, Zen Master of the Sanbo Kyodan lineage in Kamakura, Japan. The Zen style of this lineage is described in detail in *Three Pillars of Zen,* edited by Philip Kapleau. Incidentally, it was Yamada Koun who gave Kapleau access to the material that came to be published under this title, helping the latter to translate it and working with him for over six years.

In my first formal meeting with Yamada Roshi, I was given the koan "Mu" as the keystone for my practice. To make another long story short—backed by my initial glimpses into that Mystery in my teens and propelled by the habitual practice of the Ignatian Exercises in my Jesuit formation—within a few weeks of beginning Zen practice with the koan Mu came the Big Bang.

I was sitting in my room one afternoon at the language school in Kamakura, relaxing after a day-long Zen session at San-Un Zendo and a *dokusan* (formal interview) with Yamada Roshi earlier that afternoon. All of a sudden, something flashed through my whole being and over-powered me, leading to loud bursts of laughter and tears. I remember going out of my room and running up and down the corridor and up to the next floor, knocking on Father Hand's door, wanting to tell him excitedly, but not knowing exactly what to say, unable to control the laughter. One way I can describe what happened at this point is that in the flash of an instant, I *understood,* in a rather direct and intimate way, that is, *from within,* what was behind the intriguing half-smile of the

Buddha figures we see in sculptures and paintings. I telephoned Yamada Roshi's home to ask for a *dokusan,* and he gladly obliged. He called in Brigitte D'Ortchy, a long-time Zen practitioner from Germany living in Kamakura at the time, to be with him in the *dokusan* room as he asked me the usual checking questions, and then proclaimed that I had indeed experienced what in Zen is known as *kensho* (seeing into one's true, or Buddha nature).

From that point on, my practice of Zen followed the program of koan study offered in the Sanbo Kyodan lineage, which took the next sixteen years to complete under Yamada Roshi's guidance. These koans are geared to polishing one's inner eye, to keeping that experience of Mystery alive and fresh, to deepen it, to further clarify it, to enable one to see the pitfalls that can come in its wake. Through the years, Zen practice came to be for me a way of simply embodying the ineffable, infinite Mystery, with every breath, with every step, every thought, word, and deed. To put it in other words from a Buddhist context, it is a way of embodying Emptiness in every Form. Putting it in still another way, it is a mode of being and way of life wherein the Buddha's smile is manifested as none other than my own, expressed in all the events and encounters throughout my entire life.

As this experience in Zen became a guiding light in my life, a daunting theological task fell into my lap. The question came down to this: Could I continue in my Zen practice, going more deeply into the heart of Buddhism, and still be Christian? In other words, as one now thoroughly committed to Zen practice, what am I to make of my Christian heritage and identity? How do I understand the key tenets of Trinity, Incarnation, Redemption in the Cross and Resurrection of Jesus Christ? It was my great fortune, and blessing, to have been in the company of intellectual and spiritual giants such as Father Hugo Enomiya-Lassalle, Father Heinrich Dumoulin, Father Kakichi Kadowaki, Father William Johnston, and many other Jesuits, who provided the guidance and support that enabled me to wrestle with the particular issues involved in this basic question. I continue to bear this theological task, with the hope of

being able to articulate in more systematic ways in the future some of
the glimpses and insights that have come to me through the years of
wrestling with these issues. (My earlier works, *Total Liberation: Zen Spirituality and the Social Dimension* and *Healing Breath: Zen Spirituality for a
Wounded Earth*, are initial attempts in this regard.)

The Pain of the World

While teaching in the philosophy department of Sophia University in
Tokyo, Japan, I was given several opportunities to visit my home country, the Philippines, and also to travel for brief periods to Thailand,
Burma, Indonesia, India, and Sri Lanka. With the help of various Catholic
and Buddhist contacts, I was able to visit and stay in rural communities
of farmers, as well as in poor urban communities, in various Asian countries. It was these sojourns that opened my eyes to the realities of the
pain and suffering brought about by structures of oppression in our
world today.

There were many memorable and deeply moving encounters with
individuals and grassroots communities of people who were struggling
to maintain their way of life, seeking to defend it from those who would
take it away in the name of some "economic development program"
that was also in many cases backed by government military force. This
often involved the uprooting of residents from their rural communities,
with the consequent plummeting of their quality of life, not to mention
the destruction of the natural environment. I also had the opportunity
to sit in on study groups and social analysis workshops that examined
the causes of these situations of poverty and oppression and the depri-
vation of the basic human rights of so many people in the countries I visited. I would come back to Japan from these visits each time with a
clearer understanding of the structures of oppression and violence and
exploitation that characterize our economics-driven world, but more
significant, with a deepening realization of *my own complicity* in these
structures.

This realization in turn intensified the question I continued to struggle with through the years: What does it mean to live as a Christian in our world today? And one clue that I received in the process was this: To be Christian is to be called to an experience of *metanoia,* a transformation of mind and heart and of one's whole way of being. This involves no less than a radical shift from a self-centered mode of being concerned mainly with one's own gain and the protection of one's own interests, to a life totally given over to the Spirit of Christ that seeks to heal the wounds of the world. The fact that there are those who bear in their bodies the brunt of this pain of the world as victims of the violence on all levels—physical, psychological, social, economic, structural—that we humans inflict on one another and on ourselves serves for all of us as a constant reminder of the call to a veritable *metanoia.*

This clue to the answer of what it means to live as a Christian also had significant bearing on what was happening in my ongoing Zen practice, aided by koan study under Yamada Roshi. What is known as the "personalization of enlightenment," or the embodiment of the awakened way in one's daily life, involves no less than a radical transformation of one's way of life and mode of being.

A well-noted passage from Dogen, thirteenth-century Japanese Zen master, which I render in my own free translation, can perhaps help us unpack this: *To understand the Buddha Way is to understand Self. To understand Self is to forget self. To forget self is to be awakened by the myriad beings of the universe."*

In other words, the true Way involves no less than a death to that self-centered mode of being that is concerned only with its own interests and well-being—a radical turn, as one is awakened by the myriad beings of the universe, to realize that they *are* one's true self. The myriad beings of the universe include not only the physical world of mountains and rivers, but also the victims of the manifold levels of violence that characterize our twenty-first century Earth community. To be awakened by the myriad beings of the universe is to be one with the mountains and rivers, the sun, the moon, the stars, but also with the suffering and pain of one's fellow sentient beings in this concrete world of ours, and thus to live in a way that is informed and enlightened and transformed by that very suffering and pain.

This mode of being and way of life is embodied in the figure of the Bodhisattva Kanzeon [Chinese, Guanyin], whose name means "Perceiver of the Cries of the World." Kanzeon is the subject of the *Heart Sutra* and the *Kanzeon Sutra,* two well-known Buddhist scriptures that are chanted in Zen halls of all lineages, throughout both hemispheres.

Kanzeon—Encounter with the Feminine

I turn to the fourth of the encounters that have come to set the direction of my life, and that is my encounter with the Feminine. The first conscious instance of this encounter came about as I was traveling in India in the late seventies and had the privilege of concelebrating the Eucharist with an Indian Jesuit priest. At several points in the Mass, he began the prayers by invoking "God, our Father and Mother." Perhaps I need to note that having lived since my late teens in a male celibate religious community, within the male-dominant—or, one could say, male chauvinist—culture of the Roman Catholic Church, such an expression in public worship was a novelty to me. After returning to Japan, as I began to notice and reflect upon other elements in East Asian Buddhist spirituality that manifested this feminine dimension, I became more and more fascinated with and devoted to the figure of the Bodhisattva Kanzeon. As noted above, Kanzeon embodies this mystic oneness with the pain of the world borne by sentient beings, including ourselves.

In my Catholic upbringing, the Feminine was represented by the figure of Mary, the Mother of Jesus. And the figure of Mary converges with the figure of Kanzeon, as Mary stands at the foot of the Cross, one in suffering with her son Jesus, who in turn embraces all beings in their various situations of suffering.

This convergence of the two figures took place in a rather poignant way in Japanese history, during the period of persecution of Christians from the seventeenth to the nineteenth centuries. To avoid detection by the authorities, Christians displayed the figure of Kanzeon (also called Kannon) as a way of venerating the Blessed Mother Mary. Before this figure of "Maria Kannon" they prayed the Rosary and sang their holy hymns. Thus it was that the Buddhist and Christian feminine symbols for Cosmic Compassion came together in a concrete manifestation. The theological and spiritual implications of this convergence continue to fascinate me, and again I hope to be able to further articulate my reflections on this in the future. In this convergence of Maria and Kannon, and in devotion to this figure, I continue to discover very significant hints and guidelines and a source of empowerment for our common task of searching for ways of healing the wounds of the world.

But my encounter with the Feminine did not remain on the theological and spiritual level, as it found a very concrete expression when I met Maria Reis in Japan in 1987. Our conversations soon brought to light our shared interests. Raised in a Catholic family in Germany herself, she had participated in Zen retreats in that country, directed by Father Hugo Enomiya-Lassalle, one of my own spiritual mentors. At that time she was also in the process of writing her doctoral dissertation on, of all things, the Bodhisattva Guanyin (Chinese for Kannon). After nearly two years of enjoying her acquaintance and friendship as a Jesuit vowed to celibacy, I came to feel new stirrings within, which eventually led me to ask for dispensation from my Jesuit vows in the summer of 1989.

Having been blown by some strange Wind from Cabuyao, Philippines, to Tokyo, Japan, and now to Dallas, Texas, I continue to marvel at the ceaseless unfolding of these four encounters that have graced my life. Incidentally, by a twist of uncanny insight—and perhaps not by chance either—the lineage name given to me by my Zen Teacher, Yamada Koun Roshi, is Keiun, which means Grace Cloud. I contemplate with gratitude these visits of grace, looking to them for clues to certain kinds of questions posed to me by friends, colleagues, students, or by inquisitive individuals like the editors and potential readers of this volume: Are you Christian? Are you Buddhist? Are you both Buddhist and Christian? Are you neither? I may have to turn to Nagarjuna, second-to-third century Buddhist philosopher, and stand him on his head to help me find a way of articulating my answers to these engaging questions.

LOVING SOMEONE YOU CAN'T SEE

ROBERT A. JONAS

I N 1954 I am seven years old. One winter night I lie on a
feather bed in the two-story house that my grandfather built
in 1920 at the edge of a cow field in Wausau, Wisconsin. My
grandmother, Leona Radenz, sits beside me in a rocking chair. As she
turns out the bedside lamp, yellow light from the hall streams across
the dark oak woodwork and chest of drawers. I watch the light glint in
the large oval mirror that hangs above the bureau. I can just make out the
ceramic Jesus who hangs crucified on the small wooden cross beside the
mirror. His face is looking down. Maybe he can see the two black-and-
white photographs framed in tin that stand on the bureau. In one,
Grandpa is smiling in his WWI khakis, just back from two years duck-
ing German bullets in the trenches of France. In the other, Grandpa is
standing with his two sons, my uncles, Eugene and Earl, who are safely
back from the next world war.

Grandma reaches forward to pull her homemade quilt to my chin.
After she settles herself again, she begins to whisper, "Our Father, who
art in heaven…" Taking my cue, I join her in prayer. After we reach "forever and ever. Amen," we breathe together in the silence. Then Grandma
begins the prayer that she learned from her German parents, *Ich bin
klein, mein Herz ist rein, soll niemand drin wohnen, als Jesus allein*. I know
what it means: "I am small, my heart is pure. No one lives in my heart,
but Jesus alone." Some nights, Grandma offers a different prayer: "Now
I lay me down to sleep, I pray the Lord my soul to keep. If I should die
before I wake, I pray the Lord my soul to take." Tonight it is *Jesus allein*

who takes shape in my heart as Grandma gets up from the chair, strokes my forehead, and says, "Goodnight, Bobby."

Jesus allein. I know what he looks like. I've gazed at the small painting that hangs at the foot of Grandma and Grandpa's basement stairs. Jesus is a gentle, long-haired young man who holds a stray lamb. My parents may move me and my younger brother and sister from house to house and neighborhood to neighborhood. Mom and Dad may get along sometimes or they may have a string of bad days in which they stumble into the house and shout at each other late into the night. They may drink so much that their speech seems to spill out of a mouth full of marbles. They may not know where I am. I may stay at Grandma and Grandpa's house some nights and at my parents' house other nights. But Jesus is everywhere. And he'll come find me if I ever get lost. Even if someone dies (as the friendly old man next door did last year), Jesus will never die. He is like the other adults I know except that he never gets mad at me and he'll be with me even if I die tonight. Knowing Jesus helps me sleep, especially when I'm afraid or confused.

When my mind is full of bad thoughts, I repeat the prayers that Grandma taught me. Grandma can get angry with me, pinch my ears, and wash my mouth out with Dial soap. But I know that since she loves Jesus, at heart she must be as good as he is. Grandpa has a good heart, too. A few days ago he saw me playing with my steel toy soldiers, lining up the opposing sides. Without looking at me, he said, "Two hundred of us Wausau boys went to the trenches. Only twenty-eight came back. Christmas night we made a truce with the Germans and sang Christmas carols together." Anytime I want, I can go down those basement stairs and look at the picture of what holds us up. It's Jesus who stops the fighting and who takes care of everyone, no matter what side you're on. Jesus is how I know that God is love, forever.

———————

Twelve years later, in 1965, after having some "born again" experiences of Christ's joy, I enter Luther College, thinking I'll be a Lutheran minister. But the Vietnam War is heating up and I lose faith in America and in the church. I transfer to Dartmouth College, major in Government, and join a karate class. It's my first taste of Asian spirituality.

The teacher, Donny Miller, teaches us Chan (Chinese Zen) and Taoist meditation as the spiritual context of karate. I'm hooked. I attend every weekday for my junior and senior years. We break pine boards and old New England bricks with the striking edge of our hands and feet. In the winter we walk barefoot in the New Hampshire fields, bringing awareness to the exact place where the soles of our feet touch the snow. We warm our frozen feet by directing the body's *qi,* its earth energies, to that point of contact.

I've stopped going to church, not out of anger but because these new spiritual frontiers excite me. My Lutheran religious training said almost nothing about the body or nature. So I am fascinated to hear that my body is a hologram of the cosmos and of the trees, rivers, and oceans. In my spare time and over the summers, I pore over Laozi (Lao-tzu) and Thomas Merton's *The Way of Chuang Tzu.*

Nature, I am discovering, is not something "out there" to be dominated and subdued, but a part of me. A wise part of me. Moral and spiritual lessons can be learned not only from the Gospels, but even more immediately from the body, the seasons, and the trees. Earth-centered meditation and Eastern philosophy fit with the part of me that wanders aimlessly in Wisconsin hayfields listening to bobolinks and meadowlarks and that enjoys the blood rush that comes when a partridge or deer suddenly explodes out of a thicket in the woods. Having grown up as a Missouri Synod Lutheran, I know a lot about how human beings ought to treat each other. We should be Good Samaritans, respecting each person as a child of God, forgiving our neighbors and loving our enemies. But no one ever told me that there is a spiritual dimension in the expectant silence of waiting for a cedar waxwing to come back for more berries. I thought that when I sat silently on a log, waiting to hear Canada geese pass overhead, I was doing something I should be ashamed of: doing nothing. I was a good Lutheran, and doing nothing was just being lazy, practically a sin. As far as I'm concerned, at that point, I've left Christianity behind, once and for all. God is dead, but a new spirituality is opening in the East.

———

After I graduate from Dartmouth in 1969, I work as a VISTA volunteer in the inner city of Kansas City, Missouri. I teach black and Italian kids karate, introducing them to meditation and methods of peaceful conflict resolution that come from cultivating inner peace. Since most of my students are Christian, I investigate the work of writers such as Alan Watts, D.T. Suzuki, and Thomas Merton, looking for metaphors and stories that connect our meditation to the ministry of Jesus. I learn that Japanese Zen evolved from Taoism and Chinese Buddhism (Chan), and that Zen koans are questions that open the mind but have no final answer. I notice that some of Jesus' questions—such as "Who do you say that I am?"—sound like Christian koans.

But I'm learning new things about Christianity as well. Merton discusses the Desert Fathers, Evagrius, Cassian, and Gregory of Nyssa, medieval saints such as Bonaventure, Bernard, and Eckhart, and the sixteenth century Spanish mystics St. Teresa of Avila and St. John of the Cross. All new to me. My Lutheran upbringing and my religion courses at Luther College skipped these people, as if nothing significant happened in Christian theology in the eleven centuries between St. Augustine and Martin Luther. I am fascinated with this Roman Catholic world that dances with the East.

In 1973, while managing an organic vegetable farm in southern New Hampshire, I fall into a mild depression. Neither meditation nor reading seems to help; I need someone to talk to. I turn for advice to a fellow organic gardener I met at a recent conference. It turns out that Brother David is a Roman Catholic Carmelite monk who lives at The Common, a hilltop monastery near Peterborough, New Hampshire. David introduces me to St. John of the Cross and his *Ascent of Mount Carmel*.

One morning in late March, after we've walked through the

monastery gardens, David and I sit down before a fire in the small library. I trust David. He's small and rotund, and he doesn't say much. But when I talk with him, he seems completely present, and interested in my questions. There's so much I want to talk over with him. I feel as if St. John of the Cross is speaking directly to my heart and that he may be a crucial link between East and West.

I want to know if David sees any connection between Asian meditation and John of the Cross. I say to him, "I love the way that St. John weaves together his love for Christ with the Song of Songs and the deep contemplation that he calls the Dark Night. St. John seems to bring together romantic love, God's love, and a kind of Buddhist self-emptying. And then he says that the top of the spiritual mountain is *nada* or nothing. Is *nada* the same *nothing* or *emptiness* that the Buddhists talk about?"

"Well, Merton thought so. We don't know if St. John had any contact with the East. But the emptiness theme is central to the mystical Catholic and Orthodox traditions. Among academics, it's called 'negative' theology because it's about what God is *not*. God is beyond all *this or that*. It's also called *apophatic* spirituality, that is, 'without images.' God is beyond all our concepts of God, beyond all our images of God. Jews show respect for God's transcendence by writing the word without a vowel, as G-d. Probably all Christians know about the I-Thou relation, but not so many have learned the *nada* tradition. I'm not sure why. Certainly, it's there in Hebrew scripture, and in the *kenosis,* the self-emptying of Christ."

"But then it's a paradox for Christians, isn't it? I mean, we say that God is beyond this world, but also that God shows up in this world, in the flesh. It seems as if *kenosis* contradicts the Incarnation."

"Yes," David says, as the housekeeper comes in with some tea for us. David thanks her and pours me a cup of steaming English Breakfast. "In the contemplative tradition we honor the paradox of the Trinity. God is *beyond* us, Jesus is *with* us, and the Holy Spirit is *among* us. One God, but three ways of being. Mystics such as St. Bernard and St. John saw scripture as a mystical guidebook to Christian transformation. Just as God has three ways of being, we have three ways of encountering God. We come close to the first Person of the Trinity (the Father, the one whom Jesus called *Abba*) in silent contemplation, when we let all our thoughts and images go. We come close to Christ as we experience the intimacy of the I-Thou relationship in solitary prayer. And we feel the loving unity of the Spirit as we share in rituals, worship, singing, and shared prayer."

———

David and I have many more conversations over the next two years before his Carmelite provincial transfers him to another monastery. But this relationship has been healing for me and has opened up the exciting world of Christian contemplation. I decide to become a Third Order Carmelite, a lay person associated with the monastery, committed to certain daily, weekly, and monthly spiritual disciplines of prayer and liturgy. Of course, to become a Carmelite I must first become Roman Catholic. This is no easy thing.

When my parents began dating in the middle 1940s, Grandma Radenz was upset that my father was Methodist, not Lutheran. You might sing Christmas carols with your worst enemy, but never with a Methodist or a Catholic. Not being Lutheran was a sin. Prior to my parents' wedding in 1946, Grandma experienced a fit of moral righteousness and dis-invited some of Dad's Methodist relatives. A few years later, my uncle Earl and his Roman Catholic girlfriend, Beatrice, broke up several times because of Grandma's anger toward Catholics. (They eventually married anyway and sent Grandma a telegram after the wedding.) The rule about Lutherans and Catholics not marrying could have been the Eleventh Commandment. Lutherans had their feet on the ground. Catholics were lost in clouds of liturgical magic and had abdicated their moral powers to the pope.

Even though at the age of 27 I still feel the resonance of Grandma's biases within me, I cross the line and become a Catholic. While I do see value in the fierce "Here I stand" individualism and personal piety of Lutheranism, Eastern meditation has warmed me to the notion of self-surrender. St. John of the Cross validates two important aspects of my spiritual life: He affirms both my devotion to Jesus and my willingness to let Jesus go. John of the Cross shows me that a tender, even passionate, I-Thou relationship with Jesus lies hidden within our love for specific people. Certainly, one of the gifts of Christianity is that it perceives the ultimate value of I-Thou relationships because they disclose God. On the other hand, St. John also relativizes personal relationships, including our relationship with Jesus, by inviting us to enter the "Dark Night" of God's mystery. St. John's Jesus is more elusive and less predictable than the gentle shepherd, the Lutheran Jesus who saved my life when I was a child. But somehow I trust that they are still one and the same Jesus.

Until 1978 when I move to Cambridge and begin doctoral work in psychology and education at Harvard, I remain active in the Third Order of Carmelites at The Common, enjoying St. John's artful integration of love mysticism and "empty" contemplation. Another monk, Father Paul, becomes my tutor on the contemplative way. He takes me through the Hebrew Song of Songs because, he says, "in the early centuries after Jesus' death, Christian mystical theologians considered it their foundational text."

I gradually appreciate the astonishing spiritual vision of the *Song*. It depicts the loving dance of God's presence and absence, a pattern that I have repeatedly experienced in my own relationship with Jesus.

In one of our last conversations, I ask Father Paul the same question that I posed to Brother David: Is Christ's self-emptying the same as Buddhist emptiness?

"Maybe," Paul says, "but it's not emptying for its own sake. It's emptying in love, for the other. Contemplatives seek union with God's Love. But St. John of the Cross saw how we can make idols of anything, even religious things, even spiritual images and practices. Even the image of I-Thou love can get in the way of actually experiencing it. So there's a radical Night in John, a letting go of love for the sake of love, a letting go of God for the sake of God. John writes in the *Ascent* that the soul must empty itself of *all* earthly and heavenly things."

"Even heavenly things."

"Yes. Sometimes they're the hardest to relinquish. The ego sticks to them like Velcro."

"So, when the ego empties itself, we experience what Jesus did—we are unified with Love."

"Yes. John calls it a marriage."

"Do some people actually live in that state all the time? It seems impossible."

We walk along in silence for a moment, and then Paul says, "Several times in *The Song*, the soul seems to reach union. She says, 'My beloved is mine and I am his.' That's the unity.

"But then she laments, 'I opened to my beloved, but my beloved had turned and was gone. I sought him, but did not find him; I called him, but he gave no answer.' That's the absence. And both are true. On the one hand, we are made in the image of God and we are one with Christ. We are the apple of God's eye. Like Jesus, we are God's Beloved. But on the other hand, we feel incomplete. Our hearts long for all of God, not just a glimpse. But then God is gone and gives no answer."

"So, God is here and God is not here."

"Yes. As we say in Catholic theology, 'already and not-yet.'"

"This is helpful!" I exclaim. "My childhood faith left me open to a lot of guilt. Sometimes I'd feel so close to Jesus that I'd cry with joy. But then I'd pray and pray, and nothing would happen. So I'd feel guilty. Like, there must be something wrong with me. Or maybe I'm too much of a sinner and God is disgusted with me."

"St. John of the Cross would say that it is very human, very normal, to experience the absence of God. It doesn't necessarily mean that you've done something wrong. God is glimpsed but never grasped. Sometimes God communicates God's self to us most directly in the experience of God's apparent absence."

"That reminds me of the Zen saying, 'If you see the Buddha on the road, kill him.'"

"Exactly. We have to let go our ideas *about* God. St. John encouraged his novices to cultivate a steady awareness, so that they could be at peace with the alternating feelings of presence and absence, of consolation and desolation, knowing that they take place within the ongoing context of God's love. St. John of the Cross spoke of the 'living flame of love' that burns away everything that separates us from God. Thoughts and emotions come and go, but God's love is forever."

––––––––––

Ten years later, in 1988, I am four years into postdoctorate work as a psychotherapist and newly married to Margaret Bullitt-Jonas, an Episcopal priest who shares with me a devotional prayer life. After many conversations sparked by her recent seminary experience, I remember my own flickering desire to study theology and I enter the Weston Jesuit School of Theology. Most of my papers focus on the relationship between Buddhist meditation and Christian contemplation, Buddhist *shunyata* (emptiness) and Christian *kenosis* (emptying).

Throughout the 1980s I have been studying with several Vipassana and Zen Buddhist teachers. With their help, I've seen directly the moment-to-moment soap opera in my mind. I've seen what they call "monkey mind," as well as the suffering that comes when I mistake my conditioned thoughts for reality. At each step along the way, I've also sensed the elusive presence of Jesus, my teacher. When I sit in Buddhist monasteries, Christ is sitting there, too. I have faith that for Christ, Zen is another way to be with *Abba*. In zazen, Christ is listening for the voice that calls him and each one of us "my Beloved."

In my theology readings, I also discover that Christians have been meditating since the early centuries after Christ. In the fourth century, Evagrius of Ponticus teaches *hesychia,* peaceful repose that comes from being recollected in silence in God. Evagrius' student Cassian asks his monks to notice how the undisciplined mind "is assailed by storms of thoughts" but, at the summit, is still. I am attracted to Cassian's "passion for the unseen." These Christian mystics sound like Zen teachers, except that all their metaphors are rooted in the Gospel stories that permeated their daily liturgies.

At Weston, I read how successive generations of Christian contemplatives swim upstream toward God in the currents of two distinct streams of spiritual knowledge, the *kataphatic* and the *apophatic*. The *kataphatic* stream (Greek, "affirmative speech," that is, with images) stresses God's similarity to creation. It values certain thoughts, images, and feelings as revealing God, as being doorways to God. The *kataphatic* tradition trusts that God is encountered in and through the created world.

By contrast, the *apophatic* stream (Greek, "negative speech," that is, taking away images) stresses that God is radically *different* from creation. No thought, image, or concept can ultimately contain or express the mystery of God. *Apophatic* or contemplative prayer is experienced as a blind, silent love that transcends all images, thoughts, and feelings.

As I read more, I begin to feel accompanied. Many Christians have noticed the alternations of presence and absence that I find in my meditations and prayers. They confirm the inward dance of my own prayer— sometimes rejoicing in music, reading scripture, and participating in liturgies, and sometimes craving the total silence and emptiness where words can't go.

In studying the Christian mystics I learn—no surprise!—that those who are drawn to the *apophatic* are the favorites of Buddhist writers such as D.T. Suzuki, who compares zazen to the insights of Evagrius, Eckhart, *The Cloud of Unknowing,* and St. John of the Cross. When both *apophatic* and *kataphatic* are understood to be simultaneously true—that is, images, music, thoughts, and liturgies can bring us close to God but can also separate us or distract us from God—I hear an echo of Mahayana Buddhism's *Heart Sutra,* in which "form is emptiness and emptiness is form." One cannot collapse the spiritual life in either direction without losing the whole.

Throughout my seminary years, I continue my morning meditation practice. I struggle to simply be present to God in the midst of the flickering flame and my overactive imagination. I know that I'm not supposed to be thinking, but I can't help it. I'm thinking about what makes Christian meditation distinctive, and I conclude that while Christian contemplation is about "self-emptying," it is also, essentially, relational. Just as God is a oneness of intersubjective Love, so, too, are we, in our deepest being. Often, as I sit in silence, I glimpse the loving presence of Grandma Radenz, Margaret and other family members, along with Brother David, Father Paul, St. John of the Cross, Thomas Merton, and Jesus—all of them circulating in my heart. Sometimes I think it's not me who is praying but all of them. I'm simply making space for them, for that council of holy ones who are coming and going from the cavern of prayer in my heart.

———————

My last class at Weston Seminary in 1991 is a seminar on Thomas Merton that focuses especially on his responses to Buddhism. The teaching assistant is David Duncavage, who was once, like Merton, a Trappist monk. As a farewell to the class he offers to play his Japanese bamboo flute, the shakuhachi. David says, "This musical tradition is an ancient Buddhist practice called *Sui-Zen,* which means 'blowing Zen.' The goal of the Sui-Zen monk was to bring complete attention to each breath and to be so present that all ego attachments fall away in the duration of one prolonged note. They called it *ichion jobutsu,* to become Buddha in one sound. After I left the Trappists, I lived in Japan and learned to play shakuhachi. I'll play a piece that's about three hundred years old. It's called '*Kyorei,*' 'Empty Bell.'"

Then David picks up a dark piece of bamboo and brings it to his lips. After ten seconds he blows down its length, producing the most beautiful, organic tones I have ever heard. For several minutes he blows, one breath at a time, leaving a silent space between each breath. I feel that I've been inside a cage all my life and that someone has just let me out.

After class I ask David for lessons, and soon I am sitting across from him once or twice a week, alternately blowing down the bamboo and talking about the Buddhist-Christian dialogue. Almost immediately, the shakuhachi becomes the center of my daily prayer. Each morning, before my psychotherapy clients arrive, I sit with a candle, read a Psalm or a Gospel story, and then play one of the Sui-Zen pieces called *Honkyoku,* "Origin Music." The shakuhachi has become my way to be close to the Earth, listening to Buddha and breathing with Jesus.

In 1993 I establish the Empty Bell, a small retreat center near Boston. Its mission is to study and practice the Christian contemplative path and to join in dialogue with Buddhists. Once or twice a week, a community meets for one-and-a-half hour sittings. We ring the temple bell, sit in silent meditation, read the Christian scripture for the day, reflect together on the contemplative dimension of the scripture, and then pray out loud. Throughout the 1990s, we host Zen, Sui-Zen, and Tibetan Buddhists from many different schools. And, like a traveling priest who carries a satchel with communion bread and wine, I take the shakuhachi with me wherever I go. When I preach at Christian services, I blow the shakuhachi and invite people to listen to the silence between the notes and consider the simple beauty of natural things such as wind through bamboo. In this quiet listening, I say, is the secret of Christ's self-emptying love and prophetic vision.

Can one be both a Buddhist and a Christian? In the late 1990s I participate in three Buddhist-Christian retreats with a Benedictine monk, Father Laurence Freeman, and the Dalai Lama. We share many days and evenings of meditation, prayer, and dialogue in Bodh Gaya, India; Florence, Italy; and Belfast, Northern Ireland. Each time His Holiness suggests that people not practice two religions at once. He says being a Buddhist-Christian is like being a sheep with a yak's head. Better to be deeply rooted in one's own tradition, even as one learns about and makes friends in other traditions.

But as a participant in scores of other Buddhist-Christian dialogues and retreats over the last twenty years, I have heard different opinions.

Some people seem happy to be "Buddhist-Christian," because, they say, Zen is not a religion, it's simply a way to be present. One friend says that a "Zen-Christian" might train her mind to be so free of distraction that she is always present to Christ. But then, is she Zen or Christian? Does it matter?

Each day when I pick up my "Buddhist" shakuhachi, I pick up my desire to be close to Jesus. But who is he? My childhood images of Jesus as shepherd, Mother Hen, friend, protector, and savior are still meaningful for me, but the Risen Jesus has also disappeared over the horizon of my thoughts and imagination. Perhaps he has gone into that Cloud that Moses entered when he took off his shoes and ascended the holy mountain.

Buddhist meditation and my soul friendship with St. John of the Cross and other Christian mystics have introduced me to a Jesus who is continually appearing and disappearing in my most private thoughts and emotions, in other people, and in the water, trees, and rocks. He is free of any particular form, and the detachment I've learned through meditation has helped me to recognize his formless form. He is my *Heart Sutra* and, as Grandma taught me, the only one who lives in my heart.

In a time of worldwide uncertainty and suffering, we need to root ourselves in the deepest wisdom of our religious traditions. On September 12, 2001, in response to the previous day's events, I wrote the following letter to my shakuhachi community. It expresses a hope that is informed by both Buddhist and Christian insight.

> *This is holy time for the shakuhachi. What does it mean to play shakuhachi? Yes, it is only wind in the trees, only breath through bamboo. But a holiness circulates in that simplicity, a holiness that brings to light everything in our hearts.*
>
> *Honkyoku is not merely music, a flat horizon of notes strung together to produce an effect in the listener. It is not played merely for the sake of*

technical proficiency. Today it is clear to me that the stakes are much higher than that.

For those who can perceive it, shakuhachi music is the voice of the earth come to full awareness of itself. With each breath, we glimpse a love that transcends our usual mind-states of self-concern and image-management. When we blow with this larger intention, we know that the music is for others, not just for our own enjoyment.

I hope we will strive for a certain purity in our music, a prayerful quality of mercy, love, and truth. Playing shakuhachi at this time of mourning can convey a universal longing that all beings be joyful, humble, healed, and fulfilled.

THE MOMMY AND THE YOGI

SALLIE B. KING

R ELIGIOUS CONCERNS and motherhood have pushed and prodded each other almost all my adult life. This account will focus on that story. But first, a little background. Before motherhood, before adulthood, in childhood and adolescence, my religious life was one of intensive, private, individual seeking. I was born into a military family and raised as what I call a "generic Protestant"; my parents were not religious, though we did attend the combined Protestant services on the military bases where my father was stationed. My family gradually drifted away from church attendance, but I went in the opposite direction. When I was in high school, I volunteered to assist in a Protestant Sunday school class on the Air Force base where my father worked; I soon found myself with full responsibility for teaching the kindergarten class. While I enjoyed being with the children, I ultimately could not reconcile the teachings of Jesus—which seemed clearly pacifist to me—with the military base on whose land I stood as I spoke Jesus' words. I gave up teaching Sunday school.

I had two other major problems with mainstream Christianity during my adolescence. I found that I could not reconcile the idea of a benevolent, omnipotent God with the ocean of human suffering of which I was all too keenly aware. The Problem of Evil was not a theoretical problem for me; it discredited the idea of God as I had been taught it. I was unable to maintain that idea of God; I had to give it up.

Finally, as an avid student of world culture and a life-long ponderer of religious questions, I saw the earnestness with which people in all

times and places have sought answers for the mysteries, pains, and con-
fusions of life, and the gratitude with which they have accepted whatever
wisdom came their way. I came to the conclusion that a loving God could
not possibly punish people with eternal damnation simply because they
were not Christian when they had taken up the religion before them in
good faith. I was revolted by the Christianity that I heard teaching otherwise. I walked away from Christianity disgusted.

In college, my wide reading on religion and my constant pondering
of religious issues intensified. When I discovered Buddhism, it made
complete sense to me. The Four Noble Truths' direct naming and
addressing of suffering as the central problem described life exactly as I
saw it. Moreover, it did entirely without the God in whom I could not
believe, was impressively irenic in its social relations, and did not go
around denouncing and condemning people who thought otherwise.
Perhaps best of all to a questioning mind like mine, Buddhism assured
me that I need not take what they taught on their authority, but should
seek for answers myself, in my own experience. I could hardly believe
such noble ideas and practices existed. I attended some retreats and
learned how to meditate in a Buddhist manner but did not join any Buddhist organizations or establish a relationship with a teacher.

At about the same time, I also studied Christian mysticism on my
own. Christian mysticism did not present me with the problems that
mainstream Christianity had. I felt an affinity with it. I practiced what I
came to call "natural meditation," spending long hours sitting with a
silent mind, quietly watching the sunrise, the sunset, the night sky, the
ocean, a candle flame—always alone. These practices opened up for me
an experiential world that crushed all ordinary things into complete
insignificance. I never thought of these experiences as either Buddhist or
Christian; they just seemed human.

Things change. I met and fell in love with my husband, Steve. He was
a member of a Zen Buddhist organization, which I also joined. We meditated together. I attended occasional retreats. My worldview was not yet
seriously challenged.

A few years later, I became pregnant with my first child. Suddenly, as soon as I knew that I was pregnant, the world was an entirely different place for me. I no longer wanted to meditate; I just wanted to sit around and be pregnant. I wanted to read books about motherhood and eat the perfect diet for my child's health. I couldn't have cared less about meditation and the world it opened up for me. My practice stopped completely. I was entirely content as I was.

Things change more. The child arrived. Completely head over heels in love, I also knew within twenty-four hours that this was not going to be easy! A colicky baby, she had us sleeping an hour, waking an hour, sleeping an hour, waking an hour, all through the night. She also cried every evening as the sun went down for about three hours. We couldn't find a way to stop her crying, though we found that if we held her and sang and danced with her, she cried much less. We were walking zombies for weeks. Finally, as she began to settle into life and the fog began to lift, two Buddhist reflections gripped me. First, I reflected often upon what a manifestation of *duhkha* (here, the pain inherent even in the joyful) a baby is. We wanted nothing more in life than for this child to be happy, and yet it was completely impossible to keep her happy, despite our lavishing loving care upon her; she cried every day. Second, I strongly felt the need to regain some stability in my life by restarting my meditation practice; but this was completely impossible for me as well. It was all I could do to care for this child and fall into exhausted sleep whenever she slept.

Time went by. As my first child grew and a second arrived, I began to feel the inadequacy of my religious life, on two fronts. First, though I practiced meditation with my husband as best I could, it was not enough. I felt exhausted by the daily chores of academic work and motherhood. All waking hours were accounted for between work and children; meditation time was time wrenched away from sleep. It didn't seem to fit into my life very well. I would have liked to attend a meditation retreat, but it was out of the question with the small children to care for and just to be present for. I very much wanted to go, but even more strongly, I did not want to leave them. To leave them to indulge myself in a week-long retreat would have been impossibly selfish. (Many Western Buddhist parents, especially mothers, have contended with these problems.)

Second, as my older daughter entered the social world of preschool, she came home bearing strange and disturbing tales that her school friends told her of an angry God that lived in the sky and punished children if they misbehaved. I soon realized that my husband and I could "be" Buddhists all we wanted, but that living in southern Illinois, far away from any Buddhist centers, we were badly in need of religious community. If we went on as we were, our children would soon conclude that their parents were just weird; our views would never hold weight against their peers and the entire local community. Moreover, they lived in a world in which religion attacked small children with scary ideas! They needed some kind of religious "protection"—a view that would be nurturing to them as they developed and provide a sane alternative worldview with which they could repulse the aggressive and frightening one that was all around them. Buddhism just wasn't available as a public, community option in southern Illinois. I went looking for the "next best thing."

I remembered the Quakers I had encountered during my college years and began attending Friends (i.e., Quaker) Meeting. I soon decided that this was not just the "next best thing" to Buddhism; for me it was a wonderful thing in its own right, different from Buddhism, but completely compatible with it. What particularly impressed me in Quakerism was its dual focus: inwardly, on direct, personal experience of spiritual truth, and outwardly, on nonviolent social action—with a serious, sustained effort to have the outward action express the spiritual lifeblood. I decided that I wanted to take out membership in the Religious Society of Friends (Quakers) but only if I did not have to stop being a Buddhist in order to do so. My local Meeting, where membership decisions are made, had no problem with this, but I pressed them to look into the matter further. The "higher ups" at the regional level had no problem with it, either—the region already had a Methodist

Quaker and a Jewish Quaker, they said—why should there be a problem with a Buddhist Quaker? My sentiments exactly. I became a member.

For many years, I thought of this as the "easy path" in Buddhist-Christian dual religious membership. Both Quakerism and Buddhism were very flexible on doctrine, both finding religious truth to exist primarily in experience, and all verbal formulations to be provisional. The doctrines that were there seemed highly compatible: most important, Buddha Nature and the Quakers' Light Within. The moral values were highly compatible as well. Importantly, both groups seemed clear that they did not "own" religious truth. The Buddhist teachers I followed taught Buddhism as a vehicle—an excellent vehicle, but not to be clung to as absolute. They occasionally referred to aspects of other religions, particularly Christianity, with appreciation. Quakerism, while rooted in Christianity and permeated with it, recognized that the Light of truth was also present outside Christianity. On the other hand, the two seemed to have different strengths: Buddhism in its meditation practices and its profound philosophy, Quakerism in its manner of bringing spirituality into the worldly life of lay people. I concluded that where they overlapped, they were similar, and where they differed, they were complementary.

I should mention that I am not the only one who finds a spiritual affinity between Buddhism and Quakerism. I had occasion a few years ago to speak to a national gathering of Friends General Conference, the branch of Quakerism that maintains the traditional unprogrammed Meeting for Worship. As my subject was Buddhism and Quakerism, I took advantage of the occasion to ask the 1500 or so Quakers who were present to stand up if they had in some way taken Buddhism into their spiritual lives. About 85 to 90 percent of the people in the room stood up.

So for me, all was well. Quakerism was present locally, available as a community within which my children could grow and be nurtured and I could be challenged to bring my spirituality to bear on the details of my daily life. Buddhism didn't go anywhere; it was still there, touching, as far as I was concerned, the greatest spiritual depths possible to

humankind. Gradually, however, and imperceptibly at first, a discomfort grew in me.

A friend jokingly challenged me with being a fraud in the Society for
Buddhist-Christian Studies, since Quakerism is only a "marginal" form
of Christianity (as the *Encyclopedia of Religion* says). For a while, I
secretly suspected that he was right—though, when I repeated this
comment in Quaker circles, my peace-loving Quaker friends bristled at
the suggestion that they were not fully Christian. They saw themselves
at the very heart of Christianity! Gradually, I came to see just how
Christian Quakerism is.

Messages that I was receiving from Buddhism seemed more and more
incompatible with my Western thinking, as embodied in Quakerism,
and, especially, with my reflections on my experiences as a mother. And
while I was drawn to Zen because it was relatively immune from the
Buddhist attitude I will be describing, still, as a scholar of Buddhism, I
was constantly exposed to this kind of thinking in the tradition—often,
but not always, in the teachings of the Buddha himself, whom I highly
revere.

The Buddhist message I heard was this: Life is characterized by the
three marks, *duhkha* (dis-satisfactoriness), *anitya* (impermanence), and
anatman (absence of self). Attachment is what returns us again and again
to this samsaric world. The proper response to the samsaric world is
detachment. There is no ultimacy, nothing of lasting value in this world.
Or, minimally: Attachment is a mistake, because whatever we attach
ourselves to will inevitably change and slide through our fingers.

This is exactly the description of life that made perfect sense to me
in adolescence; now, however, I began to have some problems with it. It's
not that this description is not true, I thought. But, at the same time, I
have before me this infant (each one). This infant came into the world
through my husband and me. We have an absolute responsibility for this
child. Even more—I felt, more than thought—this child has been part
of my body for nine months. During one pregnancy, nauseous and unable
to eat, I watched as my face and shoulders grew emaciated, my wedding

ring became loose on my finger, and yet my belly rapidly expanded. After birth, this child and I are still physically linked. When nursing, she plugs back into my body for hours every day, for a year. She is almost constantly in my arms or on my stomach or back. Our bonding has tied me to her emotionally even more than we are tied physically: She is literally constantly on my mind. When she is sick and my holding her comforts her, I sit all day with her in my arms, not eating or drinking, not moving a muscle for fear of disturbing her. Her well-being becomes, irrationally perhaps, the first consideration—at all times, in all contexts.

Without my consciously realizing it, my subconscious worldview has changed: I have come to feel that there is ultimacy in this world. In practice, it is an ultimate good, for me, to care for this child. Nothing else matters as much; nothing else comes even close. Yet, at the same time, on the conscious level, my mind is full of thoughts of *duhkha* and *anitya,* the unsatisfactoriness of the world. Gradually, I begin to sense that the two central aspects of my life—my Buddhist mind and my motherhood—may be incompatible.

At the same time that this realization is creeping into my mind, I am constantly hearing in the Quaker world—in which I have also immersed myself—about love. In our unprogrammed Meetings for Worship, people frequently extol acts of selfless love. In our hymn singing, in our Bible study, love is a prominent theme. In our gathered silences, I have repeated opportunity to sit quietly, open, as Quakers say, to what the Spirit brings up in me. What comes up repeatedly as most important and meaningful to me, religiously and otherwise, frequently has to do with love. My mind becomes full of thoughts about love and its place in spirituality.

We are born in human form for a reason, I came to think—the form of life that we manifest has a purpose. Humans come here biologically and instinctually equipped to seek love and to give love. A child raised without love does not learn how to be fully human; we are even told that mother-child bonding (attachment) is necessary to the child's development. The reason we come to the world in this human form must make use of human capacities. I concluded that we must be here to learn more and more fully how to love.

I was also fortunate at about this time to meet a number of ordained religious who seemed to embody and radiate love. In the space of two weeks, I had occasion to visit first a Theravada Buddhist monastery and then a Catholic Trappist monastery close to where I live. Unexpectedly, on both occasions, I was quite overwhelmed by a person I met there. These two people, a Buddhist nun and a Christian monk, were by no means famous saints, and yet they were alike in their overflowing joy and gratuitous love. They seemed to have so much lightness and happiness in them that it bubbled over in goodwill, in sheer, gratuitous, unconditional, spontaneous loving-kindness. Both gave me touching gifts, deep spiritual sharing, and most of all, genuine, warm caring. I was struck by the similarity of their behavior and their way of being. The homily I heard while at the Trappist monastery was on Matthew 20, the parable of the workers in the vineyard and God's uncalculating love. I thought to myself, this is exactly the kind of love shown to me by these two religious.

Gradually, I came to see love as a fruit of the Spirit. I came to think, in Quaker terms, that the more we are able to be filled with the living Spirit, the more truly we become able to love. I came to see learning to love more and more genuinely as the point of living a human life. And while I could see similar fruits of love in my Buddhist and Christian friends, I could see this kind of language and thinking only in Quakerism and Christianity, not in Buddhism.

Buddhism doesn't talk about love in the Western sense. Compassion is often discussed, and loving-kindness. But is this equatable to love, or not? I wasn't sure. Usually in Buddhist scripture, a cool detachment seemed to be part of the picture. But cool detachment, in my experience as wife and mother, was not part of the picture of love. That wasn't what I was talking about at all. One Buddhist scripture came to mind in which a mother's love is extolled—named appropriately enough, the *Metta Sutta,* the scripture on loving-kindness:

Just as a mother would protect her only child even at the risk of her own life, even so let one cultivate a boundless heart towards all beings (*Suttanipata,* I.8).

Hmmm.

I thought: Isn't it the best part of us that we love, that we learn to forget about ourselves and think of someone else? Caring for our children drills this into us: The more we resist and try to hold out for what we want, the more we suffer! I resisted as much as anyone! Everyone who gets up night after night to nurse an infant or tend a sick child knows that the only way to survive the rigors of raising a child is to forget about oneself—just give up, let go, and accept what you have to do! Thinking of everything else you need to do or want to do is useless. Complaining or wishing it to be otherwise makes it worse. Just do it! In fact, caring for a child, loving a child, is probably the single situation in most people's lives that contributes to the development of our selflessness, our ability to put ourselves aside and think of the well-being of another. This is a Buddhist value! Wouldn't Buddhism do well to make use of this as a teaching device?

My quandary came to this: What is the place of love in this world— ordinary, familial love? It is true that nothing in this world lasts. And yet we love. And it is the best thing about us that we love; love is the only setting in which we ordinary people are able to put ourselves aside and think of the other first.

Finally, one night, I had a dream. In the dream, my husband and I were as if dead and passing through a kind of limbo or bardo. We went together through door after door, and in each place we reached we'd have a different experience. Some of them seemed as though they were meant to be frightening, but we weren't frightened, because we knew it was an illusion. Also, we weren't frightened because we were going through it together.

Finally, we got to a big, open hallway with a lot of doors radiating out from the central hub of the hallway where we stood. Over one door it said "Christians" and over another it said "Heathen." I had an immediate impulse to go through the Christian door, feeling that that was the "right" choice—in order to go to heaven! I thought the "Heathen" door would lead to hell. I thought to myself, "I'm not gonna make that mistake!" But then I started debating whether I was or wasn't a Christian: "I sort of am—but not like that!" And there were lots of other doors anyway, though I didn't see whether they had signs over them.

I was standing indecisively when someone (who seemed like a staff person of the place) showed up. It seemed that he should know how things worked, so I started asking him about the doors. He indicated that it didn't matter which door I went through, that regardless of which door I chose, I would end up in "bliss" (which clearly encompassed heaven, nirvana, *moksha* [liberation], and so forth).

I replied, "I'm not sure I want 'bliss.'"

"Oh, everyone wants bliss! No one chooses to pass it by!"

"I was happy the way I was, at home with my husband and children."

"But your husband has already passed through to bliss."

I looked around, and though Steve was still standing next to me, his eyes were vacant, and I could see that he had indeed passed through to bliss. I was mad.

"We were happy the way we were. Why'd you have to interfere?"

"Would you want to interfere with your husband's bliss?"

"No, I wouldn't want to do that. But I don't want to go over to bliss. I want to go back. I want to go back to my children." I had a vision of the two children and myself at home, sitting around together.

And I reflected very strongly, "Yes, that's what I want to do! I want to go back! I want to go back!" And that desire completely filled me—the desire to go back, the desire to be with my children, the desire to help my children, and not only my children, but all children. I saw in a flash that "my" children were only "my" children temporarily; at other times, other children were "my" children, "I" was a different "me," and indeed everyone was someone's child—"my" child at one time or another. There wasn't the slightest doubt in my mind: I wanted to go back, to live that life, knowing full well that in choosing that life over "bliss," I was choosing terrible pain and grief along with great joy.

This feeling was so strong that it woke me up. As I woke up, I thought and felt, "That was a Buddhist dream! I chose to return to this world of samsara for the sake of sentient beings!" A few minutes later, I thought, "Oh! That was a mother's dream, too! I like this life; I want to be here because I like it. And I want to be here with my children and for my children; I couldn't bear to abandon them." Later still, I thought, "How odd, if the Buddhist dream and the mother's dream are really the same." I felt that I had finally solved my fifteen-year natural koan. The mother's love, her "attachment" that keeps her bound to samsara, her gut-level inability to abandon her children who cannot make it on their own and truly need her help—these things are indistinguishable from the bodhisattva's willingness to turn away from nirvana and return to samsara for the sake of all sentient beings.

A few months later, I experienced a postscript to the dream. I was picking my daughter up after school, and as I sat in the car, I saw her coming towards me and looking at me with the sweetest, most beautiful, open, vulnerable, trusting smile on her face, and something in me snapped. I swore at that moment that I would never again vex my mind with questions about my love and "attachment" to my children. I thought, "I'm through with all that! It is the most important thing in the world. It has to be part of why we're here. Forget detachment!" Not that I ever was detached—no way! But often I had fretted about my sense that Buddhism told me that I should be detached, along with my keen awareness that I couldn't be, and my endless, internal debate over which was right. No more!

I now count the dream and my vow upon seeing my daughter's smile as among my most important religious experiences.

Imagine my feelings, then, when a few days after seeing my daughter's smile, I participated in a discussion with a group of Buddhist scholars and practitioners on some readings that included the following passage, from the pre-eminent Theravadan Buddhist commentator, Buddhaghosa:

When this being is born in the mother's womb, he is not born inside a blue or red or white lotus, etc., but on the contrary, like a worm in rotting fish, rotting dough, cesspools, etc., he is born in the belly in a position that is below the receptacle for undigested food (stomach), above the receptacle for digested food (rectum), between the belly-lining and the backbone, which is very cramped, quite dark, pervaded by very fetid draughts redolent of various smells of ordure, and exceptionally loathsome.[1]

This is the kind of thing in Buddhism that gives mothers a real pain! My child is not like a worm and my womb is not like rotting fish! Women are not fools to have children! Love of a child is indeed attachment, but that attachment is not delusion! I was repelled, but I no longer struggled to make excuses for, rationalize, or accommodate this kind of thing in Buddhism. I simply rejected it.

Life being what it is, it was not long after I settled all this in my mind that I began to confront, in a new way, my older daughter's approaching departure from home. Of course, by the time parents get to this point, we have lived with our child for eighteen or so years. All this time, day after day, it has been drilled into us by the ups and downs of family life to forget about ourselves and think of them. Now that we have finally learned, to some extent, to do that (it hasn't been easy), they're going to disappear! It is natural, inevitable, to feel wrenched. It's like a nasty joke played on us by Mother Nature to turn the tables at this late date. Or perhaps it's more like a Zen joke: You gradually, painfully learn to forget yourself, to think only of them. You gradually come to feel that they are the ultimate good, the ultimate truth. Then: Poof! They disappear! Oh yeah, what was that about *duhkha* and *anitya* again? What a great teaching device! Would Buddhism not do well to view it this way?

A beloved grown child leaving home is the epitome of *duhkha,* the pain inherent even in the joyful. An adolescent who, for some reason, is unable to move out into life is a great sorrow; it is in fact the last thing a loving parent would want. So while it pains you to see them go, the last thing you can wish is for them to stay; you want them to realize their potential and give the world what they have to give—that is the greatest joy! How much I have benefited from Buddhist insight into this situation. The *Dhammapada* is completely right and compellingly profound when it says, "'I have sons, I have wealth': thinking thus the fool is troubled. Indeed, he himself is not his own. How can sons or wealth be his?"[2] I need to hear this, over and over.

Yet the parents' mixed heartbreak and joy at seeing the young adult move on is also completely valid. These experiences and our responses to them are meaningful and important in each individual's spiritual journey. What better way to learn selflessness, love, and giving than to care for an infant? And what better way to learn letting go than to watch a grown child walk away? Yet the latter does not cancel or invalidate the former! Letting go well, in the right way, at the right time, to the right degree, is a part of love, even attached (devoted) love.

Motherhood, in its many facets, is an intense spiritual discipline. I do not need to think that my feelings and experiences with respect to motherhood are unique; on the contrary, I know they are the most common thing in the world. But I do need a religious tradition that validates those feelings and experiences. I deeply appreciate simple things in Friends Meeting like singing the words to the familiar hymn, "For the Beauty of the Earth," in which we give thanks "for the joy of human love, brother, sister, parent, child." I deeply appreciate a tradition that has lavished warm, individualized, personalized care on my child, so nurturing her that she can rise in the stillness of the gathered Meeting and give verbal ministry, give voice to the Light as she has received it. If she can do that, I know she is ready to go out into the world.

For me, this natural koan that has occupied many of my middle years has been a challenging blessing. The Quaker-Buddhist path has not been such an "easy path," after all. This natural koan, in Buddhist language, has been, in Quaker language, the Spirit leading me forward. This Great Doubt that has seized me, this questioning mind fixed in not-knowing at the confluence of love and emptiness, has been, in Quaker language, the movement of the Spirit, the presence of the sacred. I am grateful that both traditions encourage me to regard this questioning mind with respect and seriousness.

I don't believe that Buddhism, in any of its Asian forms, can fit entirely comfortably for any Westerner. Yet also in Quakerism, for me, there are irritants—the hymn lyric that gives voice to an obsolete (for me) theology, or the Biblical passage that has been the seed of a repugnant bit of Christian history. I cannot sit in complete comfort with either tradition. And yet I need both. For me, there is profound truth in both. I no longer see them as so nearly reconcilable, but more as two languages, each of which speaks with great profundity truths of the spiritual life, yet neither of which (like any language) is really translatable into the other.

In the end, all truth must be reconcilable. But I am well aware of my distance from that point. For now, the Japanese Zen poet Issa expresses my Quaker-Buddhist sentiment perfectly in his haiku, written upon the death of his child:

The world is a dewdrop,
Yes, the world is a dewdrop,
And yet, and yet...[3]

THE LIGHT OF BUDDHIST WISDOM
AND THE THREE BIRTHS

SISTER ELAINE MACINNES, O.L.M.

T HE LIGHT OF BUDDHIST WISDOM has illumined much of my life, and yet I am reluctant to start this story without a clarification. I lived in the Orient for thirty-two years and basked in its warmth almost from the time of my arrival in Japan, September 12, 1961. Indeed, I often speak about Oriental spirituality and use the term freely to cover many varying kinds and degrees of spiritual insights I now own, most of which originated during my tenure in the Far East.

Further, although I have been involved in Buddhist meditation for over forty years, I want to make clear that I know very little about the Buddhist religion. Of course, I can devise my own Buddhism, as many are doing these days, and, indeed, after his great enlightenment, the Buddha Sakyamuni apparently did not intend to start a religion. I was taught that he advocated just sitting in meditation and living a life in accord with its revealed treasures. But following his death, the Buddha's teachings were recorded and collected and later coded or made into canons, which gave ordinary people a reference point and a body of scripture to believe in. Thus we have the beginnings of what turned out to be one of the most vibrant missionary religions in the world. I respect that religion. *And* I respect the Dalai Lama who is trying to give Westerners a solid basis for their interest in Buddhism.

A few years ago in London, England, when asked to comment on the widely held view that one could be both a Christian and a Buddhist, the

Dalai Lama remarked that that was like putting a yak's head on a sheep's body. He has devoted much time and effort in his Dharamsala home to offering self-styled Western Buddhist monks an in-depth study of Buddhism. It *is* the Precepts and the Bodhisattva Vows, the Three Refuges, the Four Noble Truths, and the Eightfold Path. But it also entails a detailed ethical and moral code.

The Dalai Lama, of course, represents one of the several branches of Tibetan Buddhism. There are many other schools and sects of Buddhism; I must admit virtual ignorance concerning most of them. So the following story may have very little to do with the Buddhist religion. I see that several co-contributors have authentic knowledge and perhaps even faith and devotion, and it is *they* who will supply what is lacking here. And amongst the readers, there will be those who live as "early Buddhists" because they practice Zen meditation and live according to the wisdom of the light of satori seen in a deep experience.

Finally, let me make clear that the "light" of Asian wisdom in my life has become more incandescence than illumination. It is a heat that causes action, a propulsion that shot this violin-playing North American Catholic Nun and Zen sitter into the poverty stricken farming areas of South East Leyte in the Philippines, and later into a series of United Kingdom prisons, in service to one of the world's most forgotten group of people—namely, prisoners.

But I must not get ahead of my story. It starts, as all stories do, with my birth. Seen in terms of "Light," I seem to have had three births. The story of my openness to Buddhism began before I was born. My first birth is recorded in Proverbs, chapter 8, verses 22-31:

The wisdom of God says this
You created me when your purpose first unfolded
From the oldest of your works
From everlasting I was firmly set,
From the beginning before the earth came into being.
The deep was not when I was born.

There were no springs to gush with water.
Before the hills I came to birth.
Before you made the earth, the countryside
Or the first grains of the world's dust.
When you fixed the heavens firm I was there.
When you drew a ring on the surface of the deep.
When you thickened the clouds above,
When you assigned the sea its boundaries
And the waters will not invade the shore.
When you laid down the foundations of the world
I was by your side, a master craftsman,
Delighting you day after day,
Ever at play in your presence
At play everywhere in your world,
Delighting to be with the children of the earth.

Deleting personal pronouns, that could be a Zen poem. In any case, from the time I could think, reflect, and hear the Bible, this passage from Proverbs owned me. What attracted me to it I can only imagine, but I probably felt so at home there because:

- I came from a family that was secure (firmly set).
- Somehow in the mind of God I was indeed present before the earth and seas (I have a special lifelong sea affinity).
- When God started to move, fixing the heavens, drawing a ring for the oceans' boundaries, thickening the clouds, putting down the foundations of the world (I felt myself there most assuredly).
- All the while, I was playing around everywhere in this "becoming" world, in God's presence, whom I was delighting.
- I was delighted at what evolved in all of creation.

Christianity is good news indeed. Undoubtedly this made me able to accept the good news in Zen, which is preached in the word of silence and experience, a preaching by no-words, and continuously so, as I discovered in Japan. Eventually, I became able to perceive this, and have used it ever since, whether teaching in prisons or out.

The bottom line of the good news is, as my Zen teacher the late Yamada Koun Roshi (then head of the Sanbo Kyodan lineage in Zen Buddhism) said innumerable times, that we are all born to be mystics. One day, when a friend and I were giving a meditation workshop to twenty-four lifers at Wormwood Scrubs Prison in London, England, the silence following the sitting was palpable. Since it was a first experience for all, I took the time to tell each man individually and quietly of the teaching I had received, that we are all born to be mystics. There was not a snicker of disbelief among them. Proverbs says it as it is: "You created me when your purpose first unfolded."

My second birth was March 7, 1924, and I was soon informed that that birth date was auspicious. It was the (original) feast of St. Thomas Aquinas, a man revered for his intellect and scholarship. Although I never for a moment thought that would touch my inner being, I believed that this great saint would subsequently take an interest in me and my welfare. I also was impressed that he was said to be such an intelligent man on a scale that I could only try to imagine.

I first met him more formally when I was about ten years of age. I accompanied someone to a Catholic bookstore that still stands on St. George Street in Moncton, New Brunswick, Canada, my birthplace. There, many years ago, I discovered a large green volume, beautifully bound and imprinted with large gold letters: "AQUINAS." I remember excitedly stepping up on a footstool to reach for the book.

I flipped it open and saw in the lower right hand corner a section dealing with the five ways the existence of God could be considered. The first of these spoke about action and movement, stating (as I recall) that we can continuously see movement all around us, and that each movement is caused by some other movement. Then came the sentence, "the Prime Mover we call God."

I remember being deeply affected and impressed. Incredibly, I seemed to understand. God the Prime Mover! I closed the volume quickly and believed it with my whole heart. After all, St. Thomas Aquinas had said it! But that was all I could absorb then of a revelation of such magnitude. I must have digested it well, for it has stayed with me and been a frequent reference point in the many intervening years. Indeed, it has nourished my whole life and, as it turned out, been invaluable in my growing understanding of Zen Buddhist practices.

When I was studying and meditating with Yamada Koun Roshi at the San'un Zendo in Kamakura, Japan, the characteristic of the Sacred, the Buddha Nature, that I heard spoken of most frequently was "power." The roshi used to say that the Essential World is empty (perhaps the no-thing of nothing is a better English articulation) but at the same time full of infinite potential. He therefore most often used the reference "empty-Infinite" as an appropriate indicator of *his* experiential grasp of the Buddha Nature. Secretly, this delighted me. None of his disciples were as yet drawing parallels between Zen Buddhism and Christianity, but here was a Buddhist boldly using a Christian term, the Infinite. I teased the roshi that the word "smacked" of Christianity. He responded, "I say the Infinite, because that is how I experienced it."

Full of potential. Full of power. The source of the Prime Mover. I was on home ground. For a while it was just a theory to me, derived from Aquinas's insight, like hearing someone tell of the power of electricity. And then later I came to experience that power in itself. *That* was like touching a live wire!

In the East, one designation for that experience is the Sanskrit term *advaita*—literally, "not two"—a moment of great joy and happiness, involving no separation of any kind. *The joy of the raindrop is to enter the ocean.* Such an experience reveals to us that we belong, we are of it, or better still, engulfed in power that is sacred. In other words, "we ARE." Practicing that spirituality, we live our lives in a continuous state of be-ing, proceeding from one present tense to the next. Opening the volume of Aquinas's works when I was just ten years old initially prepared me for this.

Also in my young years, God was referred to as a father in heaven. I had a good rapport with both *father* and *heaven*. Years later, however,

during my first *dokusan* (interview) with the Buddhist nun Fukagai Gichu
Roshi, she pointed out that the specifics of father and heaven might not
be helpful in Zen practice. But I had already imbibed Aquinas's teaching
about God's inconceivability, which prevented me from accepting God's
father-hood as the only credential of the Almighty, and in consequence
I came to see that "heaven" is not only "up there" and "after death," but
also right here, right now.

I was also helped in this regard during my eight years in Rinzai Zen.
In *sesshin* (intensive retreats), Shibayama Zenkei Roshi gave excellent
daily *teisho* (a public Zen talk on a koan—a short, pithy conundrum
whose resolution can only be intuited). He would never be boxed in
with one articulation of the Great Matter. Buddhism does not seem to
be gifted with the personhood of God, but Shibayama Roshi's constant referring to the Ultimate and Nameless left me free for expan-
sion, as it were. In fact, for the roshi, a simple "It" sufficed as divine
nomenclature.

In more recent years, this has delighted me yet again. Many sisters
in the religious community to which I belong are especially sensitive
to feminine issues. They rebel at the constant masculine references to
God in so many of the Church's writings. I must admit, though, that
my suggestion to them of the Zen "It" brought no enthusiastic
response.

To paraphrase Shibayama Roshi, "It" is alive and always manifesting. I
recall the first time I heard the story oft-repeated in the zendo, about the
monk who had *kensho* (an experience of seeing one's own true nature)
while walking along a path. He suddenly saw peach blossoms in the distance, stirring in the breeze. That slight quiet movement was the needed
catalyst, and abruptly he came to the experiential knowledge designated
by the Japanese word *satori* (enlightenment). The first time I heard that
story, I knew immediately that it was both possible and had been experienced. The Prime Mover at work again! I was already familiar and intimate with a busily creative God moving all over the universe, and this
knowledge of God as the Prime Mover was empirical and not just spec-

ulative, even when I was very young. I experienced something related when I was in my early teens.

My sister and I were ill. One day, mother came into the room and placed a nursing tray on the bedside table. She had been taking our temperatures but was suddenly called away. I took the two thermometers and started to play with them and of course broke them both. There was no remorse, for I was delighted to find that I had two drops of magical mercury to play with. I soon discovered they were inclined to adhere to one another. As I held them apart with my forefingers, I could feel the tiny pull. Then as they came closer together, the pull became stronger, and finally, when in close proximity, they literally jumped together. That was a "hands on" moment...coming to know experientially...a touch of the wisdom to come. All things are verbs!

It was years before I mentally put the "Prime Mover" and the internally active mercury drops together. In fact, I thought I had completely forgotten about the thermometer event, which must have happened in the late thirties. But in 1972, when Yamada Roshi confirmed my *kensho*, I immediately surprised myself by exclaiming, "It was just like those two drops of mercury!"

Many years later, I read a parallel story of the very young Gautama. He too had had an early *advaita* (not two) experience that later held a special insight for him. His father and his nurses had taken him to watch the ceremonial plowing for next year's harvest. His father left the very young child in the care of his nurses, under the shade of a rose-apple tree. Gautama watched the plowing and, as the soil was being torn up, the young grass and the eggs that the insects had laid were being plundered. Gautama was horrified and was later to say that he felt he himself had been violated. It was an experience of identification that could sensitize the young prince towards other forms of life. It says in the Buddhist commentary that, on that day, the natural world recognized the spiritual potential of Gautama, and as the hot day wore on, while the shadows of the other trees moved, the shadow under the rose-apple tree continued to shelter the boy from the blazing sun.

Years later, Gautama was to recall these two experiences, of violation and then of cooling shelter. In the midst of his austerities, his exhausted body and mind and heart cried out for ease and coolness and direction. Suddenly he remembered what had happened that harvest day so long ago. In recalling that former feeling of devastation and identification and the subsequent cool shade of the rose-apple tree, he found himself thinking *Nirvana,* (*Nirvana* literally means "blowing out, cooling off"). It is said that he suddenly asked himself, "Could that experience of old possibly be the way to enlightenment?" Perhaps instead of torturing himself into the release of duality, he could achieve it more gently and humanely. That he did so is now well known.

When I heard that legend, I understood a great deal of it in an experiential way, and thus did not regard it as one of the many stories about the Buddha that are apocryphal. I have tried to trace my own experience of "life-the-same-as-mine-in-the-soil" and it seems to have started when I was a junior sister in St. Catharine's, Ontario, sometime in 1957. We were living temporarily in a home with a small but attractive garden, and I took pleasure in looking after it. I got the feel of earth in my hands. About the same time, I was starting to read some bits about quantum physics, and in my mind and hands I believed that the earth was alive...that in my hands its life was pulsating.

Then, some years later, when I was in Manila living at the Good Shepherd Convent on Aurora Boulevard in Quezon City, I saw it more direct and immediate. One day there was a very strong earthquake. I ran out of the building and found the gardener stretched out on the wet grass, hollering for me to get away from the building and to lie on the ground as he was. It is something to be at eye level with the earth as it heaves and belches. Suddenly there was *only* the earth, only the soil, only the good brown stuff. That realization caused me to cry out, "I *am* the earth!"

A great lesson concerning the Prime Mover and appropriateness was underlined when I first went to Kamakura. There was much discussion then among the roshi's disciples concerning a Theravadan monk who had come to Tokyo a short time before and performed outstanding supranormal feats. My memory of the occasion is that one of the monks under Harada Daiun Roshi (virtual founder of the Sanbo Kyodan) attended a meditation session led by the Southeast Asian visitor at a Tokyo hotel. Speaking of the height (or was it depth?) of his concentration, the Theravadan monk predicted that he and his chair would rise to the ceiling and remain there fifty-five minutes. This is precisely what happened. When the allotted time had passed, he and the chair he was sitting on returned to their original position. The visitor challenged all those present to show *their* degree of concentration. No one present could do anything that spectacular.

Crestfallen, the Sanbo Kyodan monk returned to his teacher. But Harada Roshi made short shrift of the problem. "Bah!" he said, "Who is he helping up there on the ceiling?"

His monk then asked, "What would you have done if you had been there?"

Harada Roshi replied, "If I had been there, I would have said, 'I'm sure you are tired after such a long trip. Here is a cup of tea to refresh you.'" And with the flowing movements that Zen teachers often use, the famous master spread out his hands and mimed the serving of tea.

Here we have two kinds of movement—one flying up to the ceiling spectacularly, and the other serving a weary traveler—both propelled by the same power of concentrated meditation. It was reported that the monk who saw this continued to hang his head, unconvinced. He still thought that levitating is the way the Buddha Nature fittingly reveals itself. But it was Harada Roshi who gave the integrated Zen teaching of the Prime Mover at work.

Zen concerns everyday stuff. Yamada Roshi for a while used to take me to task for always referring to insights and intuitions of the sacred as mysterious. For him the presence/power of the Prime Mover was a *fact,* and his emphasis on the word hinted at baldness, nothing attached, just as it is. There is a koan in *The Blue Cliff Record* about sixteen bodhi-sattvas (living saints) entering the bath and experiencing the *fact* of the water. Not only can the bath be a sensuous experience, it is also the location of the transcendent. This koan, entitled "The Bodhisattvas Enter the Bath," reads:

> In ancient times there were sixteen bodhisattvas. They entered the bath according to the custom of bathing monks at that time. Instantly they realized the "cause" of the water. "All you Zen followers, what do you understand?" One said, "Subtle touch, very clear, accomplished Buddhahood dwells here."

So water is eminently a place of rendezvous with the Prime Mover. It is no wonder that Canada's environment-friendly scientist David Suzuki has said that life is animated water.[1] One frequently finds such parallels between cultures and between religions, too. It was this kind of parallel that helped me in my struggle to come to terms with the Japanese word *kokoro*. There is no one-word equivalent, although it usually appears in a dictionary as "mind." Some of my Japanese friends and acquaintances who were quite proficient in English rejected that interpretation. There is nothing in "mind" that suggests the angst, the feeling, the nostalgia of *kokoro*. But, having long experienced St. Augustine's restlessness, I was able to grasp some of the intensity and spiritual longing so natural to an Oriental mind.

When my own personal journey had become more focused after I entered the convent, that inner point of feeling found light in the Pauline phrase "I live, now not I but Christ lives within me" (Galatians 2:20). I do not know or remember how I came to be attracted by that phrase and can only say that it seemed to be given as gift. Of course I desired earnestly to know it experientially, and at the same time I was equally determined to discover how I was going to practice it.

It is perhaps only natural to assume that I gradually came to see the Divine Indwelling as central to my personal spirituality, but Christianity seemed to point me in the direction of mystery and fervor, which posed an object. Even the phrase Divine Indwelling seemed to have boundaries—as though God had a "place" within my body. In Novitiate, at the beginning of my formal spiritual training, I was not satisfied with this intimacy. The inner angst was being drawn irresistibly to something deeper.

Then one day I read *One With Jesus,* a small book by the Belgian Jesuit Paul de Jaeger. He wrote of his experience with the aforementioned aspiration, "I live, now not I but Christ lives within me." He said that he came to realize that the Divine Indwelling is not intimacy but identification.

Identification! When I read that, my head-world and heart-world exploded from two to one, or—as Zen masters say—"not even one." The joy of the raindrop is to enter the ocean. Total identification. Now, how to practice that? How to make it my lived spirituality? Where would I find a teacher? There was not one in the convent I had entered, nor among the visiting priests who were our spiritual directors, nor in the books offered as possible helps. There seemed to be nobody in North America who could help. I wondered if perhaps I would have to learn it through osmosis, or by direct heavenly intervention.

Then I arrived in Japan on my first mission assignment, and on Mount Hiei in Kyoto, I met my Buddhist monk friend Horisawa Somon. His first question was "How do you pray?" I soon discovered he was inquiring about body position, and he thoroughly rejected my very Western dismissal of that subject as an unimportant aspect in meditation. Within a matter of days, I met Father H.M. Enomiya-Lassalle and eventually the Buddhist Rinzai nuns, who taught me to let meditation take over my entire being—body, mind (*kokoro*), and breath. And on that glorious day in December 1972, the connection was made, and intimacy became identification.

When the raindrop enters the ocean there are no boundaries. There is just the ocean. It is a moment of great joy. The "fit" is perfect and open to all. It is one, it is not even one. It just *is.* Christian Zen masters will say, "Come and taste."

Identification starts to become available when we enter the world of silence. I have asked myself hundreds of times over the past seven decades whether or not silence was part of my Catholic prayer life. I cannot say "no." Contemplation was always held up as an ideal, and I understood contemplation to be silent prayer. I knew I was encouraged to enter silence, and sometimes felt that I had been gifted to do so for short periods.

But after entering a *zendo* and learning to sit in a specific body position, adjusting the breath in a certain manner, and keeping the mind at one with the breathing, I became aware that silence in Zen is quite different from any kind of silence I had practiced heretofore. In fact, after forty years of this discipline, I wonder if silence is the most apt articulation of entering a deep state of consciousness. We certainly start with silence, but after a while, the practice takes over.

And then in some indescribable way, the circle becomes complete. Silence brings one to a deeper state of consciousness where IT takes over and our perception of the phenomenal world drops away. The great Japanese sage Dogen Zenji described this state as the "falling away of body and mind." At that point, and in that place, one perceives that the Absolute Power, the Originating Power, is all pervading, and for that split second, not only activates life, but also lives it.

Of all the points in my interweaving of Christian and Buddhist facts, the following is most central. As said before, for me it started in that rendezvous and fascination with the Pauline phrase "I live, now not I but Christ lives within me." It gradually came to light in Zen as I saw the parallel in Dogen's teaching that every effort at non-thinking lessens egostrength, and the Sacred Power within can then act spontaneously and appropriately without hindrance. My own breakthrough came at one specific moment, December 6, 1972.

I had been in Japan for eleven years, eight of which had been at Enkoji in Kyoto sitting with the Rinzai Buddhist nuns. *Joriki* (the special power that builds up in meditation) had been accumulating, and *makyo* (an abrupt eruption on the surface of the consciousness) broke through. At that time, I was helping Father Lassalle at his new Zendo, *Shinmeikutsu* ("Cave of Divine Darkness"), in western Tokyo. Even while overseeing the kitchen and telephone, I had considerable time to meditate, and one day I noticed a radio playing in the grounds. But later I was assured that no radio had been on. The following day, I noticed it was audible only when I was sitting.

One afternoon, drowsy in the heat, my head nodded, and one of the rookie monitors rushed up just when the radio was playing its loudest. Without any indication of his intention, he gave me a couple of good whacks with the *kyosaku* (encouragement stick). Immediately, the music burst into loud, majestical organ chords, seemingly of heavenly origin. The sound filled the entire universe. It lasted only a few minutes, then gradually disappeared, and I never heard it again. But I knew its message. So did Father Lassalle.

When I spoke to him in the evening about that manifestation, the old Jesuit advised me to go to another teacher soon, since *makyo* is an indication of deep sitting. He was thinking of Yamada Koun Roshi, a layman who was gaining an admirable reputation for having a particular charism of bringing sitters to *kensho.*

Sesshin retreat is a kind of hothouse during which we sometimes experience a deeper than usual state of consciousness, *sanmai* in Japanese, or *samadhi* in Sanskrit, and also the eruptions called *makyo*. A good teacher may then confront the disciple with a koan. The jousts between student and teacher gradually free the sitter from intellection and start the sitter "moving," as the Zen masters say. If the time is ripe, we leave the intellectual process and are catapulted into intuiting the essence. The interviews at which this jousting takes place are called *dokusan,* and the small room becomes a battlefield of sorts. The teacher and disciple develop a sparring relationship that can trigger the *kensho* experience of enlightenment.

It happened for me in December 1972, on the fourth day of the annual *sesshin* when Japanese Buddhists celebrate Shakyamuni's enlightenment. At the early morning *dokusan,* the roshi discerned that I was moving. Later, I was bothered by something he said in the morning's *teisho* and then again in a subsequent *dokusan.* I asked to speak with Father

Lassalle, who was also making the *sesshin*. I had become afraid. The old priest spoke to me most kindly and said the experience I was apparently approaching would break down the feeling of separation, which is very strong in us Westerners. He said the roshi was trying to strengthen my faith in the *Oneness* of the Kingdom and God by bringing me to that experience. "Be perfectly honest and open with him. Trust him. He is a great master."

After supper on the sixth day, I stretched out on the *tatami* matted floor, reached for my New Testament, and opened it where I had inadvertently put a card from Father Lassalle. The first sentence that hit my eye was, "This joy, this perfect joy, is now mine." I couldn't help but smile.

That evening, *dokusan* with the roshi was uneventful, but he brought me into the concrete-me more fully. I returned to my place in the *zendo,* looked at the "me" that seemed to be ensconced in a hard shell. Suddenly, the very core of that shell burst open. Its lovely contents shot out into every part of my being. I was inundated until there was no me left. No boundaries anywhere. How beautiful and clean and pure…born into this world of the Infinite…belonging and fitting and home-ing! How utterly perfect. My heart was bursting in gratitude at this third birth. Indeed, this joy, this perfect joy, is now mine.

Eventually this experience became for me the basis of that enigmatic designation, spirituality. Of the many definitions available, the one most apt in my life has been articulated by Father Ronald Rolheiser: "Your spirituality is what you do with the fires that burn within you."[2] The steady fire within has propelled me through many decades of activity. I am now at the advanced age of 77, *biju* in Japanese, designated a year of joy and happiness.

It is with considerable confidence and deep gratitude that I can follow the pattern the golden thread of my life story has woven. The Prime Mover is the Oriental weaver, and the design an eternal pattern spanning East and West.

LIVING IN GOD'S GRACE

TERRY C. MUCK

B Y ALMOST ANY MEASURE, I am a conservative Christian. Billy Graham is one of my life's heroes. I belong to and read scholarly papers at the Evangelical Theological Society. I teach in the E. Stanley Jones School of World Mission and Evangelism at Asbury Theological Seminary. I used to edit *Christianity Today*. I believe every word of the Apostles' Creed. And I believe that what God did by sending his son Jesus to die on the cross for humanity's sins is what makes it possible for all humanity to have hope for both present and future salvation. In today's Western religious climate, that's conservative.

Yet when I stop to enumerate the factors that have contributed to my remaining a conservative Christian for all of my adult life, one of the most important factors has been the teachings of Buddhism.

I know that for many who read this essay that last statement calls into serious question my claim to be a conservative Christian. I know that, and I also know that there have been times in my life when I would have shared that suspicion. I don't any longer. Although I do consider what I have just said to be an irony of major proportions, I don't consider it impossible to be a faithful Christian and yet to be beholden to another religious tradition for some of the depth and vitality of that Christian faith. In the paragraphs that follow I would like to make that case.

An Optimism of Grace

The first step in making such a case, at least from a Christian's point of view, is to believe wholeheartedly in what some Wesleyan scholars have called the optimism of grace.[1] Put simply, the optimism of grace refers to a belief and a disposition to look at the world in the belief that God has always and everywhere been active. As the Psalmist said, "If I go up to the heavens, you are there; if I make my bed in the depths, you are there" (Psalm 139:8).

Of course, one does not have to look at the world with this kind of hopeful expectation. Sin and evil sometimes seem as pervasive as the effects of God's grace. In a century filled with two world wars, several genocides in the USSR, Germany, Cambodia, and Rwanda, and grinding poverty everywhere, it is just as tempting (and rational) to look around and say, "I go up to the heavens and evil is there, I descend to the sea and am awash in sin."

However, I have consciously chosen not to view the world in this way. I stand with John Wesley, who observed, "God acts everywhere and therefore is everywhere, for it is an utter impossibility that any being created or uncreated, should work where God is not."[2] While not minimizing or turning a blind eye on the sin and evil in the world, I consciously choose to look always and everywhere for the evidences of God's grace: In everyday events. In the physical beauty and awe-inspiring power of the world. And in people—especially in people.

Understanding the world in this way has important consequences. First, for me at least, it forces me to understand that religion is primarily about people. One of the lasting contributions Wilfred Cantwell Smith made to the study of religion was his claim that in the end religion is about people. He did not gainsay the importance of ideas, because they are the carriers of the spirituality that characterizes us all. He certainly left open the possibility of revelation. But to understand the world's religious scene, one is always driven back to people: What do you believe, my friend? By what principles do you order your life? What is your experience of God? As Smith put it, "The study of religion is the study of persons."[3]

Second, the optimism of grace has led me to conclude that the religious person is a curious person. Questions have consumed my adult life. I am curious. I am fascinated by the spiritual life of individual human beings. At times this curiosity has perplexed those nearest and dearest to me. When I kept inviting the Jehovah's Witness missionaries back to our home because I was intrigued by the conversation, my mother fretted. My dad never quite understood the "comparative religion thing." My dean wondered why I visited several Christian Identity militia camps one summer and subscribed to all their periodicals, surely landing both me and the seminary on several FBI surveillance lists.

What to do with this curiosity? My understanding of the optimism of grace has enabled me to channel it to good ends. When I meet people of other religious traditions (and of my own), I am not looking to discover sin and evil. Instead, I am looking for the way God is working in their lives. I like the image given to us by Lesslie Newbigin: In every human being, Christian or non, there is at least a spark of the original *imago Dei* (divine image) still smoldering. Why not seek it out and fan it?[4]

Which leads to a third implication: Attitude is as important as accuracy. It is arguable that the biggest problem with interreligious interchanges today is not the *fact* that we may disagree over some very important issues. As big an issue is the *attitude* with which we hold on to these ideas and what that attitude leads to in terms of relationships with other people.[5]

The questions to ask are these: Does the way I hold my religious beliefs lead to the objectifying of the other person, reducing him or her to nothing more than the philosophical effect of his or her religious ideas? Does the way I hold my religious beliefs close me off to finding new and rich expressions of God's grace as manifest in other people?

If I hold my beliefs with hope, with the expectation of finding God everywhere, I am not thereby assured of pleasant exchanges with everyone. Others may not approach me in reciprocal fashion. But my chances of a positive interaction are greatly increased. And I become part of God's story of redemptive kingdom building, which is simply unearthing the presence of God's witnesses in the world, no part of which has ever been left without that witness.

Submission to God's Will

Submission to God's will is what keeps the optimism of grace from degenerating into a Pollyanna-ish view of the world, into wearing rose-colored glasses. There are other ways to check overly naïve optimism, of course. One is a runaway concept of the pervasiveness of sin. This produces a line of thinking that my father called "worm such as I" theology, after the line from the old hymn "At the Cross."[6] Unfortunately this line of thinking runs so counter to the intent of the optimism of grace that it is like introducing a computer virus onto your hard drive—it erases everything else, especially the sense of the goodness of God's creation. So I don't choose this path.

Alternatively, we can rely on our own good sense to curb the potential excesses of optimism. Unfortunately, on most days we do not possess adequate good sense to accomplish the task. As human beings left to ourselves we seem bereft of a "governor," a warning that we are going too fast for conditions. If some optimism is good, then more optimism is better, and total optimism is best.[7] Or so we think.

Thus we need outside help with maintaining a realistic level of optimism. Sometimes we turn to moral codes, sometimes to canon law, sometimes to doctrinal expressions. All these can be good, but only if seen as operating in the larger context of God's will. And this is where submission enters the picture.

Submission is not a very popular idea in our culture. As a concept it has been hijacked by the power mongers, some of them religious, and used as a subterfuge to exercise their control. By appealing to submission, evils such as totalitarianism, authoritarianism, and patriarchy have been perpetrated in the name of religion. Yet in discussing these obvious evils, we should not throw the baby of submission out with the bath water of misuse.

I learned submission from reading Calvin. Actually I shouldn't say it that way, because I think part of the reason submission can become oppressive is that we focus on it as if it is an initiating act instead of a response to God's truth. If seen as an initiating act, submission becomes distorted, twisted by pride in our religiosity. Properly understood, submission is an instinctive response to God's sovereignty. This is how Calvin saw it: "We yield to God's mercy.... We must think humbly of ourselves before God."[8] When we see God as sovereign creator and ourselves as the created being, then submission is the proper, pre-programmed response.

In our culture, women have perhaps the toughest time with submission. So pervasive has been the male insistence on surrogate submission—to church leaders instead of to God, to male leadership instead of to God, to human ideals instead of to God—that a proper, just sense of submission is extremely difficult to embrace.

Still, I believe it is the "A" response to our recognition of God's sovereignty. As a response to God, it engenders great fruit: humility, joy, structured freedom. Combined with an optimism of grace, it shapes an attitude toward life and the world that opens us up rather than closes us down.

In my personal case, submission to God's will is what turned a vocation into a call. My curiosity about the world's religions made me early on want to choose the vocation of scholar of religion. God called me to ministry. Like Samuel, I heard the call but could not identify the voice (1 Samuel 3). Identification would only come with submission. When I submitted, I identified the calling voice as God's. My curiosity about the religions rose above a vocation and was transmogrified into a calling.

I can remember as if it were yesterday my original intrigue with the religion called Buddhism. I was intrigued because it seemed at first to be the antithesis of a religion based on submission to God's will. The Buddha was explicit in saying one should not practice because he told them to but because one tried it and liked it.[9] I wanted to know more. As I studied, I found that the Christian concept of submission to God's will was not a blind nihilism—and that submission, if understood as egolessness, was a central part of Buddhism.

Thus, my enrichment from Buddhism began early. Once I had determined to embrace God's universal presence, both temporal and spatial,
and submit to what I understood to be God's will—gracious activity
toward everyone—my interest in and study of Buddhism had to fit into
that pattern. I have not been disappointed with the results.

The Teachings of Gautama Buddha

Let me set the context. I decided to study the history of religions at
Northwestern University. On arriving, I found myself in good hands.

Edmund Perry was the founder and chair of the department. By the
time I arrived, he was inching closer and closer to retirement after an
academic career devoted to training students for the scientific study of
religion. Yet he believed that such a study was not done by de-religioned
automatons, but by people of religious convictions. Edmund was a
Methodist clergyman from Georgia who never lost his passion for the
Church. He taught and modeled for me many, many things, not the least
of which was how to combine scientific detachment and Christian commitment.

Walpola Rahula was a Theravada Buddhist *bhikkhu* (monk) from Sri
Lanka who would have found it unthinkable that he should have to be less
a monk in order to be more a scholar of religion. He too modeled for
me how to combine religious commitment and religious studies scholarship. In addition, he taught me that religious activism could be engaged
with one's scholarly integrity intact. He was such an activist in Sri Lanka
on behalf of both education and a *bhikkhu*'s participation in political life
that he was at various times *persona non grata* there.[10] He taught me about
Buddhism, and he taught me about life.

Now let me relate some content. Elsewhere I have written about lessons I have learned from Buddhism, especially regarding soteriology and
morality.[11] In this essay I would like to rehearse for the reader two further areas:

The Buddhist teaching of *anatta* or no-self. This is perhaps the most distinctive of all the Buddha's teachings.[12] It has taught me much about human anthropology and psychology. Simply put, *anatta* teaches us that there is no permanent essence to individual human existence. In Christian terms, the Buddha denied that there was such a thing as an enduring human soul. This seems in direct opposition to the orthodox Christian teaching that there is an enduring, essential human soul. And unlike some other discrepancies between the teachings of Buddha and the teachings of Jesus that turned out to be more apparent than real, this divergence persists. The difference struck me as profound when I first studied Buddhism thirty years ago, and remains a profound difference today. What to do?

First, acknowledge the difference.

Second, continue to study. My study of *anatta* has taught me a great deal about my understanding of the human condition. The Buddha made his case this way: He analyzed the individual human being into its constituent parts. He found five: material elements, senses, perceptions provided by the senses, analysis of these perceptions into patterns of thought and dispositions, and actions prompted by those patterns of thought and dispositions. Once the analysis into five constituent parts is done, the Buddha said, nothing is left. And since the five elements themselves constantly change as the materials age and sense perceptions reflect a constantly changing context, nothing is permanent *(anicca)*. Thus, there is no eternal soul as Christians understand it.

The teaching of *anatta* was elaborated by the Buddha's disciples in two ways. The Buddha's more philosophically and psychologically oriented followers expanded and elaborated on the Buddha's basic teaching, mainly by further analyzing the five categories into more and more subdivisions made up of categories of sense perceptions, dispositions, habits of mind, and possible actions in response. The Buddha's more practice-oriented followers developed these teachings into a variety of meditative practices called insight meditation.

Third, ask how this teaching affects our theoretical understanding—in this case, our Christian theology. I was a psychology major in college

and seminary, and I considered graduate study in psychology before settling on religion. I am passably familiar with most modern psychological systems and know of nothing as sophisticated in terms of a typology
of the human psyche as what the Buddha taught. What the Buddha and
his early followers did in terms of analyzing the human psyche is comparable to the current genome project, the mapping of human genes.

As a Christian, I have found this analysis to be enormously illuminat-
ing. Without embracing the Buddha's motivation for this teaching (the
doctrine of *anatta*), it has expanded my understanding of the pinnacle of
God's creation, the complex human mind. Further, "thinking on these
things and pondering them in my heart" has taught me lessons regarding human motivation that do fit into my Christian conception of what
it means to be human.

My Understanding of God's Creative Acts

I don't know if that understanding, however, would ever have been as
rich as it has become if I had not had the privilege of living in a Buddhist
culture for an extended period of time. In 1976 I received a Fulbright-
Hayes grant to do my Ph.D. dissertation research in Sri Lanka. I went,
I experienced, I grew up.

My theoretical understanding of *anatta* and insight meditation took a
quantum leap toward wholeness when I met Buddhists for whom *anatta,
annica,* and Vipassana (insight meditation) were second nature. I was
reminded of the subtle nature of the effects of religious doctrine. Just as
not all Christians who embrace the doctrine of grace are gracious, so not
all Buddhists who embrace the teachings of no-self are selfless.

Living in Sri Lanka, however, forced me to examine my own understanding of the interfaces between Christian faith, Buddhist teachings,
and interpersonal relationships. Interpersonal relationships, I began to
see, are not a peripheral subject when it comes to the study *and* practice
of religion. They are at the center of all the issues. So I had to sort
through all my Christian theological issues first:

Do you or do you not, Terry, believe that God made every single human being in the world? Yes.

Do you or do you not, Terry, believe that God made each and every one of these human beings in his image? Well, yes, I do.

Do you or do you not, Terry, believe that the *imago Dei* still has residual effects on all human religious behavior, especially in the area of the urge to seek God, what Calvin called the *sensus divinitatus?* I surely do believe it.

Do you or do you not, Terry, believe that God has commanded (and we are to obey) that we love our neighbors (even our enemies) as ourselves in word, thought, and deed? Yes, I believe it.

In the light of these affirmations, I was forced to come to what were for me some revolutionary decisions concerning Buddhism and Buddhists. It seemed clear to me that given the above, all the Buddhists I met were created by God, made in his image, and seeking him. Buddhism was not some wily snare of the devil, as C.S. Lewis had led me to believe in the *Screwtape Letters,* [13] but was rather the product—at least in terms of human motivation—of Buddhists sincerely seeking to know God.

I knew, of course, that Buddhists would not put it this way; indeed, I intuited that many Buddhists would probably be offended by my expressing this in this way. But it was very important for me as a Christian to spell out these doctrines with their implications because, if all this were true, then my attitude toward Buddhism and Buddhists would have to change from what I was taught. I had been taught that Buddhists were godless evildoers and pagans and barbarians. *Pagans and barbarians* were words usually said with such disdain that one felt the very humanity of these people was in question.

Historic Christian doctrine, however, taught otherwise. These were children of God, seeking him. Instead of being dismissive and confrontational with these people and this teaching, was I called to come alongside them, have fellowship with them as fellow children of God, and talk about our common search for God?

This was a big change to consider. It went against my training. It went against the prescriptions of my fellow scholars, who saw such thinking as dangerously unscientific. It went against the understanding of most Buddhists, who saw me as an untutored sentient being, eyes covered with the dust of ignorance, in need of the *buddhadharma* (the Buddha's teaching).[14] To be honest, even today, twenty-five years later, there is not a lot of call for this kind of thinking in our world. Fellowship and cooperation in the search for God are sometime ideas that are usually overwhelmed by the more operative waves of confrontation and competition.

Yet I think that to be a good Christian you must believe and practice these things. You can only go so far in being a good Christian by being a good Christian in the Church. From there you must take a leap and do all the things you do among Christians with others. This is becoming more and more important as we spend more and more of our time in the presence of others.

The Practice of Dialogue

But the world is set up otherwise. The world and its competitive systems are set up to control and conquer. So in order to begin to reshape the world into patterns of cooperation and fellowship we must intentionally set up situations, artificial constructs, that enable us to practice in experimental situations that will hopefully become new cultural patterns of interaction. Such is the practice of interreligious dialogue.

I joined the Society for Buddhist-Christian Studies in 1980. Actually, I attended the first organizational meeting in Anaheim, led by Fred Streng and John Cobb. I have been a member ever since. I attend the annual meetings. I have served on the board of directors, been chair of the nominating committee twice, and for the past five years been editor (with Rita Gross) of the Society's journal, *Buddhist-Christian Studies*. I have read papers at the Society's meetings and have become good friends with a core group of people dedicated to fostering this type of interaction. It has been wonderful.

Of course, it has not been unequivocally wonderful. Interreligious dialogue in today's West, particularly in academia, has weaknesses. I can think of two major ones. First, it is an artificial construct. It is unreal. We behave at these meetings in ways foreign to everyday life and to the way that the vast majorities of the world's people behave. We are in some senses like little children who dress up in mommy and daddy's clothes pretending to be adults when we know we are still children. Not that this should surprise us. We knew that in order to change cultural patterns we would have to set up some pilot projects that would succeed and show people the value of what we are doing.

Second, "cooperation and fellowship" are tough nuts to crack. We too quickly idealize them, set them against "competition and control," and thereby lose their essence. That is, cooperation is not the antithesis of competition but its complement, the attitude and approach that makes the exchange of ideas (by its very nature a "competition" exercise) a mutually beneficial search for truth. A couple of things can happen when you attempt to totally eliminate competition in favor of cooperation. You might become hypocritical, denying that you are competitive even as you attempt to defeat the forces of fundamentalism. That is, you simply become a closet fundamentalist preaching the dogma of cooperation. Or you might give up on the search for truth altogether in favor of a kind of naïve relativism.

We struggle with both of these tendencies in our Society, but I think we usually win the battle on both fronts. We cope with the first through the simple acknowledgment that we are in some senses "artificial," but intentionally so, in attempting to offer the wider world a different and, we think, better way. We cope with the second by attempting to strike a balance with what one might call "cooperative competition."

Can this type of interaction be reconciled to the teachings of conservative Christianity? I think so. I think you really find out what you believe (the full, deep meaning of what you believe) in the give and take of conversation.[15] It doesn't happen easily, it doesn't happen safely. It doesn't happen by burying our talents in the sand, but by investing those talents in the interactions of the world's religious people. The fellowship we are seeking is not a static détente, but a dynamic movement of active, engaged people everywhere moving as a group toward God.

Will the practice of interreligious dialogue as currently exercised continue to model for us the way toward the future to which the religions call us? Perhaps. Since it has been such a rewarding experience for me, I am tempted to say I hope so. But something tells me that that might not be the best thing. If the Society for Buddhist-Christian Studies continues to be the center, then that means that we are not moving the culture along toward cooperative competition, the true fellowship of all God's children. So although that might continue to be personally rewarding, it would be a functional failure.

I dream of a society where cooperative competition becomes the norm, not a hothouse flower. Where everyone sees themselves as part of a humanity-wide search for human liberation/salvation/release. The good must be graciousness, selflessness. The goal must be truth. The goal must be God.

The Experience of the Holy Spirit

It is not a very neat solution, is it, to say that the goal must be God? "Goal" begs for "means of attainment" and "means of assessment." God is amenable to neither. God can't be a goal.

What can be described in God terms (and goal terms), however, are the things we do in order to reach out to God. Our goal, you could say, is to do those things that lead to witness of God. Can we be evidences, however small, however imperfect, of what it is like to seek God? Can our resolve to be more and more holy, indeed to move toward total subjective holiness, contribute to the world's understanding of God?

Christians are adamant that such a move, leading to such a witness, can be made, but only if God initiates it and—through the Holy Spirit—empowers it. Perhaps Buddhists would take issue with that description, perhaps not. But the extent to which Christians see or feel the Holy Spirit working in our lives, the lives of others, and in the social systems we set up is the extent to which we are faithful Christians.

I suspect that of all the things that I have said in this article, this may be the most revealing of my conservatism and the most out of step with our current culture. Religion at the core is a transcendent enterprise. It of course speaks to biology and psychology and sociology and philosophy and theology. But those are in the end all human enterprises and to be judged as such. They only become religious when they are understood to be under the umbrella of the indefinable transcendent.

This is a frustrating position to hold, but I am convinced it is an absolutely determinative one. Without it, religion is effectively reduced to human rationality and becomes indistinguishable from the human sciences. With it, we have reason for the hope that is within us. This is the irony. Reason may become more rational without the transcendent, but it loses its focus or truth. With the suprarational, reason rises above itself, finds its proper context, and becomes what it was meant to be—the defining characteristic of God's recurring creative act, humanity.

Although Buddhists and members of other religious traditions may be uncomfortable with the particulars of this definition, my experience has been that talk of God being active throughout the world through something called the Holy Spirit finds resonances with religious seekers everywhere. Among Christian theologians, I think John Wesley expressed this idea with as much clarity as anyone: The world swims in an inexhaustible reservoir of divine grace. We only miss it when we take our being for granted. The minute we pay attention, grace can be quickly identified.

There is a great deal of talk about common ground in the emerging disciplines and practices that surround interreligious interchanges. Various attempts have been made to locate this common ground. Some have said that the transcendent we all seek is the same, that is the common ground. Some have said that it is the end product of the search—salvation/liberation/release—that is the common ground. Some have said that it is the searching—ethics, the campaign for justice, concern for the poor—that is the common ground. Some have said that it is only in the process of conversation itself that we find the common ground. Although these are the major suggestions, there are also others. But none of them quite measures up. If they are not so general or diffuse as to be practically meaningless, they are so specific to human control as to be unconnected to the divine.

True common ground must be connected to the divine, yet a common experience of religions everywhere. Christians call this the Holy Spirit. The belief that someone somewhere has and is making provision for us seems to me to be the most helpful and least arguable of all common ground proposals. I believe that it leads to a much needed commodity: hope.

I believe that the Christian gospel gives us hope. That what God did through Jesus Christ is determinative for the whole world, not just the Christian club. So although I have learned much from Buddhism and in several ways define myself over against its teachings, I am not a Buddhist.

Can there be any more important product in the world today than hope? Is anyone else providing it? The hope of human reason, the driving force of the Enlightenment, evaporated among all but the most credulous, decades ago. The hope of scientific progress has been shown to be a two-edged sword. The hype of human security in material health and wealth has not spawned more hope but growing despair.

The Christian faith, properly taught and understood, has a simple product, a product called hope. The irony of the product is that it is given away, not sold. It abrogates the law of supply and demand. The more it is sought, the more there is. And it becomes real to people not when they compete for it but when they cooperate with the hopeless in its search.

That is why I'm a Christian. It's why I teach in the E. Stanley Jones School of World Mission and Evangelism. It is why I love all the world's people, no matter what their religion, and it is why I eagerly have fellowship with them. It's why I am so hopeful. You cannot dispense hope while pretending you don't have any.

ON BECOMING A BUDDHIST CHRISTIAN

MARIA REIS HABITO

T HE OTHER DAY, just as I entered the house, arms full of grocery bags, the telephone rang. "This is Colleen O'Connor, calling from California. I am writing an article on Guanyin and Mary for the *Dallas Morning News,* and I would like to ask you a few questions. Do you have a few minutes, or should I call back later?"

I stared at my grocery bags, trying to figure out which items would need to go into the refrigerator. Compared to the groceries, Guanyin and Mary seemed quite removed from my life right now, but then again, the refrigerator seemed just as out of reach at the other end of the kitchen. So I might as well answer Colleen's questions.

She asked me why I thought there was such a growing interest in Guanyin among Westerners. I answered that people are increasingly looking for a feminine dimension of spirituality, and that both Guanyin, the Chinese goddess of Mercy (in Japanese, Kannon or Kanzeon), and Mary, mother of God, are figures who embody this dimension of unconditional love and boundless compassion. I imagine that if Colleen had posed this same question to one of my Buddhist nun friends in Taiwan, they might very well have answered it quite differently. They would probably have said that it is not we who are looking for Guanyin, but that it is really Guanyin who is looking for us, reaching out to us. And could the renewed interest in the Virgin Mary among people of various religious backgrounds not also be explained in the same vein?

During the course of our conversation, Colleen related to me that she had looked for statues of Guanyin in San Francisco's Chinatown and that she found them quite unfamiliar, strange. "Did you not feel that way when you encountered Guanyin for the first time?" she asked me curiously.

This question is what brings me right to the heart of the topic of this article, "On Becoming a Buddhist Christian." My first encounter with Guanyin took place more than twenty years ago in Taiwan, where I studied Chinese language and culture from 1979 to 1981. Like Colleen, I one day stood in front of a graceful and mysterious figure clad in a white flowing robe who reminded me of a Madonna. This figure, however, was not displayed on the shelves of a bustling store for religious items, but rather sat delicately on the main altar of a small hermitage in the quiet hills surrounding Dragon Lake near Ilan in East Taiwan. "Shih-fu (Master), who is that?" I asked the Buddhist Master, who had lighted incense and then bowed in front of the figure that was softly illuminated by flickering candlelight.

"Can't you see?" he replied gently. "That is you!"

———————

What am I? Who am I? Are these not the very questions that send many of us on a religious search? In my case, this answer from Shih-fu hit like a bomb, unleashing these questions in a powerful way. What does he mean? I asked myself over and over. What is my connection to this figure he calls Guanyin? What does he see that I don't?

This encounter with Guanyin was not my first encounter with Buddhism. In the summer of 1978, when I had just graduated from high school, my mother took me on a two-week trip to Taiwan. Our host there was Father Joseph Wang, a Roman Catholic parish priest in the coastal town of Keelung and now also auxiliary bishop of Taipei. One day, he took us to see a "special friend" of his, a Buddhist nun who had made a vow to spend fifteen years in meditation in one small room and to eat only what lay people would bring her to support her practice. Now the vow was fulfilled, and the nun had come out to be available to visitors. Buddhism was then very unfamiliar to us, and on the way to the hermitage my mother and I talked about how strange this lady must be to make a vow of this sort. When we arrived, a lively nun of about sixty years of age came toward us with a huge smile.

Greeting us warmly, she asked, "Are you Catholic like Father Wang?" When we nodded somewhat hesitantly, not knowing what to expect, her smile grew even bigger and she replied: "Buddhists or Christians —it does not make the slightest difference. We are all brothers and sisters."

Her open-mindedness and spontaneity instantly wiped out the inner prejudice and reserve that I had brought to this encounter and inspired me so much that I wanted to learn more about Buddhism. And so I returned to Taiwan in the following summer and enrolled at the language school of the Taiwan Normal University in Taipei.

––––––––––

I met Shih-fu for the first time in the spring of 1980. Yang Kao-rung, a philosophy student who lived in the same dormitory as I at the time, and who knew of my interest in Chinese religion, one day invited me to join him on a trip to visit a Buddhist master. "Master Hsin Tao is only about thirty years old," he told me, "but his spiritual power is already immense. He is able to answer all your questions not only about this present life but also about the lives before that—your previous incarnations."

When we had climbed the last steps up to the hermitage and arrived at a shady terrace overlooking the lake and its green surroundings, Master Hsin Tao just emerged from the kitchen with a teapot in his hand and invited us to join the other guests at the patio table. He served us tea as Yang Kao-rung introduced me to everybody present. I was relieved when the focus of attention shifted away from me and back to the conversation that the other guests had been having with Shih-fu, as everybody called the Master. His gentle voice and face seemed somewhat familiar, but then I had never before seen eyes as radiant as his. I sat quietly contemplating the beauty of nature around me, when all of a

sudden everybody started talking to me at the same time. Yang Kao-
rung finally explained the commotion to me: "Shih-fu says that there is
a very deep *yuan* (karmic connection) between you and him." Seeing my
puzzled look, he added, "*Yuan* means a relationship, a connection from
a previous life." A "previous life"? I was not inclined to believe that there
was anything like that, and moreover, what connection should there be
between me and a Chinese Buddhist hermit? Shih-fu seemed to read my
thoughts, because he said, "Do you think that you are here for no reason?
Everything has a reason, a cause. That is also the meaning of *yuan*."

Looking back on my life, I had to agree that I had come to Taiwan for
a reason, a cause, and there were many links in the causal chain of events
that had led me up to this encounter with Shih-fu. One of them even
included a "previous existence," namely that of my maternal grandfather
who had fought in the Boxer war and brought home a Chinese teapot
and cookie box that fascinated me when I was growing up. And of course
there were my parents, who had taken care of a young Chinese priest
during his stay in Germany when my mother was expecting me. The
brother of this priest was Father Wang who had invited us to Taiwan the
previous year. What Shih-fu called *yuan,* I called providence—guidance
by God, in which I trusted.

It was time to leave. Shih-fu accompanied us back to the bus station
and confounded me again with his words: "You are a tree that can bring
rich fruit. Therefore I want to plant your roots in fertile ground." But my
roots were already planted—in the ground of Christianity. Again, Shih-
fu seemed to read my mind because he said: "I was born in Burma. When
I was still very small, I lost my parents in the war. I was thirteen years
old when I came to Taiwan with the army. Because I had seen so much
suffering and pain during the war, I was looking for answers to my questions in religion. At that time, I went to a Christian church for two
years and also read the Bible. But this did not help to answer my questions or to let go of my inner conflicts. When I was fifteen, I started
meditating on my own and discovered for the first time a path to inner
peace, to letting go of suffering. This path is the teaching of the Buddha.

This is what I want to pass on to others." When it was finally time to board the bus, Shih-fu invited me to come back as often as possible for further conversations.

On the way back to Taipei, I asked Yang Kao-rung again about the meaning of *yuan*. In answer, he recited a Chinese saying: "With *yuan*, people will come together from a distance of a thousand *li*. Without *yuan*, they will not meet, even if they stand in front of each other." So in this sense, *yuan* is an inner affinity between people that exists because of their fate. Or, in other words, it is a condition that enables people to encounter one another. In the Buddhist view of things, fate is something that we have created ourselves through our deeds, through karma. Was I ready to open up to this encounter, to accept Shih-fu's invitation to further dialogue? The note in my diary for this day—which, unknown to me then, would give my whole life a very definite direction—ends with this sentence: "I have to go back and speak to him again. I only hope that I can stick to this intention and not lose sight of it."

One rainy afternoon in October 1983, I climbed up the winding path to Ling-jiu mountain, which is named after Vulture Peak in India, where the Buddha preached the *Lotus Sutra*. To continue his ascetic practice of at least eighteen hours of meditation a day, Shih-fu had chosen a cave in this remote spot, which has a magnificent view of the beautiful Taiwanese east coast. His meditation practice had become impossible at the Dragon Lake Hermitage, because people kept coming in ever increasing numbers to ask for his advice.

"Have you returned this time to become my disciple?" Shih-fu greeted me. I was slightly taken aback at his changed appearance. He was so skinny as to be all bones, with a long beard and a wild mane of hair hanging down to his shoulders. Only the radiant expression of his eyes had remained the same. Leading me to the cave, Shih-fu briefly explained that he looked the way he did because he was practicing a form of Tibetan meditation that entailed only liquids for food and did not allow for the cutting of hair. "Really, I want you to become my disciple this time." Shih-fu repeated his initial request when we sat down in the cave. "You have always understood me better than many others, and I'll need your help in the future." My help? In the future? "I will be traveling all over the world, and I want you to be my interpreter," Shih-fu answered my unspoken question. "You can help me to reach so many people who are looking for a spiritual path." I hardly trusted my ears. Why would Shih-fu, who had spent the last decade as a hermit practicing meditation in solitary places travel "all over the world"? Was he serious?

It was true that, after my two years of language study, I was now able to understand Shih-fu better than I had at our initial encounter on that spring afternoon in 1980. Even though at first I had returned to visit him only very hesitantly because each visit proved to be such a spiritual challenge, gradually I had come to accept these challenges in the trust that I was not all alone in this. Providence, which had led me so far away from everything that was then known and familiar to me, would not abandon me—or would it? At times it seemed indeed that I was completely losing ground, and I remember especially one night where I had a dream or a vision—I don't know what to call it. I woke up in tears, sensing that literally everything, the whole universe as I had known it so far, had fallen apart. Who was I? Who was God? What was the purpose of life? Heaven had fallen down, and everything was shattered, dark, and obliterated—except for my pain and confusion. And yet the sun was shining outside like every other day, as if nothing had happened.

"Come." Shih-fu led me outside to a terrace overlooking the ocean. The rain had stopped and the clouds had dispersed. The setting sun now lit the sea and sky on fire. "Do you see how all-encompassing heaven and sea are? I want your heart and mind to become just as all-encompassing, just as free of hindrances. Only then will you be able to grasp emptiness—true emptiness, not the concept of emptiness that is spinning around in your head. True emptiness means that your mind has no hindrances and your thinking no loopholes. If your mind is free from the hindrances created by clinging to notions of I, me, mine, then it will completely open up to the truth. Then you will live not for yourself, but for all beings in trouble and pain. Then you will truly possess the wisdom and compassion of Bodhisattva Guanyin."

He looked at me smilingly and added, "But now, your mind is not free of hindrances. Even as you look at the sea, your thinking is not free of notions of I."

"What notions?" I asked, slightly upset because I thought that I had consisted of pure listening and gazing.

"You believe that you cannot become my disciple because you are from a different cultural background, a German and Christian one, right?" I had to admit that I had been thinking that.

"Listen," Shih-fu said, "the fact that you were born in Germany has to do with your karmic connection. It has given you intelligence and a German, logical way of thinking. All this is good for the study and practice of Buddhism. Religious practice is like learning. It requires intelligence. Without intelligence it is difficult to grasp the whole truth. But you also need positive *yuan* to help you. That is what you need to have built up through many existences." "However," he finished encouragingly, "to open up to truth completely, you need to learn not to make an image of yourself. Don't cling to your German 'I' and to your Christian notions. Don't make them into hindrances on your path, but let them help you instead."

That night I shared the wooden floor of the small temple building next to the cave with two young nuns, Fa-hsing Shih and Liao-yi Shih, who had recently followed Shih-fu to the mountaintop. I found it difficult to go to sleep, and when I finally did, I was startled by a strange dream in which I saw six moons revolving around each other in the endlessly arching midnight-blue sky. The light of the moons was so intense that I almost could not bear it, but neither was I able to move my gaze away.

The next morning, Shih-fu greeted me and asked, "Did you dream anything? Dreams often contain a message," he continued, looking at me attentively, "and therefore I always ask my students on special occasions about their dreams. The special occasion today is that you will formally become my disciple. This is a step that will strengthen the karmic connection between teacher and disciple. Even if you never return to me in the future, this connection will continue to exist and to help you. It will make sure that you will always have the very rare and precious opportunity to encounter the teaching of the Buddha."

After I told him about the six moons, Shih-fu stood up excitedly, saying that this dream was a good omen and that I should follow him to the temple now. I did so, very surprised by the fact that my resistance and confusion of the morning had suddenly turned into sheer joy.

"Can you bow before the Buddha?" he asked me, as we arrived in front of the altar. He explained: "Buddha is not a god, but a teacher who has opened up for us the path to the wisdom of our own heart and mind. Bowing to the Buddha and taking refuge means that we honor the enlightened nature of our heart and mind, and that we entrust ourselves to the Buddha within us. Bowing to the Dharma, the teaching of the Buddha, means that we bow to the true form of all existence. Bowing to the Sangha, the community of disciples, means entrusting ourselves to the pure way of life in which every thought and act is an expression of our true nature, the wisdom of our heart."

While I repeated the Triple Refuge ("I take refuge in the Buddha; I take refuge in the Dharma; I take refuge in the Sangha") after Shih-fu, my knees started to shake more and more. Suddenly I heard Shih-fu say to the nun Fa-hsing, "The statue is moving!" I looked up at the white Guanyin statue but could not detect anything because I was shaking myself. Shih-fu, however, was convinced that the statue had moved, and he took this—together with my dream—as a sign that I would be able to progress on the spiritual path. I was given the Dharma name Hui-yueh, meaning Moon of Wisdom, and a certificate that I had become a lay disciple. And with that, I was a freshly hatched Buddhist Christian.

How does the story continue from there? Did I live up to the high promise that through so many signs was given on the day of my lay ordination? Am I a Moon of Wisdom? Certainly not, if you ask my two boys' opinion on the matter. Florian, who is nine years old, will easily tell you that his mom does not understand what is "really cool"; and Benjamin, eight years old, described me in a first grade essay in his Japanese grade school in Kyoto as "itsumo okotte iru" (always upset). Do I still have visions? Yes, but they are mostly of laundry that needs to be done, dinner that needs to be put together before or after soccer practice, of piano and violin that need to be squeezed in between homework and play, of video games that need to be avoided, etc. The list is long and rather mundane. Wouldn't I have done better to stay in a mountain cave pursuing enlightenment?

In fact, I took very much to heart Shih-fu's words that the practice of meditation is even more important than the study of scriptures, and I started sitting on my own. Rather miraculously, in that same year 1983 I was led to my first Zen retreat, under the Jesuit Father Enomiya-Lassalle at a Franciscan monastery. I continued my practice under his guidance until I met Yamada Koun Roshi in Japan in 1987. Yamada Koun had been Father Lasalle's teacher and had also trained many of the other Christian Zen teachers who are now leading Zen groups in many parts of the world. Both Father Lasalle and Yamada Roshi had strengthened in me the confidence that it is also possible for Christians to practice the way of enlightenment. The way of enlightenment is a path of purification in which we gradually let go of all ego-centered ways of thinking, feeling, and being, in order to become completely transparent to the working of grace, or—to put it in Buddhist terms—to the wisdom and compassion of a Buddha.

When I did the first Zen retreat under Father Lassalle, I was still trying to figure out whether I should return to Shih-fu and become a Buddhist nun. "Oh, but you do not automatically get rid of your ego by simply entering a monastery," Father Lassalle advised me on this question, "and besides, aren't you a Christian?" Wasn't I a Christian? That was the very question I kept asking myself as well, because other than having been baptized and raised Catholic, my relationship to God was not clear to me at this point. I felt attached to the Catholic culture that I had been raised in; loved the cathedrals of Strassburg and Metz that my parents used to take us to so frequently when I was growing up; couldn't imagine myself without the music of Bach, Mozart, Widor, or Vierne; would find it sad to live without the Easter and Christmas liturgy. But was that enough to be called a Christian? Should there not be a direct, tangible experience of God? I had been taught that God is love. But did I know this deeply, not just theoretically? And what is more, did I love God with my whole heart, soul, and strength, and my neighbor as myself? No, I could not honestly say that, because I was too full of questions and doubts about everything, including myself. God is love. What does that really mean?

I struggled with this issue during many of the subsequent Zen retreats and especially during one retreat with Father Lassalle in Shinmeikutsu, Japan, in the summer of 1987. After one particularly intense sit, something happened that completely resolved my mental and bodily tension and—like the encounter with Shih-fu—changed my life forever. I cannot describe it other than to say that I was touched by grace, enveloped in a love so gentle and so clear that tears of joy and repentance streamed down my cheeks. How could I have been so blind for so many years of my life, not realizing how loved I was and how everybody else was loved just as much? I felt like shaking up the whole meditation hall, getting people off their cushions and shouting at them: "Why are you sitting here so gravely? Don't you realize that God loves you? Get up and dance with joy!"

After this experience I passed without difficulty all the initial koans that check on an enlightenment experience. Yamada Koun Roshi later confirmed my experience.

My student life in Japan continued until the end of 1989, when I finished my dissertation on the Great Compassion Mantra of the Thousand Armed Guanyin. The importance of this mantra in the Buddhist tradition has been compared to that of the "Pater Noster" in Christianity.

In 1987, a year of grace, I met Ruben, who at the time was also a Zen student of Yamada Roshi and a Jesuit priest teaching at Sophia University. He eventually decided to leave the Jesuits, and in 1990 we were married at Southern Methodist University, where Ruben now teaches World Religions at Perkins School of Theology and serves as Zen teacher at the Maria Kannon Zen Center. Our sons Florian and Benjamin were born fifteen months apart in 1991 and 1993, changing our lives in ways we could not have imagined before. Gone were the quiet evenings at the Zen center and the peaceful hours of early morning meditation that I had been used to for more than ten years. I was so overwhelmed by the new demands of double motherhood that I developed insomnia after the birth of Benjamin. Just getting through the day was sometimes so difficult that I then desperately wished myself back into a mountain cave. Enlightenment seemed such an easy task compared to this! But Shih-fu seemed far removed from my life at that point, and I sometimes wondered if our karmic connection was not depleted.

However—to make a long story short—Shih-fu's prediction that he would be traveling all over the world has come true. Since the early 1990s, he has been engaged in a project to build in Taiwan a Museum for World Religions as a vehicle for interreligious interchange, and he has traveled widely in countries all over the world to promote this project. I am now his interpreter whenever time allows. For example, we went to the 1999 Parliament of the World's Religions gathering in Capetown, South Africa, and to the United Nations Meeting of Religious Leaders in New York. At these and other meetings, Shih-fu speaks about his vision that the way to achieve peace in this world is to encourage mutual respect, cooperation, and love among the religions, and he introduces the museum as a concrete step towards the realization of this vision.

For me, each of these trips—as interesting and exciting as they may be—brings a new set of struggles: How will Ruben and the children cope during my absence? How will I manage my difficulty sleeping and still be a good translator? What will I do if I don't understand? I am after all not a professional translator and have not lived in a Chinese-speaking environment since 1981, and so on and so forth. It seems that no matter what I do, doubts, anxieties, and fears keep raising their ugly heads and voices in the night. Is this simply part of the human condition? Or is it just part of my condition? If so, how shall I deal with it?

Maybe this is where I am most a Buddhist Christian. If anticipatory worries about a business trip for the museum, a syllabus to be developed, a class to be taught, an article to be written, or just anything at all, prevents me from fully being present in the here and now, I start reciting the Great Compassion Mantra. As Shih-fu explains it, "The recitation of this mantra liberates heart and mind from all outside entanglements and lets it return to its origin." And what could the "origin" of heart and mind be, other than what Buddhists call "emptiness" and what Christians call God? There are times when I would rather pray the "Our Father" or the "Hail Mary" than recite the Mantra, but the effect is similar, in that the words eventually give way to stillness. Like every other being, I would rather "Don't worry, be happy," but I find that the emotional states experienced as worry, anxiety, sadness, or melancholy help to draw me closer to God, help to make me more aware of my complete dependence upon God. My experiences in Zen have removed any previous doubts about the presence of God, but they do not mean that I have lived "happily ever after." I don't know if that is possible, or even desirable. It seems that we need a certain dose of suffering to keep in touch with God and with the people around us, to develop the compassion of Guanyin in ourselves, to become loving and merciful like Mary.

When we were living in Kyoto not long ago, our sons Florian and Benjamin were given preparatory instructions for their First Holy Communion by an elderly American sister who was very kind but not very experienced in dealing with young, inquisitive children. For the first class she brought a picture of an orthodox Jewish man wearing a scripture box on his head and started asking the children what they saw in this picture. When all the details were detected and described, the sister commented, "We are all like this man who carries the knowledge of God on top of his head. Children, what we have to learn is to put the knowledge of God from our head into our heart."

Benjamin, just six years old, jumped up from his seat, looked the sister straight in the face, and demanded innocently, "How???"

There was no answer.

Growing up Catholic, I was not told how to put the knowledge of God "from our head into our heart" either. It is probably assumed that this will eventually happen quite naturally, through the liturgy, the Eucharist, the music, the celebration of the Church feasts. But if it did really happen that way for everyone, there would not be so many people who leave the Church because it fails to address their spiritual needs.

Growing up Catholic, I was never concretely challenged to put the knowledge of God from my head into my heart until I met Shih-fu and later Father Enomiya-Lassalle and Yamada Roshi. Shih-fu was also the first one to question seriously my very knowledge and understanding of God.

Even though my life seems still very far away from its conclusion, I need to conclude this article. And this is what I have to say at this point in my life: My encounter with Buddhism and my close connection to my Buddhist teachers, Shih-fu and Yamada Roshi, have not uprooted me from Christian ground. On the contrary, my Buddhist teachers, together with Father Enomiya-Lassalle, have done everything possible to fertilize these roots and to let them grow stronger and deeper. They have taught me how to water them and how to deal with the weeds. They have taught me how to put the knowledge of God from my head into my heart. My deepest gratitude to all of them.

PART THREE:

*Perspectives on
Jewish and Christian
Encounters
with the Way
of the Buddha*

———————

A Sociological Perspective

INTERFAITH ENCOUNTER AND RELIGIOUS IDENTITY:
Sociological Observations and Reflections

E. BURKE ROCHFORD, JR.

W HEN I WAS about eight years old, I faced a frightening experience. I stood with a number of my friends in front of a *non*-Catholic Church, poised to enter. For reasons I no longer remember, we had come to this church on an organized visit. As a Catholic, I felt I was on the edge of betraying my Church and myself. I didn't know exactly what would happen should I enter this church, but I knew that I was placing myself at risk. Feeling an unspoken peer pressure, I passed through the doorway, worried and uneasy. Afterwards I felt relief to emerge unharmed, but still I had a nagging feeling that something "bad" awaited me.

As I think of this story, I feel a strange sort of embarrassment. Yet, as a young Catholic boy, I had learned that such encounters represented threats to my Catholic faith and identity, even if I didn't know exactly why. It seems appropriate for me to reflect on this story now, although I haven't done so in many years. The memory emerged as I began to explore the issues in this paper. Many of us grew up with strict barriers around our faith and frightening implications for crossing over them. Yet today a breakdown of the traditional structures of separation has opened the religious arena to interfaith exchange, dialogue, and encounter.

Thirty years ago the question of how someone in the U.S. could somehow be engaged both as a Christian *and* as a Buddhist, or as a Jew *and* a

Buddhist, would have likely met with blank stares, or words of disapproval.[1] After all, it was naturally assumed that people were *singularly* Jews or Christians—or, less likely, Buddhists, Muslims, or Hindus. Academic treatments of interfaith encounter have often paralleled popular opinion. Relying on conversion models, interfaith encounters were interpreted narrowly in terms of their transformative potential: Jews and Christians either became Buddhists, or they steadfastly resisted challenges to their faith. Yet as we have seen in the personal narratives in this text, people are practicing elements from more than one religious tradition, and some have crafted *dual* religious orientations and even identities. In what follows, I explore the encounter between Buddhism and Christianity. In particular I draw attention to the varied ways that individuals have sought to negotiate Buddhism and Christianity and the consequences this has for their religious identity and everyday actions.

Religious Identity and the Encounter with Buddhism

My discussion here will draw upon a series of group interviews I conducted in August 2000, at the Society for Buddhist-Christian Studies Dialogue Conference in Tacoma, Washington. In addressing the effects on Christian identity of encounter with Buddhism, I want to begin by making a distinction between what I take to be interfaith dialogue and interfaith encounter. I see interfaith dialogue as an attempt to build empathetic *understanding* of a religious "other." It is a form of mutual exchange that favors a stance of "objective distancing." Interfaith encounter, on the other hand, leaves open the possibility of *personal* change and transformation. To encounter a faith different from one's own means to engage actively in portions of its theology, morals, ethics, or practices. The result is that one's own religious orientation loses its taken-for-granted quality and becomes subject to conscious and critical assessment and perhaps reformulation. I make this distinction because those interviewed for this study are Christians who in various ways have been *changed* by their encounter with Buddhism. [2]

Perhaps the most striking finding emerging from my interviews is the attempt by most to retain the uniqueness of each tradition, even as they seek to combine religious beliefs and practices from each. Thus, those I spoke with largely reject the idea of blending Buddhism and Christianity into a "new" personal religion. They turn aside the very idea that their religious worldview and practices result from integrating and synthesizing elements of the two traditions. Rather, each tradition represents separate threads that inform and nourish their spirituality *individually*. As two of my interviewees commented:

> ...these are [religious] practices and disciplines which are in my case rather complementary. I think of them as having different strengths. I don't want to blend things, because I think each has its own integrity that I completely respect.

> So what I do *not* feel is that I am a Buddhist-hyphen-Christian who is blending the two. I feel that I function as different individuals. But I know that the other one is there. I remain aware of both. *[Interviewee's emphasis.]*

These comments suggest that Buddhism and Christianity stand side by side in consciousness; that one is both a Christian *and* a Buddhist. The two traditions, unique in practice and theology, are experienced as complementary and yet not to be syncretized.[3]

But how is it possible for Buddhism to complement Christianity rather than challenge it? Moreover, what elements of Buddhism complement Christianity? Rabbi Schachter-Shalomi helps in responding to the first question. He suggests that the Buddhism exported to the West comes without a great deal of moral and ethical baggage. It also has arrived without the rich culture of its Asian homeland. Buddhism, as we find it in the West, has been "stripped" of those elements that might otherwise bring it into conflict with Judaism or Christianity or, for that matter, with Western culture more generally.

220 BESIDE STILL WATERS

Virtually everyone I interviewed found reason to mention that Buddhism's understanding of suffering has been both spiritually and practically useful to their lives. Moreover, this understanding complemented their Christian beliefs. Note, in the following quote, how Buddhist ideas about suffering are combined with Christian imagery:

> At the level of everyday ethics I think there is practically no difference, that they support each other.... But Buddhism is more aware of the pain and suffering especially of non-human life than a lot of the Christian tradition.... In times of personal difficulty they both help each other but in different ways. Buddhism helps me to see the insubstantiality of any joy or suffering so as not to be attached to it. And then Christianity would often give the warmth to it.

Not surprisingly, those I interviewed were at least sporadic practitioners of Buddhist meditation, or they had been in the past. In fact these practices had drawn many to Buddhism originally. As an Asian Buddhist practitioner commented, "Usually Christians derive influence from Buddhism in terms of practice. They have a harder time moving away from their doctrinal core."

Although we see a conscious and active attempt to align Buddhism with Christianity, it remains unclear what this means for people's religious orientation and identity. Can we reasonably assume, for example, that the people who refer to themselves as "Christian-Buddhists" in fact lay claim to a dual religious identity? My interviews revealed three more or less distinct adaptations or orientations to Buddhism, which I discuss below.

Buddhism as "Intellectual Work"

Three of the people I interviewed expressed the view that Buddhism was useful to them primarily as an intellectual framework. Buddhism helped them to understand the social world, certainly, but it also informed their own scholarly work in critical ways. None of the three admitted to having an active Buddhist practice, apart from engaging Buddhist ideas to further a larger intellectual project. As one of them commented, "I don't really care about Buddhism or Christianity very much except to the extent that they are useful. And I find that the *Lotus Sutra* is enormously helpful for me given my love for the world. It helps me relate to the world." Another stated, "I can identify myself as *neither* Buddhist or Christian. Just that they are two wonderful paths. Because my life has always been nomadic, I suppose it is nomadic intellectually as well. I can participate in and find great value in [both] without necessarily being completely committed to either one of those paths."

Also, Buddhism can have a more pragmatic value: Buddhist thought and interpretive categories can be used to rethink the intellectual meaning of Christianity. In this way, Buddhism becomes an interpretive lens akin to broad disciplinary theories that provide for alternative understandings of the social and physical worlds. Using Buddhism in this way largely preserves the integrity of Christian categories without destabilizing them. Unlike the other two orientations discussed below, this encounter with Buddhism appears to have little influence on personal religious identity or practice. Yet it must be acknowledged that the intellectual work involved requires an understanding of Buddhist ideas and consciousness.

Buddhism and the Deepening of Christian Faith

Traditional ways of thinking suggest that, when faiths collide, commitments to an existing religion are jeopardized. Alternative religious ideas and practices are viewed as "contaminating," "polluting," and "destabilizing" of an existing faith. Yet a sizable portion of those I interviewed told a different story. Rather than being corrosive to their faith, the encounter with Buddhism *deepened and enriched* their understanding of Christianity, as well as their identity as Christians. In other cases, Buddhist practice served to reinvigorate commitment to a dormant or even rejected Christianity. Thus, the encounter with Buddhism became a means to becoming a "better" Christian, as the words of two of my interviewees show:

> It is my perception that people who live in both Buddhist and Christian worlds are by and large either one or the other. I am firmly Christian. That is, Christianity is my way. But I have a strong Buddhist side....I went into Zen and picked up the discipline. I went deeper and deeper into it but every step that I took opened up Christianity for me. I went back to the text of the scriptures and they were like a different book....Buddhism forced me to go back and ask what is the foundational experience of Christianity. I found that my roots are built out of the Christ resurrection experience. But I came to understand that through Buddhism.

> From my earliest life and imagery there is someone who is eternal, who loves me....It is the place I go back to when I am desperate. It is the place that I trust. Other Christians know that place within themselves...because I suspect that many of them, whatever Church they go to, somewhere along the line they glimpse the presence of what we call the Holy Spirit. Or Jesus, Christ's presence....But I did a lot of Buddhist sitting for ten years. I had Zen teachers. I have a daily Zen practice...[yet] it is really Christ that I want to show up. Christ presence. That is my only role in life, is to become Christ presence. Let it become Buddha for others.

Perhaps surprisingly, the encounter with Buddhism also provided a path back to Christianity for some of those interviewed. An atrophied or discarded Christian identity was reenergized through the spiritual focus of Buddhist practice. One man recounts how time spent in a Korean Buddhist monastery reawakened his relationship with Christianity.

I had studied [Buddhism] for about four years on my own. I was living in South Korea in a monastery. That is when I picked up the Bible and read it all the way through. And it really healed a lot in my relationship with Christianity. I had just had a gradual disappointment with Christ. And I had less and less energy in terms of going to church. I healed myself in reading the Bible.... I realized that for myself Christianity is part of who I am. It is part of my culture, what I had grown up [in] and therefore a part of me. I feel that I can't deny it.... Christianity is part of who I am.

A full-time Western practitioner of Buddhism had a similar, though perhaps more dramatic experience. Years earlier she had given up the Christianity of her youth as being "too narrow," yet fifteen years after committing herself to a Buddhist way of life, she reunited with Christianity. In a time of personal crisis related to her Buddhist practice she found comfort in a Christian Church, where she was baptized. During this difficult period she remained committed to her Buddhist practice. A subsequent Zen teacher commented upon hearing of her turn to Christianity in that moment of crisis, "This is Zen coming to America." As she said, "He thought this was really something. Because I had been practicing [as a Zen student] 'giving up.' But, that it had happened in a church, he thought was really something." She summed up the experience and its meaning for her:

What a gift that after so many years of Zen practice I could find Jesus in my heart. I didn't exactly know what this meant. Everybody I know said, "Oh, it is this great conversion experience." But it wasn't. I didn't leave the *zendo*. I was back on my cushion every day, but with something new in here *[pointing to her heart]*. And so that was a great gift.

Unable to "fit in a parish church," this woman joined and remains active in the Society for Buddhist-Christian Studies. There, she says, "I began to get support for sitting with Christ and as a Zen practitioner."

As we see here, the practice of Buddhism, whether intentionally or not, can affirm and indeed invigorate an existing religious identity. Yet there are other instances where encountering Buddhism results in a shift in religious consciousness and identity.

Dual Religious Identity

Some who encounter Buddhism *do* align its beliefs and practices alongside their Christian faith. As one interviewee put it, "If you are following more than one path, but in a very serious way, then you *are* those two religions." This involves a fundamental recrafting such that Buddhism and Christianity form an equal partnership in religious identity.

> They are always co-equal in my thinking. They go hand in hand, really.

> *EBR: But what does "co-equal" mean?*

> In my daily thinking, in my religious thinking, both sides get equal time. Christianity doesn't get 100 percent.

It is here where we can genuinely speak of a *dual* religious identity. Separate religious paths and frameworks are joined together in consciousness and find expression in the world of everyday life.

Although Christianity and Buddhism are generally experienced as complementary, each also offers at least somewhat "counter-definitions of reality and identity."[4] As one of my interviewees observed, "There are times when I think Buddhism and Christianity are so similar as to be the same. And yet at the same time utterly different." For, in fact, each has its own "sense of ultimate grounding"[5] with an accompanying mode of discourse and "attendant rules and grammar for putting things together."[6] As this implies, crafting a dual Christian-Buddhist identity represents a social and psychological *accomplishment* as much as a religious one. Buddhism isn't just *added* to consciousness in a straightforward way. Rather, "ideological work"[7] is required. Consider the attempt of one woman to understand "love" from a Buddhist perspective. Note, too, how she attempts to gain this understanding by placing a Christian perspective on "love" *within* a Buddhist framework:

> What I am struggling with now is how to understand love in a Buddhist framework. It doesn't fit. And this is something that I care about very much. I am attached to it, as they [Buddhists] say. *[Laughs.]* I can't make sense of love as we understand it in a Christian framework from within Buddhism. I guess that is where I am really struggling right now. I understand the Christian notion of love of the other and everything that comes with it in terms of ethical appeal. I am just not sure where that would fit within Buddhism.

As this woman's struggle aptly illustrates, attempts to align Buddhism and Christianity are neither simple nor always successful. For some, repeated attempts to align the two traditions may lead to choosing between them, as we have seen in the case of those who reassert their Christian identity. Others may ultimately reject their Christian faith in favor of conversion to the Buddhist Dharma. Few, I would guess, successfully negotiate a dual identity as both Christians *and* Buddhists. The sheer difficulty of this is highlighted by the following comments.

> When I was going through a period of wondering which way I would jump—the Buddhist or Christian—I felt I wanted to jump both ways. And I felt I couldn't do that. That was quite disturbing. However, the situation solved itself when I realized that I was framing the question incorrectly. It is not whether I should be either Buddhist or Christian but it was why should there be a conception of an "I" that can only be one way or the other.

Because from a Buddhist perspective the "I" is not inherently existing so it doesn't have to go one way or the other. And from Christianity, the redeeming self is Christ rather than the old Adam. And presumably Christ has no problem with this. So then it wasn't my problem and I gave up. It is just the same if you were to get a Buddhist and a Christian on two chairs and have them talk and say, "Well isn't that interesting?" And they are getting along well, or they are not getting along well. But it has been productive for them to meet. We say in diplomatic circles that we had a productive meeting.

Yet the question remains as to how those with a dual religious identity function in the realm of everyday experience. A partial answer is suggested by one of my interviewees who commented, "Sometimes I think as one; sometimes I think as the other." But *when* does one think and act from within one or the other framework? I want to suggest that *dual religious identities are by necessity context-driven identities. A situated self* awaits the individual within the differing contexts encompassed by social interaction.[8] Essentially, different social contexts invite either a Buddhist or Christian self that, in turn, directs an appropriate response.

In the case of worship, one can readily engineer a context ready-made for a specific religious expression. A person can enter a church or temple, for example, with the full expectation that the appropriate framework will emerge. As one of my interviewees acknowledged, "When I am at Mass, as I was this morning, I am not really thinking of the Buddhist thing, although Buddhism goes through my mind. But when I am doing *sadhana* [realization practice], or going to a Buddhist place, I don't have any central image of there being a God." In other situations of worship, appropriate contexts may need to be created. This can be seen in the attempt of one man to organize distinct places of worship in his home. The very placement of his shrines symbolizes his dual identity as both a Christian and a Buddhist:

During meditation or prayer practice it has to be one or the other.... In the house I have just moved into I have set up the three shrines in one room, though they are separate. Exactly how I will configure the room later on is not too clear. I would like them to be as if they were three separate rooms, so they don't start blending.[9]

Yet social life is far more uncertain and less subject to being so neatly organized. In the course of a day contexts change, often unpredictably. Of course, the majority of contexts we face in everyday interaction are "ordinary" and draw on commonsense knowledge. Yet other situations are more complex and draw on broader personal orientations and elements of the self. Here we are able to see how context makes differing demands on dual religious identities:

There was a case when I was chair of my department and I had to confront something important. And I am a pretty easygoing person but this was something that was going to be difficult. The word came into my mind, the Quaker practice of "speaking truth to power." And I knew I had to do that. And that is a tradition; I have learned it because I have submitted my mind to this training and it became a tool that was very useful to me. Usually, I think more often as a Buddhist, because I look at the world in terms of suffering and action to relieve suffering. This is sort of the fundamental big picture framework that I am inside of.

Another man contrasts Christian and Buddhist ideas about "judgment." He then tells how he used a Buddhist framework in an attempt to stop logging operations in the national forests:

When I grew up as a Christian, I grew up thinking about judgment. How powerful a thing judgment is.... It is aggressive and separating. Judgment leads to violence....The Buddhist stream reminds us of how ubiquitous judgment is. It is everywhere and not to take it personally. To me that is one of the greatest gifts from Buddhism.... I found it very powerful to be sitting with some Western [U.S.] senators, who I find loathsome in terms of their attitudes toward the earth. But instead of fighting with them, and judging them, I am looking for *upaya* [skillful means]. I am looking past the [judgmental] thoughts I have about them. Instead, I am asking myself, "Where is the effective word that I can say? Where is the effective connection I can make, or pressure [to exert]?" It is the detachment in social action situations.

In another example, Sallie King writes compellingly in her essay about her life as a mother and the shifting relevance of Quaker and Buddhist thought in her development as a parent. When her children were young she concluded that her "Buddhist mind and my motherhood seem to be incompatible"—incompatible because she found the Buddhist concept of detachment conflicted with the deep love she held for her young children. Without rejecting Buddhism, or even the concept of detachment, she "came to think in Quaker terms," giving emphasis to love as a spiritual ideal. Years later, when her children approached the age of leaving the family household, the Buddhist idea of detachment found new meaning. But as she also acknowledged, "letting go" of an older child was itself an act of parental love.

Religious Boundaries, Identity, and Hothousing the Spirit

Rabbi Schachter-Shalomi reports that in his own religious life he has moved away from creedal religion to embrace more experiential forms of spirituality that engage the heart and the soul. Using the Buddhist concept of *upaya* as a model, he finds himself searching for the "skillful means to awakening." This search has taken him far afield from his own Jewish roots to Buddhism and beyond in order to locate the "skillful

means of hothousing the spirit." Echoing this sentiment, one of my interviewees stated:

> My identity is a spiritual seeker. Whether it is Christian, Bud-
> dhist, Hindu, whatever. I don't really care. I am a spiritual
> seeker.... I am really open but I am a Christian.... So I make a
> distinction between religion and spirituality. It is the popular dis-
> tinction today, and I agree with it very much. Religion is a *con-*
> *cretized* spirituality. My concretized spirituality is mainly being a
> Christian. *[My emphasis.]*

We live in an age where spirituality is less likely to be *concretized* or
contained within single traditions. In the presence of an increasingly
diverse spiritual marketplace, many of the mainline traditions have
themselves become less exclusive and more tolerant of religious pluralism. Nathan Katz in his essay notes that at one point in his spiritual journey he was encouraged by his rebbe to continue his Buddhist meditation
practice at the Naropa Institute. Upon arrival at the Institute, the resid-
ing lama admonished him to observe Shabbat as his Saturday meditation
practice. It is precisely this lowering of structural barriers by both old
and new religions that has greatly facilitated interfaith encounter. As we
see so vividly in the life stories presented in this book, it has also reshaped the very nature of the religious quest, and the form and meaning of religious identity.

TO LEARN AND TO TEACH:
Some Thoughts on Jewish-Buddhist Dialogue
ARTHUR GREEN

I T WAS CIRCA 1970 that I received a call from Fordham University's Center for Spiritual Studies asking me to participate in a day-long seminar of spiritual teachings from several traditions. The theme of the day (it was a bright spring day, in fact, as I recall it) was to be "The Seasons of the Year in the Spiritual Traditions," and there were to be speakers from the Christian, Jewish, Hindu, and Buddhist traditions. I shared the platform with Brother David Steindl-Rast, a well-known Benedictine monk and author; Swami Satchidananda, founder of Integral Yoga; and the head of the New York Zen Center, whose name (perhaps tellingly) was and is unknown to me.

Brother David spoke very beautifully about the journey from Christmas to Easter, the passage from birth to death to resurrection, taking them all as metaphors to describe stages in the spiritual life. I did something similar, speaking of the fall and spring festival cycles as holy periods of rebirth for the individual and the people. I talked in highly personal terms about coming out of Egypt and the journey to Sinai. My feeling was that I too had done pretty well.

When the swami's turn came, he chatted smilingly and lovingly with the audience for a few minutes, and then asked us to join him in chanting. Judging by the look on his face and those of his disciples (who were quite numerous in the audience), he offered us a quarter-hour taste of pure bliss. Then came the turn of the Zen teacher. He got up and said, "I have fifteen minutes; we will sit." And he then proceeded to do so, again providing a very direct and unmediated experience in which all could take part.

After the event was over, I chatted with Brother David. "Why," I asked him, "do we Westerners keep our spiritual treasures so hidden?" How is it that one could have a dozen years of Jewish or Christian education and never be exposed to the simple things we were saying? Even after they were said, how great was the distance between the telling and the experience itself? Why could we not learn from these Eastern teachers, just opening our hearts to share our religious lives with people in a direct and unmediated way, without insisting on so many prior layers of learning, faith commitment, and ritual observance?"

"You Jews think you've got it bad?" he answered. "Look at us Catholics—we even insist on commitment to a life of *celibacy* before we'll open the box and share our greatest treasures!"

A great deal has changed in the third of a century since that encounter. My teacher Abraham Joshua Heschel used to complain in those days that we totally lacked a Jewish *devotional literature* in English, books the seeker could read for inspiration and encouragement along the path. Now there are hundreds of such books on the market, both translations of classical sources and new compositions written specifically for this generation. Some of them are even quite good. Kabbalah, once the secret wisdom of Judaism, is being taught everywhere, even to non-Jews, let alone to Jews with no prior knowledge of, or commitment to, the exoteric aspects of tradition. "Jewish meditation," once the province of a most arcane corner within Kabbalistic and Hasidic circles, is now being taught at Ys and centers all over the country. More books on "Jewish meditation" have been written in the past twenty years than in the preceding thousand.

Mostly, I believe, this is "good for the Jews." (Yes, I cringe plenty at seeing some of the more superstitious elements of "practical Kabbalah" marketed to the innocent New Age audience. I understand they are selling "holy water" blessed by the rabbi, at a center not far from here, and I am duly horrified.) There is indeed a rich and wonderful spiritual language to be found within Kabbalah. If it can be distilled and remixed to work for the current age—and I too am trying my hand at that—both the practitioners and the Jewish people as a whole stand to gain. Loyalty to Judaism in our day, a time of living in a truly open society, will have to be based on love and attraction to Judaism rather than on guilt or fear. And this love will come about because the language of Judaism *works* for us, because it stirs our emotions, satisfies our minds, and lifts our spirits. The teachings of Jewish mysticism, especially those of the Hasidic masters, were designed to fill just that role in the spiritual revival movement of an earlier generation. It is time to look to them, both as a source of learning and as a model for our own creativity, in an hour when spiritual revival is once again central to our agenda.

But there is great difference. All the past sources of Jewish mystical teaching belong to an exclusivist time and tradition. They were written under the rule of religious interaction as a zero-sum game. If my religion is true, yours must be false. If the teachings of Judaism are profound, those of the other faiths—usually Christianity and Islam, the traditional "rival" religions—must be more shallow, distorted, or downright untrue. The notion of a universal religious truth that transcended the boundaries of tradition was not generally accepted within Jewry, and surely not by the mystics.

Of course this Jewish denigration of other religions has to be understood in historical context. Jews lived for nearly two thousand years as barely tolerated minorities in societies and states that defined themselves as either Christian or Islamic. There were great variations in the degrees of persecution from one place or time to another, to be sure. But "tolerance" was the best Jews could hope for from the general society, and religious teaching always depicted Judaism as a somehow inferior or incomplete religion. The hope of teachers and leaders in the two would-be "successor" traditions to Judaism often led to active campaigns aimed at conversion. These had more success in various periods than is generally known or admitted. The historical powerlessness and exilic condition of the Jews was marshalled as "evidence" of their religious error. How could one imagine that God would abandon His chosen people and leave them to such a lowly status, unless they had gone wrong in some deep and essential way? To counter this Christian and Islamic supersessionism, Jews increasingly asserted their exclusive claim to truth, cried out their wounded hearts to God, and longed for the redemption that would prove their vindication.

But the claims of exclusiveness on all sides masked the true situation. Both Islam and Christianity were deeply indebted to Judaism. Each in its own way was based on ancient Jewish teaching, including but not limited to the Hebrew Bible text itself. The Jews also adopted many practices and ways of thinking from the surrounding cultures. There were ways, quite naturally, in which eastern European Judaism was typically eastern European in its folk beliefs, veneration of holy men, casual intimacy of prayer as "conversation" with God, and so forth. The same could be said of North African or other Jewish communities. "As the Christians are, so are the Jews" is a Yiddish folk saying that goes back to medieval Germany, reflecting a certain degree of truth.

There have also been sources of knowledge and understanding that come from outside the three monotheistic faiths and that have shaped and influenced all of them. The greatest example is medieval philosophy. The teachings of Aristotle were well known in the Middle Ages. Those of Plato were thought to be known also, but these were actually neo-Platonic writings of the fourth to sixth centuries. Both of these bodies of teaching, coming from outside the Judeo-Christian-Islamic world, were taken to be sources of truth by such great authorities within the traditions as al-Farabi, Maimonides, and Thomas Aquinas. They in fact provided the basis for the best-known theologies of all three traditions for many centuries. In more recent times, both Jewish and Christian theologies (Islam had by then turned away from the modernizing West) were composed based on the teachings of Immanuel Kant and G. F. W. Hegel, the leading figures of continental philosophy in the eighteenth and nineteenth centuries.

During the past fifty years, due to a process that can be subsumed under the category of "globalization," Jews and Judaism are for the first time coming into significant encounter with the religious teachings of the Far East, especially those of the Hindu and Buddhist traditions, in all their many and varied manifestations. These contacts are different from those with Christianity and Islam in two important ways. First, there is no reason for defensiveness or hostility. These are not traditions in whose name Judaism was ever suppressed or persecuted. Nor are these traditions that ever claimed to supersede Judaism or asserted that its time was past. The Jewish-Buddhist and Jewish-Hindu dialogue may take place in an atmosphere that is free of the long-standing resentments and the struggle to overcome ancient feelings of competitiveness that mar Jews' dialogue with Western religious partners.

But these are also religions that are not based on the Judaic model. When engaging in dialogue with Christian and Islamic partners, we can assume a shared legacy of the ancient struggle against polytheism and the rejection of what our shared traditions called "idolatry." The Hindu and Buddhist ways of dealing with such sensitive questions for Judaism as monism/monotheism/polytheism and abstract faith/graven images make the contact with them problematic in an entirely new set of ways.

Large numbers of Jews, along with a great many other Western seekers, have been drawn to various forms of Eastern religious teaching over the course of the past half-century. These people are in no way to be blamed or condemned for having "abandoned" their Judaism. If there is any fault to be found in the failure of honest seekers to find their way within Judaism, it may lie more with us, the rabbis, Jewish teachers, and educators. We did not speak the right spiritual language. We were unable, despite both knowledge and goodwill, to "open up" pathways within Judaism for these many seekers. Ours is a highly intellectualized tradition, one in which it has long been assumed that the sincere seeker will have a knowledge of language, texts, and practices. Lacking these, and often frustrated at feeling like an "outsider" to their own heritage, it is no surprise that so many Jews have turned elsewhere.

Of course we long to welcome these seekers home and pray for their return to the Jewish spiritual fold. We do so not because Judaism has the only truth, or because ours is the best or only way to seek God. We long for their return because we love them and need them. The souls of Israel are viewed from within our tradition as one single great soul. All of us stood together at the mountain; all of us were there in the soul of Moses as he entered the heavens. To see so many Jews alienated from our Torah is to lose a part of ourselves, to know that we are less than whole. Our loss is more painful because we see that these are not Jews deaf to the call of the spirit. There are too few such Jews within our little community, always called "the smallest of all the nations." These Jewish seekers are our fellow heirs to a great legacy. We are generous inheritors, and would be happy to share it with them, to have them join with us and enrich us with what they have learned along the way. Some indeed have returned to Judaism by way of a journey through the East, and our shared Jewish life is richer for their presence.

Life in this open society calls for a new sort of interfaith dialogue, one that takes for granted a mutual respect and admiration. This has to be characterized by a true sense that God's single, unifying presence is to be found in each human soul, in all of humanity's languages and cultures, and in the forms of every religion. We celebrate difference, to be sure, and are not looking to obliterate distinctions or to combine all religions. Missionary efforts should be completely rejected in the context of this new dialogue, as should a shallow syncretism that does not respect diversity or the need to preserve distinct identities. But the preservation of one faith's distinctiveness should never demand the price of denigration of others. In that spirit, the traditional religious genre called "apologetics" needs to be challenged and redefined, since such works usually set out to prove the superiority of one faith-path above all others.

The purpose of dialogue in this post-triumphalist context is mutual edification. We wish *to learn* and *to teach,* to gain wisdom from others that will (sometimes through challenge) deepen our own quest. We also want to share with others what we think is wise and universally applicable from within the storehouse of our own traditional wisdom. We recognize that there are great tasks that face us all as fellow inhabitants of this planet, tasks that will require cooperation across lines of tradition if they are to be accomplished. None among these is more urgent than the changing of human attitudes toward the natural world in which we live and of which we are a part. All religions need to pool their wisdom to create a profound change in human behavior with regard to our planet and the use of its resources.

But let us go back to learning and teaching. What is it that Judaism needs to learn in such a dialogue among religious teachings? And what do we believe we have to offer that might be of use to others, even those whose language remains far from our own? The approach to this pair of questions requires a balance of humility and self-respect. We need to acknowledge that we are all somewhere along the path, that none of us has the entire truth. In this sense we can all stand to learn from others. Each of our journeys is likely to be helped by the support and encouragement we receive from one another. At the same time, we should each realize that certain distinct values and teachings are brought forth so clearly in our own traditions that these might be of help to others as well. We should be willing to teach these in the course of dialogue, but without needing or demanding of others that they share our commitment to them.

In this spirit, I want to share two thoughts on each side of the ledger. These are not exhaustive, but will provide a model of my best hopes for the great potential of Jewish dialogue with Eastern religions.

In the context of Jewish-Buddhist and Jewish-Vedanta dialogue, we could profit much from discussion around the theme of monotheism and monism. Judaism's biblical legacy is one of struggle against polytheism. The deities of the Near Eastern pantheon, first "defeated" by the greater power of the God of Israel, are depicted by the later Biblical authors as non-gods, mere "sticks and stones." The powers formerly attributed to these gods are now all included within the One. The most telling expression of this change is the Hebrew term for "God" itself: *elohim* is a plural form, a collective entity that contains all of the divine powers.

Like all great cultural struggles, the ending of this one was not entirely clear or simple. The Bible, and later Judaism with it, inherited a great deal from the very milieu against which it struggled. The residence of God in the "heavens," the metaphoric trappings of royalty, and the image of God as cosmic judge are all derived from Babylonian and Canaanite myth. The need to see God as an all-powerful divine Person may itself be rooted in this ancient legacy of battle against the heathen.

For more than a thousand years, Jewish theologians have lived in tension with this biblical legacy. The medieval rationalists (with some earlier precedent) first fought against anthropomorphism, insisting that biblical descriptions of God in human terms, whether physical or emotional, were not to be taken literally. Moses Maimonides (1135–1204) represents the high point of this long process. Next came the Kabbalists, who opened up the floodgates of imagination to infinitely varied images of God. Biblical descriptions took their place within a dazzling array of nature imagery, daringly erotic discussions of love within the godhead, and awareness of God as a mystery that was at once revealed and hidden within both world and Torah. Here it was the *variety* of images and their rapid flow into one another that were to keep one from idolatrous over-attachment to a single way of depicting God.

Kabbalah, as a form of mysticism, also included some monistic or pantheistic tendencies, reaching toward a notion of God as universal soul, present throughout the world and manifest in all creatures. This direction was followed further by some of the early Hasidic masters, who read Judaism in highly panentheistic ("all is God, but God is infinitely more than the sum of all that is") or acosmic ("there is *only* God; all else is illusion") terms. Nevertheless, these same masters were unwavering advocates of traditional Jewish folk piety, including its most blatantly anthropomorphic expressions. For such teachers there was no contradiction between addressing God in Yiddish as *tateh in himl* ("daddy" in heaven) and describing "Him" as the cosmic Nothing that underlies all forms of being.

How are we to understand this process? Are we in the course of a long, slow evolution from theism to monism, parallel to the earlier shift from polytheism to monotheism? Or is there some value to keeping a monistic faith "garbed" within theistic language? Here it would be valuable to dialogue with other traditions that also embrace both monistic philosophies and countless tales of gods and spirits. The balance among these is different in each tradition, and indeed it varies (as it does in Judaism) from one school or teacher to another. So too are the historic legacies and contexts of these discussions quite distinct. Nevertheless, we might have much to learn from Eastern discussions of "the one and the many," or the ways in which both a highly abstract theology and a rich legacy of myth are considered to be "true."

Judaism's devotion to personalistic religious language has another side, however. This is one that I would place in the "teaching" column, a value I would hope to share with others. The most basic ethical claim of Judaism is that every human being is created in the image of God. This idea, clearly expressed in Genesis' account of creation (Genesis 1:26-27; 5:1-2), was proclaimed by the early rabbinic sage Ben Azzai as the most basic rule of Torah. It is because we proclaim each person to represent God's image that we Jews consider each human life to be ultimately precious and unique. This leads us to the commitment to care for each person. We are obligated to work to bring about the circumstances that will allow every human being to become fully realized as God's image. Our prophetic tradition calls upon us to obliterate hunger, disease, and degradation of human beings, to institute justice and equality, all in the name of faith in God's image.

All this, perhaps the best that Judaism has to offer, is tied to our personalistic view of God, of whom we are a mirror image. Yet the question must be faced: Are we in God's image, as seen from within tradition, or is the anthropomorphic God a projection of our image, one we should seek to overcome? Our attraction to a more abstract theology is serious and long-standing. But we fear setting aside the personalist language of our teachings and prayers, lest we undercut the great humanizing and ethical power they have wrought. This interlocking network of thoughts, images, and commitments could be greatly enriched in the course of East-West dialogue.

The other pair of notions I would like to propose for such a learning/teaching dialogue has to do with silence, inner tranquility, and rest. One of the great blessings of spiritual life everywhere is its demand that we remove ourselves from slavery to the treadmill of a life devoted to industry, commerce, and acquisition. Ranging from brief daily periods of meditation to weekly Sabbath days to long periods of monastic silence, nearly all the traditions show us ways to restore our humanity by means of slowing down our busy pace.

Such teachings are much needed and appreciated in our day, perhaps more than ever before. One reason, I believe, why meditation has attracted so many in the contemporary West is that we live in a time of tremendous speeding up of consciousness. The shift to electronic media, the possibility of nearly instant contact with people anywhere on the globe, the implied insistence in such means of communication as fax and e-mail that they be attended to immediately, all leave us with a sense of collective breathlessness. This feeling is so widely shared in our culture that we barely notice it. But the need for signposts of one sort or another that will remind us to "SLOW DOWN AND LIVE" has taken on a new urgency.

Judaism's response to this cry is of course the observance of the Sabbath, the weekly "day off" that is meant precisely to save us from the dulling effects of unceasing labor. The insistence that we separate completely from the commercial culture is especially helpful as a restorer of values. Elsewhere I have suggested some key ground rules for a contemporary Shabbat, designed for those who want to preserve the spirit of the holy day without being devoted to the entire regimen of Sabbath laws. The Sabbath has been one of Judaism's great gifts to Western civilization. In our day that gift has to be renewed, not in the spirit of rigid "Sunday blue law" legislation, but as one to be accepted voluntarily and reshaped in response to our contemporary needs. A Shabbat without computer, without television, indeed altogether without "screens" that keep our eyes drawn to them rather than to one another, might in itself be a great contribution.

But we Jews could stand to learn something in this part of the dialogue as well. Ours is a highly verbal culture; Jews typically love—and are good at—matters that involve words and language. The ideal thing to do on our day of rest, according to traditional Jewish values, is to pray at greater length and to study words of Torah. Rabbis preach on the Sabbath, because Jews have time to listen. We are just beginning to learn, however, how words themselves can create a treadmill, and that true rest should involve periods free from words, even from verbal thoughts. The deepest part of Shabbat relaxation might free us from enslavement to our own thoughts and fantasies, not only from external forms of servitude. The recent growth of interest in meditation within Judaism, including both the import of techniques from elsewhere and the revival of ancient Jewish practices, bears witness to this.

Here I am suggesting that the values taught by the old/new culture of Western Buddhism are deeply compatible with Judaism. Both civilizations offer ways to realize the same goal of liberating the spirit. Both recognize the importance of setting aside a special time for devoting full attention to this task, while understanding that the real goal is to transform all of life, to turn even the most ordinary moments, toward higher consciousness. Each has powerful and well-tested ways of achieving this goal, standing at the very center of two great religious civilizations: meditation for Buddhists, Shabbat for Jews. What could be more appropriate (and consistent with both traditions' great respect for wisdom) than to embrace this new encounter as a rare and wonderful opportunity to learn from one another?

It is in this spirit that I welcome the present volume. It is illuminated by the shining spirit of the seekers whose life-stories fill its pages. Rather than offering a theological treatment of issues in the East-West dialogue, it is a series of testimonies to the enriching of Westerners' lives through their exposure to sacred teachings that come from another corner of human experience. Breaking through walls of cultural distance and alienation to learn from others, while still respecting our own selves and the traditions that shaped us, will lead us all to a deeper appreciation of what we Jews know as *nishmat kol hai,* the single spirit that inhabits and unites all of life. May we grow together in awareness and in opening our hearts to respond.

An Appreciation of Christian Appreciations of Buddhism's "Still Waters"

WILLIAM R. BURROWS

T HE AUTHORS of the essays collected in *Beside Still Waters: Jews, Christians, and the Way of the Buddha* show how the Way of the Buddha has deeply influenced their lives. In reading their accounts, it strikes me that in the Gospel of John, Jesus is portrayed as the key to rebirth (John 3:1-11) and the light of the world (1:9 and 8:12). Yet in this book we have a number of Christians finding in the Buddha rebirth into a deeper life and a quiet illumination that casts light upon the ways they trod. The Buddhist Way has become a way to deepen their practice of the Christian Way. At first blush, this may seem odd. At a deeper level, I think it not odd at all.

Had Christian thought developed in different directions, the doctrine of God might have evolved so that the primary analogy for God would have been *energeia / vis* (energy) rather than *eimi / esse* (being). The primary analogy for who Jesus was in his post-incarnational existence might have been *phos / lux* (light), recalling Buddhist images. Please forgive me for going into Greek and Latin and adverting to innumerable theological controversies in the Western tradition. The point I seek to make is that Western theology might well have developed Christian self-understanding in terms of God as the power and energy of being and Jesus as the light wherein we see the inner meaning *(logos / ratio)* of the dynamic that is world process. Had such analogies been the ones that exercised the minds of the

Christian tradition's great thinkers, the intrinsic mystery of both energy and light might well have led Christians to greater openness to the mystery of life as a whole. Christians then would not have thought it odd at all to find light in other traditions. Indeed, in much of early Christianity, Christians were finding illumination on the meaning of the Christian Way from Greek philosophy and from Zoroastrian literature and ritual. So these accounts may signal that we are returning to the habits of a more mature, less dogmatically cramped age.

The authors in this volume have found themselves going deeper into the mystery of life through the encounter with the Buddhist Way. I have been inspired by the manner in which their crossing over, as it were, into the Buddhist Gospel, has brought them back to a new appreciation of the Christian Gospel. In passing, I should add that I sensed the same dynamic in the Jewish authors. But the key point of the crossing over and the return is that it is not just a once-and-for-all event. They keep going back and forth.

John Cobb, for instance, is not a young man any more. Yet his chapter shows a man who is constantly on the bridge—not just the bridge between Buddhism and Christianity, but also the bridge between religion and science. As a University of Chicago man, he was introduced via the study of Whitehead to science as a spiritual force. Cobb's long immersion in the Buddhist-Christian dialogue and his deeply textured sense of religion not just as doctrine but as embedded in history and culture make us aware of the obstacles we face. I myself am a student of Cobb; although I have never taken a course from him, I wrote my licentiate thesis at the Gregorian University on his thought (in 1970, when he and I were both much younger!). His essay in this volume does us a great favor. He has been deeply affected by Buddhism, and Buddhism has entered into his theological work in a way that is, I think, unique in Western theology. Yet he brings to the fore a dimension not accented by any other author: that Buddhism, Christianity, and science are ambiguous and imperfect instruments for the salvation of this concretely troubled planet.

Robert Jonas's essay is a classic in the history of religious conversion. It reminded me of an occasion when I heard a South African Pentecostalist preacher cry out, "God has no grandchildren!" He meant, of course, that in conversion the neophyte becomes a child of God. No matter how much Jonas's rural Wisconsin, Lutheran family may have wanted him to become a Christian *on their terms,* it occurred in a different way—initially via friendship with a Catholic contemplative, and yet he appears to have completed the exorcism of the ghosts of early Christian dogmatic rigidity only under the influence of Buddhism.

Elaine MacInnes, who was "reborn" first as a Christian in childhood, had no dramatic reconversion, it would seem, but rather experienced a steady deepening of her inner life, then Buddhist illumination, and ultimately identification with Christ in a mode of consciousness she learned in Buddhism. She rests in that identification in a way that goes beyond the dogmatics of either tradition, but is mediated in their respective mystical texts. That sense of quiet "resting in truth" pervades MacInnes's essay.

These men and women have moved beyond the legalism of Western theology's cramped definitions of nature, person, hypostatic union, and sin and its removal by sacrifice to a new view of life-as-mystery. In the teachings and practices of Buddhism, they have discovered depths in Christianity that they never before suspected were there. Ruben Habito is liberated from the vision of a "God-up-there" watching and waiting for him to sin, and he achieves it through insight into Einstein's theory of relativity and what it means for a beam of light. All at once, the need for a being who is patterned on our perception of a rational person without the limits of a body are gone. Habito does not use my analogy from the Greek Fathers of the Church, of seeing God as energy, the power that enables whatever is to be while itself transcending all that "is." But Habito had an experience of God as a "Presence," beyond and within the very stars, "manifesting itself in and through those stars, as it was manifesting itself in my own bodiliness, in and through each breath and each heartbeat, each step." That experience liberates him from using solely anthropomorphic analogies of God. But it was in Zen that he began to understand the smile of the Buddha as a way of embodying the Mystery. A theologian, he seeks to understand the relationship between the two lights of his life. He finds that point of integration, not in the abstractness of a premature conceptual reconciliation of doctrines, but rather in the concreteness of inner experience in contemplation, where the feminine dimension of God—represented by Mary and the Bodhisattva Kanzeon—help him to discover empowerment in "searching for ways of healing the wounds of the world."

As a theologian, like Ruben Habito, I too am driven to conceptualize, and I have also learned that in the silence of contemplation, when the mind stops trying to categorize but instead is willing to dwell in Mystery, a reconciliation occurs that goes beyond concepts. My suspicion is that Habito's story is particularly useful for Westerners. Our culture drives us—indeed, the rationalism that is so central to both our religious and scientific traditions compels us—to think that we need explanations and words rather than an acceptance of our finitude and the mysterious way Reality will speak to our inward parts without concepts.

Yet it is exactly that dwelling in peace while being fully occupied in the world that Habito and his wife Maria have been led to by the Way of the Buddha, going beyond carrying "the knowledge of God on top of [the] head" and moving it "into the heart." Maria's essay, moreover, reveals a dimension that other essays do not: namely, the problem of living everyday life in a way that is consistent with the depth we experience in profound illuminations. Her children bring her back to a reality many intellectuals and "spiritual *virtuosi*" avoid. The woman who has traveled the world to help a leading expounder of Buddhism make his message clear knows also that something as small as buying groceries for the family has meaning to the one who is mindful.

Sallie King found herself troubled by the incompatibility of the Christian dogma of God as benevolent and all-powerful and the "ocean of suffering" of which she was becoming increasingly aware. For her, Buddhism's explanation of suffering in relation to the Four Noble Truths made sense and did so without the God in whom she could not believe.

But in meditation she found a form of Christianity that she could not so easily reject. In the Quakers, she found a form of Christianity that some mainstream Christians felt was marginal, but which taught her that "the more we are able to be filled with the Living Spirit, the more truly we become able to love." Yet the language of love is not central to Buddhism, at least not in the Western sense of the word, and here she begins to understand that the detachment taught by Buddhism makes her more able to love others-as-others than do the Western, clinging forms of love. One senses here how the dialogue between East and West illuminates her life in ways that being monoreligious would not.

In Terry Muck, one finds an Evangelical Christian witnessing not just to Christ but to the Buddhist Way. I should confess before going farther that Terry and I meet often in Christian missiological circles, and we meet also in places inhabited by members of the scholarly American Academy of Religion. (Although we have never explicitly talked about it, I think our experience is somewhat akin to cross-dressers meeting at the office in one dimension of life and then in the demimonde of another part of their life.) Terry's essay breathes a "hermeneutic of generosity," which is to say, an attitude born of the belief that, if God is God, then God is at work everywhere. And then it is the task of the religious frontier-crosser to discern how God has been working. He speaks of an "optimism of grace" that has survived visits to right-wing militia camps and visits from proselytizers of new religious movements. Yet he is also aware of the danger of what David Tracy has so aptly called "lazy pluralism" in a culture that has become so politically correct as not to want to offend anyone. Terry's essay, because we are both theologically fairly conservative, is the one I came to read wondering how he would bring that conservatism together with the liberality of spirit necessary to consider the Buddhist Way as true light. He does so first by showing how Buddhist teaching illuminates areas in which Christian teaching is relatively undeveloped. Second, he ran up against the hard edges of both Buddhist and Christian suspicion of the authenticity of the other. And he came away

believing that the way of dialogue was one wherein "cooperative competition," not static, side-by-side admiration, is the norm.

Terry's essay, I want to suggest, is particularly important because it
embodies the experience of religious plurality. It knows both the
strengths and the weaknesses of each side of the Buddhist-Christian
divide. Most importantly, he realizes that Buddhism and Christianity
compete in a dynamic world. In my experience, the refusal of academics
to realize that competition is as much a part of life as breathing and making love is one of academia's grossest forms of self-deception. The question is not how to stop the competition, but to understand what sort of
competition is healthy!

The question raised by all these essays, when one introduces the issue
of competition among religious traditions, needs to be asked in terms of
the core vision of their founders. Neither the Buddha nor the Christ was
a lazy pluralist. Both taught that the world was enmeshed in sin and/or
delusion. Both offered a way to move from false consciousness to true
consciousness. And if they taught anything, they taught that the consequences of false consciousness are dire.

For the Buddha, the acquisitive self is fooled by the illusion that somehow it (the self) is permanent. Desire untutored by insight into the uni-
versality of suffering and how it can be overcome leads to fundamental
misconception about the nature of reality. The Buddha teaches a Way of
detachment and reengagement. Ultimately, illumination frees the self
from inauthentic existence and impels the enlightened person back into
the passing world of becoming, to carry out the deeds of compassion.
This is, of course, an unscientific summary of Buddhism, and it will make
no sense to those who have not spent a good deal of time letting it have
an impact on the inner person, purifying the self of illusion. The point,
though, is that the Compassionate One was serious about this as *the* path
of release and salvation.

For the Christ, there are two complementary insights. The first is into
one's creaturehood and God as the ground and power and destiny of
both the human and the whole of existence. The second is insight guided

by the Spirit into the insufficiency of the human being to save itself from the fate of sin and death. Faith in the teaching of the Christ is less belief in concepts than it is entrusting oneself to the Way of Jesus to experience life reached through the Easter experience of new life in the Spirit of God. To the extent one allows the Spirit to lead one in this life, one experiences what Sallie King called the ability to love. That love is not clinging love, but *agape,* a love that de-centers one from one's self. One senses in the New Testament, too, a deep seriousness about the fate from which Christ wants humankind liberated.

What sort of competition do I see Christianity and Buddhism engaged in? Not like that between Coca Cola and Pepsi Cola. Nor like that between Mercedes Benz and Lexus. Indeed, if one has gone deeply into the dynamics of the teaching of the two great Founders, the attempt to vanquish another is hardly an appropriate analogy for their relationship to each other. At another level—the philosophical or apologetic—neither tradition will strike a conceptual knockout blow over the other. Each appears to me, rather, to exhibit the character of a great work of art. Each can be analyzed with many learned words, but finally at a deeper level, religious traditions do not need to be in a struggle or competition with other works of art.

Rather, the competition in which I think the great traditions represented in this book are engaged is the race to bring light to those who live in darkness. In other words, the competition is to help those who are spiritually asleep to awaken to their inner natures so they can live more authentically in the world and attain their ultimate destiny. When I had finished reading all the essays in this book, what I felt most deeply was the need for compassionate "missionaries of light" to help our secularized and unbelieving fellow humans enter into the circle of light cast by the life, the power, the presence, the field of force that can empower those who open themselves to it.

There is much talk about the religious search in our day. We praise "seekers." This book tells the tale of people who have actually found something.

CALLING, BEING CALLED

NORMAN FISCHER

T HE WORLD SEEMS to have become passionately interested in religion. You can't turn on the television, open a magazine, or hold a conversation without some reference to it. Even the current and drastic "war against terrorism," which has sprung up as suddenly and terrifyingly as the World Trade Center buildings collapsed, is waged in reference to religion—or at least to some distorted and misguided sense of it. But the new passion for religion, though it certainly includes fundamentalisms that seem to be throwbacks to the past, also sounds a note not heard before.

There's an important distinction that reflects this, the distinction between religion and spirituality. The word religion, it seems, stands for established traditions; it stands for doctrine and belief, rules and proscribed practices, rites and rituals, the authority and sanction of tradition and the past. Religion is weighty; this is good—weight brings gravity—but it is also bad—it pulls you down, making it harder to fly.

Spirituality is something else. It's about experience, about feeling. It's personal and heartfelt. It involves practice and belief to an extent, but the emphasis is on what happens and how it feels rather than on what is supposed to be performed and how that is supposed to be understood and interpreted. If the center of religion is the church, the scripture, the doctrine, the structure, the center of spirituality is the person, the feeling human heart. The strength of spirituality is the lightness and sensitivity of its reality—if you are open to it, it's there for you, as real as a breeze. But its lightness is also its weakness—yes, it helps you fly, but you might just keep going. Lacking the ballast of tradition, spirituality tends to float us off high into the clouds, where we can easily lose track of ourselves. Clearly then what we are after is a combination of these two elements. We want a religion that holds us and deepens us, along with a spirituality that lifts us and feeds us the food we need.

A religious tradition is like a long deep conversation that has been going on for hundreds or thousands of years between committed and intelligent individuals who have developed over that time a set of terms and experiential processes to enhance and shape the conversation. Given the length of time involved, the skill and talent of the interlocutors, and the subtlety of the vocabulary, the results are powerful. However, the very coherence of the conversation makes for a problem: it is, of necessity, limited. Anything that doesn't fit into the stream of the conversation, that can't be expressed in the normative vocabulary, simply doesn't exist. It can't be thought. It must be left out. If you want to join in the conversation, you have to let those parts of yourself that don't fit, that can't be included in the dialogue, fall away. You simply must ignore them, exercising a powerful and unhealthy repression, or just as powerful and unhealthy a deception. Either way, it is a struggle. In the end, the only honest thing to do, and the only possible thing, really, will be to walk away from the conversation.

The fact is that several centuries of science, a century of psychology, and two centuries of free market democracy have completely changed us. Education, social mobility, and a barrage of ideas and unheard of experiences have made us all multiple people. We are walking contradictions. We have developed so much, understood and experienced so much, and admitted so many feelings and desires into our lives that we are completely confusing individuals. We change families, relationships, careers, places we call home, with alarming frequency. We take classes, receive certifications, study piano, do yoga and *tai qi* (tai chi), and go to support groups and therapy.

Inside, we have borne witness to so many impulses and thoughts, so many conflicting desires and images of ourselves, that we can barely sort

them out. It's too late for us: we simply don't fit into those old conversations any more—there is too much that spills out over the borders.
Spirituality honors all this multiplicity and gives us permission to articulate it. Spirituality gives us a unique avenue toward what's deepest in
our hearts. It's my view that now the traditions need to recognize and
honor the variety of people's spiritual needs and experiences. Rather
than rejecting people for being unable to fit into the conversation, or
harshly or gently trying to jam them into its confines, the traditions
need to continue to affirm the value of their conversations, but at the
same time be willing to step outside them to reach those who are standing there because that is where they truly belong. From the point of
view of religion, spirituality can seem lightweight, flakey, intellectually
vacuous, self-centered. No doubt it is all of that much of the time. But
there is also something real, something strong there that has to be
acknowledged.

The world is a wound. It has always been so and is so in our time
when certainties seem so hard to come by. Spirituality isn't just a passing interest—it is a vital source of healing, perhaps the most fundamental source of healing. If the religious traditions don't accommodate
people's spontaneous and heartfelt spirituality, regardless of how odd it
may seem, they will lose all that they have established over the generations. Opening to spirituality will challenge religious traditions to the
core. It will renew them.

My own path has been neither spiritual nor religious. This is a strange
thing for a Zen Buddhist abbot who practices Judaism to say, but it's
true. Although I grew up an observant Jew, and found that entirely sat-
isfactory as far as it went, I quickly forgot about it as soon as I became
an adolescent, when a passion for truth, for the real, began to consume
me. It simply never occurred to me to seek answers in Judaism, or in any
other religion for that matter. In fact, to me, religion seemed the opposite of what I was interested in. I was consumed with questions. As far

as I could see at the time, religion either provided pat answers that were completely irrelevant (Christianity) or it didn't bother to provide answers since there seemed to be no questions other than just getting along and surviving (Judaism). So I was living, I was thinking, I was plunging into my life looking for what was real. And I left religion far behind, never gave it another thought. Spirituality seemed silly. I sought experience in any and all forms.

It was with this in mind that I sat down on my Zen meditation cushion for the first time about thirty years ago. I wanted to find out what would happen if I plunged myself as deeply as I possibly could into my own experience. That this led me inevitably to spirituality, and through that to religion, was completely unforeseen. It took me several years to accept that, to let go of my prejudices and be willing to let myself be the person that I had become. I finally have done that, but I hold the whole thing pretty lightly. I consider my identity and my social role to be my cover story. Everyone needs a cover story, a serial number and an address, otherwise how would you move about in the world? But for all of us, the real story is beyond telling.

I bring all this up because I think it is the underlying theme of the essays in this book. In various ways, all the authors encountered religion, grew up within it, and then later, through chance, travel, or conscious exploration, were awakened spiritually. Still later they found various pathways toward folding that spirituality back into a religious life that they could actually live day by day. They found a way to reenter the conversation, on a new footing, with more honesty and liveliness.

The ostensible theme of this book—the encounter, within people's lives, of Judaism/Christianity with Buddhism—isn't quite right. Religion is what you grow up with. You are acculturated into it. Religion's conversation can't exist without a cultural frame, and in the end it nearly becomes that frame. When you grow up in a culture you necessarily become it. You breathe it in the air of your city or town, you speak and hear it in the language all around you. Religions co-create the cultures they are embedded in—which is to say they are both products of those cultures and creators of them. Whether you actually practice a religion or not, it is there in your culture and you absorb it.

Spirituality, on the other hand, is not culturally determined. It comes on you all of a sudden. Its essence is the open feeling of liberation from cultural constraints. This is why it is so often easier to find spirituality by chance, or through a personal crisis, than through normative religious practice within your own tradition. And it's why it is easier to find spirituality in a tradition you are not culturally embedded in, that appears fresh, shining, unfamiliar, new.

For the authors of this book, Buddhism was more a catalyst toward spirituality than a religious tradition, with all the weight of custom and institution that that implies. This is the beauty of religion and of human culture in general: Since it isn't anything in and of itself, it can function differently in different people according to conditions. If the authors of this book had been Asian Buddhists encountering in some significant and personal way Judaism or Christianity, the situation would be reversed, Buddhism appearing as an opaque if nostalgic religion in need of reformulation, and Judaism or Christianity as jarring opportunities for personal awakening. The stories in this book are stories of spirituality encountering religious sensibility and waking it up.

Still, since the form this encounter takes involves these aforementioned traditions, it's important to take a look at some salient points within them. The first and most obvious of these is the existence of and relationship to God, central to both Judaism and Christianity and entirely absent in Buddhism.

Buddhism is not only nontheistic, it is atheistic. That is, it is not merely disinterested in the idea of God; it insists rather on denying this idea as counterproductive. It would not be too much of a stretch to say that Buddhism, whose purpose is the elimination of deepest human suffering, sees the root of that suffering in the very idea of and faith in God. The setting up of something permanent and external that one would adhere to no matter what—you could make a case for the fact that Buddhism sees this sort of attachment to "a self, a soul, or a person" as the root of all evil. (In Zen Buddhism, however, there's more the sense that the assertion or denial of anything—including the existence of God— is the root of all evil; therefore you could say that Zen is agnostic, rather than atheistic.)

But if no God, then what? The human and the trans-human. The flow of reality. Freedom that sees suffering and the end of it through a systematic spiritual path. As many of the writers in this book have pointed out, Buddhism appears to be very rational. It makes a diagnosis and proposes a protocol for healing. No leap of faith, no supernatural belief, no required obedience to a God on high whose commands are unquestioned and ineffable. Just recognize the problem and go about addressing it. Find out for yourself whether the treatment works.

This is very appealing to the Western mind conditioned by the scientific and psychological perspective. It's curious how the historical trajectory goes: The assertion of One God as omnipotent and involved in history, the human as God's chief creation and partner, made in His image, leads to the affirmation of the supremacy of the human journey on Earth and therefore to the celebration of human intelligence, which leads to an explosion of human knowledge, which leads to the death of God (who seems to depend on and demand human subservience and ignorance—don't eat the fruit of that tree!), which leads to alienation and trouble, which leads to the attractiveness of a religious doctrine (Buddhism) that has nothing to do with God.

So this is the strength of Buddhism—that it offers a religious path that leaves out that which we feel uncomfortable about. This frees us up to follow Buddhism's program, which always includes meditation practice, something immediate and effective—an essentially spiritual practice.

In this volume Zalman Schachter-Shalomi points out that meditation practice can be found in Judaism (it can be found in Christianity too) but that it is too hard to access there because it requires, more or less, a knowledge of Hebrew and various other specific traditional Jewish skills. Basic Buddhist meditation does not. It requires only a body and the willingness to sit it down and let it breathe for a little while. Simply doing that for an hour or a day will probably yield more immediate spiritual rewards than many years of prayer—at least for the unprofessional, untrained, modern secular person who prays. And simply doing it with some intensity for some period of time will yield (as the testimonies in this volume of Ruben Habito and Maria Reis Habito and Elaine MacInnes attest) powerful mystical experiences that can be utterly life changing. (Despite the fact that spiritual experience is essentially extra-cultural, its expression and appearance is not; I find it interesting that in this volume the "Buddhist" experience of Christians sounds like those of the Christian mystics, while the "Buddhist" experience of Jews sounds Jewish.)

So Buddhist meditation, exactly because of its unfamiliarity to Westerners, exactly because of its atheism, exactly because of its immediacy and lack of prerequisites, yields a spiritual experience for Western people. And it is my sense that although the numbers of Buddhists in the West may still be small, there are probably many millions of people whose lives have been spiritually revolutionized by some form of practice that has been influenced by and sustained by Buddhist forms of meditation.

And yet, ultimately this spiritual experience, though essential, isn't enough. As several of the essays in this volume suggest, childhood conditioning isn't so easily dismissed. To call it childhood conditioning is already to reduce it to something tamable and trivial. In fact (and I am thinking here of the magical snake-like Hebrew letters that as a child Rabbi Alan Lew saw deep in his grandfather's black satchel), the religious experiences that we have as children may be the most profound and far-reaching events of our lives, and their effects may be deeper and more long-lasting than all the subsequent study and practice we do—at least as deep and as long-lasting as the ecstatic and colorful spiritual experiences we might have as adults.

From an external point of view, childhood experiences are simply childish. If we strip them of their aura, looking only at their content and explainable meaning, they aren't much. We can easily dismiss them as nostalgia. We know we have to evolve beyond them. But you can't strip them of their aura—they are all about aura, all about feeling. Our childhood experiences take on the force of archetype in our lives, imprinting us religiously. I still vividly remember the people who populated the synagogue of my youth. I remember them not as ordinary people (though I have of course come to realize their ordinariness) but as polestars of my world, images around which my sense of the real was and is still constellated. It has occurred to me more than once that despite all the changes I have lived through, all my meditation and study, I am probably not very different in my essential character and understanding and approach to life from the people in that small community where I was raised. Not because I choose to be that way, but because I, like the rest of us, am inevitably living out an adult version of my earliest dreams— even though, on an mature, conscious level, those dreams died in me long ago, as I passed through adolescence and began forming my life according to what I have learned and lived. Growing up is a shock. Childhood dreams can't stand the light of day, and the loss of them is real and drastic, even though, inside you, they remain and propel you forward.

You could say that the stories in this book are about what it is like to feel the loss of the early religious dream, and then to find a new one, and with it in hand to make the return journey to childhood, reawakening all its wonder and spiritual power, but now inspired by a new adult sense of what it means to be a human being.

One makes this return trip not, I think, out of a sense of longing or nostalgia, or even as a concession to conditioning, but because one finds that the new spirituality one has found is missing something. Again, these stories all suggest that while Buddhist meditation practice is valuable, even life changing, on a continuing basis for many—absolutely necessary for a full and deep spirituality—it can also be, at least for some Westerners, lacking.

Again it is Rabbi Zalman who points to this best. Passion, soul, is missing, he says. Meditation practice is important, maybe essential. But in the end it isn't heartfelt enough—at least for our authors.

I have spent a good deal of time over the last several years working on my own versions of the Psalms (recently published as *Opening to You: Zen Inspired Translations of the Psalms*). I did this because the poems fascinated me. They were passionate examples of what's best in Western lyric poetry (indeed they are the origin of it), torrents of words addressed to that most sought after and most elusive of all beloved ones: God. The Psalms are love poems, full of feeling, full, especially, of longing. It has been my own experience, as well as the experience of many of the people with whom I have worked over the last few decades of spiritual practice, that although meditation practice awakens so much within us, and satisfies so much for us, it leaves some corners still crying out for warm contact.

If Buddhism is strong on liberation and self-realization, it is weak on relationship. Buddhism and Buddhist meditation can guide us to a profound straightening out of mind and heart. But then what? Something in us wants to reach out to others, to be released into relationship with what is around us, above us and below us. I take God to be the expression of the passion and wonder of that longing for relation that is expressed so eloquently in prayer and poetry. The need to call out. The need to be met and answered.

I do not say that all people, or even all Western people, need to pray or need to relate to that which we have always called God. But for someone who has been imprinted from childhood with such a feeling for calling out and being called to (as the authors of this book were, all of them) it may well be that the integration of Buddhist spirituality (or a human spirituality that has been awakened through an encounter with Buddhism) into childhood religion is not a choice but a necessity.

Another point. Calling and being called to must come from the depths of the heart. Although we might find such calling made in and reinforced by community, in the end it depends on an enriched and silent heart. Both Judaism and Christianity are traditions of the book, of the text, of language, song, praise, argument, and stated belief. But in order to call out, there has to be an open space of silence to call out into, and Buddhism has provided that for Western people, too long used to the color and shape of the world, and to the ways we have of describing it to ourselves. God can't hear us and we can't hear God as long as there is too much noise. Each word of every prayer, each moment of relation to what's beyond ourselves, must be surrounded by and nurtured in silence. Poets know this. I will end this essay with my own version of a poem of Judah Halevi, the eleventh-century Spanish Jewish poet.

After Judah Halevi

Where do I find you in your hiddenness?
And where do I not find you?
Your brightness covers the ground like a carpet, like ice, like dust
Inside my heart you are moving yet you curl out to space's edge
Till time doubles back on itself folding my past into an endless future
Hinged on the point of now
Towers of trust, sun rays over the sea: these words fall for failure to evoke you
And no sanctuary contains you
Distant as the Himalayas, you are nearer than my breath
My mouth speaks you, my pen writes you, my thoughts express you
My longings and fears likewise limn your shape who feeds me—it's you I eat
I call, you are in the call
When I walk out to meet you
You walk in toward me
They say you're unseeable
But who hasn't seen you?
The stars contain your dread
Soundlessly

NOTES

Introduction

1 As quoted in Sidney Piburn, ed., *The Dalai Lama: A Policy of Kindness: An Anthology of Writings by and about the Dalai Lama* (Ithaca, New York: Snow Lion), p. 65.

2 *Christian Theology and Inter-religious Dialogue* (London: SCM Press, 1992), pp. 78–79.

The Garden in the Middle

1 My article about this experience, "Teaching Judaism in Thailand," is published in Volume 2 of *Approaches to Modern Judaism*, edited by Marc Lee Raphael (Chico, California: Scholars Press, 1984).

Interview with Rabbi Zalman Schachter-Shalomi

1 Robert Aitken, trans., *The Gateless Barrier: The Wu-men Kuan (Mumonkan)* (San Francisco: North Point Press, 1990), p. 94.

The Mommy and the Yogi

1 Buddhaghosa, *The Path of Purification (Visuddhimagga)* XVI: 37, trans. Bhikkhu Nanamoli (Singapore: Singapore Buddhist Meditation Center, no date), p. 569.

2 Walpola Rahula, trans., *What the Buddha Taught*, Rev. edition (New York: Grove, 1974), p. 127.

3 Quoted and discussed in the Pat Enkyo O'Hara contribution to Chagdud Tulku Rinpoche et al, "Prayer 2000," *Tricycle* 9:3 (Spring 2000): 75.

The Light of Buddhist Wisdom and the Three Births

1 See David Suzuki, *The Sacred Balance* (Vancouver & Toronto: Greystone Books, 1977).

2 See Ronald Rolheiser, *Seeking Spirituality* (London, Sydney, & Auckland: Hodder and Stoughton, 1998).

Living in God's Grace

1 I first ran across the phrase "optimism of grace" in Howard Snyder's *The Radical Wesley and Patterns for Church Renewal* (Eugene, Oregon: Wipf and Stock Publishers, 1996), p. 146. When I asked Howard about it, he said he thought he got it from Albert Outler, but he didn't give me the reference. Since then, I read a similar concept captured by the phrase "optimal grace" in an article by my colleague Jerry Walls, published in *Heaven: The Logic of Eternal Joy* (Oxford: Oxford University Press, 2002), p. 37.

2 John Wesley, "On the Omnipresence of God," in *John Wesley's Sermons: An Anthology*, ed. Albert Outler and Richard Heitzenrater (Nashville: Abingdon, 1991), p. 525.

3 Wilfred Cantwell Smith, *Religious Diversity* (New York: Crossroad, 1982), p. 142.

4 Lesslie Newbigin, *The Gospel in a Pluralist Society* (Grand Rapids, Michigan: Eerdmans, 1989).

5 This is the point of Dale Cannon's book, *Six Ways of Being Religious: A Framework for Comparative Studies of Religion* (Belmont, California: Wadsworth, 1995).

6 Isaac Watts and Ralph Hudson, "At the Cross," *Worship and Service Hymnal* (Chicago: Hope Publishing, 1957), p. 66.

7 The person who has been most helpful to me in seeing the totalitarian predispositions inherent in religion, especially in religious language, is Kenneth Burke. See especially *The Rhetoric of Religion* (Berkeley: The University of California Press, 1970).

8 John Calvin, *Institutes of the Christian Religion* 3:12:6, trans. Ford Lewis Battles (Philadelphia: Westminister, 1960), I:760.

9 The Pali phrase "ehi passiko" means "come and see," and many Buddhist scholars have considered it the *locus classicus* of Buddhism's human freedom. I think there is much truth to that use of the phrase, but I have also been intrigued that Jesus likewise used the phrase "come and see," in the gospel of John (1:39), to encourage people to come and see where he lived. Clearly, though, it is much more than an invitation to see his lodging place, it is an invitation to try what he stood for.

10 Rahula's experience as an activist and monk is interestingly recounted in a recent book by H. L. Severiratne, *The Work of Kings: The New Buddhism in Sri Lanka* (Chicago: University of Chicago Press, 1999).

11 Terry C. Muck, "The Role of Autobiography in the Comparison of Salvation and Nirvana," *Buddhist Christian Studies* 12 (1992): 183–89.

12 See Steven Collins, *Selfless Persons: Imagery and Thought in Theravada Buddhism* (Cambridge: Cambridge University Press, 1982).

13 C.S.Lewis, *Screwtape Letters* (HarperSanFrancisco, 2001), pp. 6–7.

14 From the Mahasatipatthana Sutta, trans. Maurice Walshe, *Thus I Have Heard: The Long Discourses of the Buddha* (London: Wisdom Publications, 1987), p. 335.

15 I remind my students of German theologian Martin Kahler's wise comment that all theology is mission theology, that is, all of our theological pronouncements are the result of contact with people of other religions and ideologies.

Interfaith Encounter and Religious Identity

1 One of the people interviewed for this study said it was a great relief when he found out in the early 1970s that a few Buddhist scholars and graduate students were actually practicing Buddhism. For years, he had refrained from acknowledging his growing personal commitment to Buddhism. When he revealed his Buddhist identity to teaching colleagues at his new university, however, he encountered considerable discomfort on *their* part. "I would have been better treated by my colleagues had I said that I was gay—because they had a methodology for knowing how to deal with gay people. And they were careful to treat them fairly and objectively. But to say that you were a Buddhist—they just didn't know how to deal with that. It made them very very uncomfortable."

2 Five group interviews involving three to five people in each group were conducted in this study. Of the eighteen people interviewed, only two were not college professors and/or religion scholars. All

but two of those interviewed in some way identified themselves as both Christian and Buddhist. The two exceptions claimed a Buddhist identity, although both had practiced Christianity in the past. While relying primarily on my interview data, I also make occasional reference here to the personal stories found in this book.

3 Although most of those interviewed were quick to dispute the idea of blending, a few thought otherwise. As one commented, "I guess I am the oddball because I think they [Buddhism and Christianity] merge, and I am nourished by both." A Buddhist practitioner who had been reawakened to Christianity used the imagery of "layering" to describe the relationship between Buddhism and Christianity as they existed within herself. As she stated, "Everything comes up through two layers. There is the Christian layer, which was put there from childhood. Then there is the layer of Buddhist practice, the years of practice that comes from sitting and a commitment to serve the Buddhist Dharma as a teacher. My emotional stuff goes through both of these." It is also worth noting that—by contrast—followers of various "new age" spiritualities blend a variety of religious ideas and practices, thereby ultimately creating what can only be called a "new" religion.

4 Peter Berger and Thomas Luckmann, *The Social Construction of Reality* (Garden City: Anchor Books, 1967), p. 166.

5 Max Heinrich, "Change of Heart: A Test of Some Widely Held Theories about Religious Conversion," *American Journal of Sociology* 83 (1977): 653–80.

6 David Snow and Richard Machalek, "The Convert as a Social Type," in *Sociological Theory,* edited by Randall Collins (San Francisco: Jossey-Bass, 1983), pp. 259–89.

7 Bennett Berger, *The Survival of a Counterculture* (Los Angeles: University of California Press, 1981).

8 Erving Goffman, *Encounters: Two Studies in the Sociology of Interaction* (Indianapolis: Bobbs-Merrill, 1961), pp. 96–97.

9 The third shrine is an "earth-centered altar."

SUGGESTED READING:
An Annotated List

The Dalai Lama (Tenzin Gyatso). *The Good Heart: A Buddhist Perspective on the Teachings of Jesus*. Boston: Wisdom Publications, 1996.
> An important book on the dialogue between Buddhists and Christians, by the well-loved Tibetan Buddhist leader who won the Nobel Prize for Peace in 1989.

Davis, Avram, ed. *Meditation from the Heart of Judaism: Today's Teachers Share Their Practices, Techniques, and Faith*. Woodstock, Vermont: Jewish Lights Publishing, 1997.
> In this book twenty-two Jewish rabbis and teachers of meditation discuss their spiritual journeys. Many describe how Asian meditation has deepened their appreciation of the Jewish tradition.

Friedman, Maurice. *Touchstones of Reality: Existential Trust and the Community of Peace*. New York: E. P. Dutton, 1972.
> Friedman, a pioneer of Jewish-Buddhist dialogue, gives a fascinating account of his spiritual journey to the East.

Kamenetz, Rodger. *The Jew in the Lotus*. HarperSan Francisco, 1995.
> A poet's rediscovery of Jewish identity in Buddhist India. Includes a wonderful, full account of the historic meeting between Jews and the Dalai Lama in Dharamsala in 1990.

Linzer, Judith. *Torah and Dharma: Jewish Seekers in Eastern Religions*. Northvale, New Jersey: Jason Aronson, 1996.

A scholarly treatment of American Jews involved in Asian spirituality. Especially valuable for its in-depth, perceptive chapter
on Jewish-Buddhist encounter.

Mitchell, Donald W., and James A. Wiseman, eds. *The Gethsemani
Encounter: A Dialogue on the Spiritual Life by Buddhist and Christian Monastics*.
New York: Continuum, 1997.
   An account of the extraordinary encounter between Buddhist
   and Christian monks and nuns at Gethsemani in July 1996.

Nhat Hanh, Thich. *Living Buddha, Living Christ*. New York: Riverhead
Books, 1995.
   By one of the most respected teachers of Buddhism in the West
   today. Explores the affinity between the teachings of the Buddha
   and the Christ.

Teasdale, Wayne. *The Mystic Heart: Discovering a Universal Spirituality in
the World's Religions*. Novato, California: New World Library, 1999.
   A wonderful exploration of the mystical dimensions of the religions of the world.

Teshima, Jacob Yuroh. *Zen Buddhism and Hasidism: A Comparative Study*.
Lanham, Maryland: University Press of America, 1995.
   The only book-length comparative treatment of Hasidism and
   Zen Buddhism, written by the Japanese disciple of Rabbi Abra-
   ham Heschel. Based on original Hasidic and Zen Buddhist texts.

Additional Reading

Aitken, Robert, and David Steindl-Rast. *The Ground We Share: Everyday
Practice, Buddhist and Christian*. Boston: Shambhala, 1996.

Boorstein, Sylvia. *That's Funny, You Don't Look Buddhist: On Being A Faithful Jew and a Passionate Buddhist*. HarperSanFrancisco, 1997.

Boorstein, Sylvia. *Pay Attention, for Goodness' Sake: Practicing the Perfections of the Heart—The Buddhist Path of Kindness*. New York: Ballantine Books, 2002.

Chodron, Thubten, ed. *Interfaith Insights*. New Delhi: Timeless Books, 2000.

Cobb, John B., Jr., and Christopher Ives, eds. *The Emptying God: A Buddhist-Jewish-Christian Conversation*. Maryknoll, New York: Orbis Books, 1990.

Coleman, James William. *The New Buddhism: The Western Transformation of an Ancient Tradition*. Oxford: Oxford University Press, 2001.

Cooper, David A. *Entering the Sacred Mountain: Exploring the Mystical Practices of Judaism, Buddhism, and Sufism*. New York: Bell Tower, 1994.

Cox, Harvey. *Turning East: Why Americans Look to the Orient for Spirituality—and What That Search Can Mean to the West*. New York: Simon and Schuster, 1977.

Cox, Harvey. *Many Mansions: A Christian's Encounter with Other Faiths*. Boston: Beacon Press, 1988.

Eck, Diana L. *A New Religious America: How a "Christian Country" Has Become the World's Most Religiously Diverse Nation*. New York: HarperCollins, 2001.

Fischer, Norman. *Jerusalem Moonlight: An American Zen Teacher Walks the Path of His Ancestors*. San Francisco: Clear Glass Press, 1995.

Fischer, Norman. *Opening to You: Zen-Inspired Translations of the Psalms*. New York: Viking Press, 2002.

Glassman, Bernie. *Bearing Witness: A Zen Master's Lessons in Making Peace*. New York: Bell Tower, 1998.

Gross, Rita M., and Terry C. Muck, eds. *Buddhists Talk about Jesus, Christians Talk about the Buddha*. New York: Continuum, 2000.

Habito, Ruben L. F. *Total Liberation: Zen Spirituality and the Social Dimension*. Maryknoll, New York: Orbis Books, 1989.

Habito, Ruben L. F. *Healing Breath: Zen Spirituality for a Wounded Earth*. Maryknoll, New York: Orbis Books, 1993.

Heifetz, Harold, ed. *Zen and Hasidism: The Similarities Between Two Spiritual Disciplines*. Wheaton, Illinois: Theosophical Publishing House, 1978.

Ives, Christopher, ed. *Divine Emptiness and Historical Fullness: A Buddhist-Jewish-Christian Conversation with Masao Abe*. Valley Forge, Pennsylvania: Trinity Press International, 1995.

Kadowaki, J. K. *Zen and the Bible*. Maryknoll, New York: Orbis Books, 2002.

Kasimow, Harold, and Byron Sherwin, eds. *No Religion Is an Island: Abraham Joshua Heschel and Interreligious Dialogue*. Maryknoll, New York: Orbis Books, 1991.

Keenan, John P. *The Meaning of Christ: A Mahayana Theology*. Maryknoll, New York: Orbis Books, 1989.

Keenan, John P. *The Gospel of Mark: A Mahayana Reading*. Maryknoll, New York: Orbis Books, 1995.

Kennedy, Robert E. *Zen Spirit, Christian Spirit: The Place of Zen in Christian Life*. New York: Continuum, 1995.

Knitter, Paul F. *Introducing Theologies of Religions*. Maryknoll, New York: Orbis Books, 2002.

Lai, Whalen, and Michael von Bruck. *Christianity and Buddhism: A Multicultural History of Their Dialogue* (translated by Phyllis Jestice). Maryknoll, New York: Orbis Books, 2001.

Lefebure, Leo D. *The Buddha and the Christ: Explorations in Buddhist and Christian Dialogue*. Maryknoll, New York: Orbis Books, 1993.

Lew, Alan. *One God Clapping: The Spiritual Path of a Zen Rabbi*. New York: Kodansha International, 1999.

Lopez, Donald S., Jr., and Steven C. Rockefeller. *The Christ and the Bodhisattva*. Albany, New York: State University of New York Press, 1987.

Lubarsky, Sandra B. *Tolerance and Transformation: Jewish Approaches to Religious Pluralism*. Cincinnati: Hebrew Union College Press, 1990.

MacInnes, Elaine. *Light Sitting in Light: A Christian's Experience in Zen*. San Francisco: HarperCollins, 1996.

MacInnes, Elaine. *Zen Contemplation: A Bridge of Living Water*. Ottawa: Novalis, 2001.

Morinis, Alan. *Climbing Jacob's Ladder: One Man's Rediscovery of a Jewish Spiritual Tradition*. New York: Broadway Books, 2002.

Piburn, Sidney, ed. *The Dalai Lama: A Policy of Kindness: An Anthology of Writings by and about the Dalai Lama*. Ithaca, New York: Snow Lion Publications, 1990.

Porterfield, Amanda. *The Transformation of American Religion: The Story of a Late-Twentieth-Century Awakening*. Oxford: Oxford University Press, 2001.

Schachter-Shalomi, Zalman. *Paradigm Shift: From the Jewish Renewal Teachings of Reb Zalman Schachter-Shalomi* (edited by Ellen Singer). Northvale, New Jersey: Jason Aronson, 1993.

Seager, Richard Hughes. *Buddhism in America*. New York: Columbia University Press, 1999.

Sherwin, Byron L. *Crafting the Soul: Creating Your Life as a Work of Art*. Rochester, Vermont: Park Street Press, 1998.

Sherwin, Byron L., and Harold Kasimow, eds. *John Paul II and Interreligious Dialogue*. Maryknoll, New York: Orbis Books, 1999.

Teasdale, Wayne, and George F. Cairns, eds. *The Community of Religions: Voices and Images of the Parliament of the World's Religions*. New York: Continuum, 1996.

Teasdale, Wayne. *A Monk in the World: Cultivating a Spiritual Life*. Novato, California: New World Library, 2002.

Walker, Susan, ed. *Speaking of Silence: Christians and Buddhists on the Contemplative Way*. New York: Paulist Press, 1997.

About the Contributors

SYLVIA BOORSTEIN is a cofounding teacher of Spirit Rock Meditation Center in Woodacre, California, and teaches retreats and workshops nationwide in mindfulness and *metta* (loving-kindness) meditation. She is the author of several books on Buddhism and mindfulness practice, including *Pay Attention, For Goodness' Sake* and *That's Funny, You Don't Look Buddhist: On Being a Faithful Jew and a Passionate Buddhist*.

WILLIAM R. BURROWS is the managing editor of Orbis Books, Maryknoll, New York, where he oversees acquisitions in the areas of interreligious interchange, Christian mission, and history. He holds a licentiate in Theology from the Gregorian University and a Ph.D. in Theology from the University of Chicago Divinity School.

JOHN B. COBB, JR., professor emeritus of the School of Theology, Claremont, is a prominent process theologian and pioneer in the Buddhist-Christian dialogue. He is author of *Christ in a Pluralistic Age*, *Beyond Dialogue*, and many other works.

NORMAN FISCHER is the founder and teacher of the Everyday Zen Foundation and co-director of Makor Or, a Jewish meditation center in San Francisco. His latest book is *Opening to You: Zen-Inspired Translations of the Psalms*.

ARTHUR GREEN is a professor in the Department of Near Eastern and Judaic Studies at Brandeis University. He has taught at the University of Pennsylvania and served as dean and president of the Reconstructionist Rabbinical College. He is the editor of *Jewish Spirituality* and the author of *Tormented Master: A Life of Rabbi Nahman of Bratslav* and *Seek My Face, Speak My Name: A Contemporary Jewish Theology.*

RUBEN L.F. HABITO is a professor at the Perkins School of Theology, Southern Methodist University, and is a Zen teacher in the Sanbo Kyodan tradition. Among his books are *Healing Breath: Zen Spirituality for a Wounded Earth* and *Total Liberation: Zen Spirituality and the Social Dimension.*

ROBERT A. JONAS is the director of The Empty Bell contemplative center in Watertown, Massachusetts, a spiritual director, and retreat leader. He is author of *Henri Nouwen* and *Rebecca*. His CDs of shakuhachi music (Sui-Zen) are called *Blowing Bamboo* and *New Life from Ruins* (www.cdfreedom.com/robertjonas).

NATHAN KATZ is professor of Religious Studies at Florida International University. Among his dozen books are *Buddhist Images of Human Perfection*, *The Last Jews of Cochin* (coauthored), and *Who Are the Jews of India?* He is coeditor of the *Journal of Indo-Judaic Studies.*

SALLIE B. KING, professor of Philosophy and Religion at James Madison University, is the author of *Buddha Nature,* coeditor of *Engaged Buddhism: Buddhist Liberation Movements in Asia,* and is co-clerk of Valley Friends (Quaker) Meeting.

ALAN LEW is a founding director of Makor Or, a center for Jewish meditation, and rabbi of Congregation Beth Sholom in San Francisco. He is the author of *One God Clapping: The Spiritual Path of a Zen Rabbi*.

SANDRA B. LUBARSKY is associate professor of Religious Studies and director of the Master of Liberal Studies Program on Sustainable Communities at Northern Arizona University. She is the author of *Tolerance and Transformation: Jewish Approaches to Religious Pluralism* and coeditor of *Jewish Theology and Process Thought*.

SISTER ELAINE MACINNES O.L.M. has written six books about her involvement in Zen, including *Light Sitting in Light: A Christian's Experience in Zen* and *Zen Contemplation: A Bridge of Living Water*. She is a roshi of the Sanbo Kyodan lineage in Kamakura, Japan, and has taught meditation in and out of prisons for over twenty-five years, in the Philippines, England, and recently in Canada. In 2001, she was named an officer in the Order of Canada, which honors Canadians for exemplary achievement.

RICHARD G. MARKS, professor of Religion at Washington and Lee University, is author of *The Image of Bar Kokhba in Traditional Jewish Literature* and "Abraham, the Easterners, and India." He is currently at work on a book on the history of Jewish perceptions of Asian religions.

TERRY C. MUCK, professor of World Religions at Asbury Theological Seminary, is author of *The Mysterious Beyond: A Basic Guide to Studying Religion*, coeditor of *Buddhists Talk About Jesus, Christians Talk About Buddha*, and coeditor of the journal *Buddhist-Christian Studies*.

MARIA REIS HABITO is the director of International Programs for the Museum of World Religions in Taiwan. She is the author of *Die Dharani des Grossen Erbarmens des Bodhisattva Avalokitesvara mit Tausend Handen und Augen,* author/editor of *Weisheit und Barmherzigkeit—Dharma Master Hsin Tao,* and has written scholarly articles on Guanyin.

E. BURKE ROCHFORD, JR., professor of Sociology and Religion, Middlebury College, is the author of *Hare Krishna in America.* He has been studying the Hare Krishna for twenty-five years and is completing a book on marriage, family, and change within the movement since the 1980s.

ZALMAN SCHACHTER-SHALOMI holds the World Wisdom Chair at Naropa University. He has written widely on aging, Judaism, and Asian spirituality, and is the leading spokesperson for the Jewish spiritual renewal movement.

SHEILA PELTZ WEINBERG is on the faculty of the Metivta's Spirituality Institute for Rabbis and Spirituality Institute for Cantors and has served for seventeen years as a congregational rabbi. She is the author of "Meditating as a Practicing Jew" and "Judaism as Transformational Practice."

ABOUT THE EDITORS

 HAROLD KASIMOW is the George Drake Professor of Religious Studies at Grinnell College in Iowa. His works on interreligious dialogue have been published in China, England, India, Japan, Poland, and the United States. He has lived in Thailand and Japan and has been involved in Jewish-Buddhist dialogue since the 1960s. His most recent books are *No Religion Is an Island: Abraham Joshua Heschel and Interreligious Dialogue* and *John Paul II and Interreligious Dialogue*, both coedited with Byron Sherwin.

JOHN P. KEENAN is professor of Religion at Middlebury College and vicar of St. Nicholas Episcopal Church in Scarborough, Maine. He has published translations and studies in Yogacara Buddhism, and has employed Mahayana Buddhist philosophy in works including *The Meaning of Christ: A Mahayana Theology* and the forthcoming *The Letter of James: Everyday Practice for Everyday Christians*.

LINDA K. KEENAN has lived in Japan for several years and taught Japanese language and literature at Middlebury College. She translated Buddhologist Minoru Kiyota's autobiography, *Beyond Loyalty: The Story of a Kibei,* and contributed "En the Ascetic" to *Religions of Japan in Practice.*

INDEX

About Wisdom

Wisdom Publications, a not-for-profit publisher, is dedicated to preserving and transmitting important works from all the major Buddhist traditions as well as related East-West themes.

To learn more about Wisdom, or browse our books on-line, visit our website at wisdompubs.org. You may request a copy of our mail-order catalog on-line or by writing to:

Wisdom Publications
199 Elm Street
Somerville, Massachusetts 02144 USA
Telephone: (617) 776-7416
Fax: (617) 776-7841
Email: info@wisdompubs.org
www.wisdompubs.org

Wisdom is a nonprofit, charitable 501(c)(3) organization affiliated with the Foundation for the Preservation of the Mahayana Tradition (FPMT).

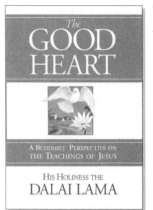

THE GOOD HEART

A Buddhist Perspective on the Teachings of Jesus
His Holiness the Dalai Lama
224 pages
Cloth: ISBN 0-86171-114-9, $24.00
Paper: ISBN 0-86171-138-6, $15.95

The Dalai Lama provides an extraordinary Buddhist perspective on the teachings of Jesus, commenting on well-known passages from the four Christian Gospels including the Sermon on the Mount, the parable of the mustard seed, the Resurrection, and others.

"Arguably the best book on interreligious dialogue published to date. One does not say such things lightly, but in a very real sense this is a holy book." —Huston Smith, author of *The Illustrated World's Religions*

MEDITATION FOR LIFE

Martine Batchelor
Photographs by Stephen Batchelor
168 pages, ISBN 0-86171-320-8, $22.95

"This exquisite book combines stories, instruction, and practical exercises from three Buddhist traditions: Zen, Theravadin, and Tibetan. Along with chapters on meditation, ethics, and many other aspects of the path, Batchelor has included chapters on inspiration, the role of a teacher, and bringing meditation into our daily lives. She has written this guide to basic and more advanced practices in language accessible to anyone, including non-Dharma practitioners. Complementing the text are photographs that help us discover the beauty of things as they are by Martine's husband, Buddhist teacher and writer Stephen Batchelor. Highly recommended." —*Turning Wheel*

ZEN AND THE KINGDOM OF HEAVEN
Reflections on the Tradition of Meditation in Christianity and Zen Buddhism
Tom Chetwynd
224 pages, ISBN 0-86171-187-4, $16.95

This provocative and very human work is the story of one man's skeptical first encounters with Zen Buddhism and how it led him to the rich—but largely forgotten—Christian tradition of pure contemplative prayer. Chetwynd explores the surprisingly Zen-like teachings of the Desert Fathers and other Christian meditation masters whose practice stems from the very first Christian communities—and perhaps Jesus Christ himself.

"An excellent publication that presents the personal and direct interface of Buddhism and Christianity. Part One, 'Zen Experience,' has all the dynamics and inspiration of genuine experience and is well worth the price of the book. Part Two, 'Christian Meditation in the Light of Zen,' traces the story of Christian meditation and its line of teachers right up to the present. ...The quotations given are outstanding.... Part Three goes into practical details about Christians doing Zen, giving concrete suggestions for practice. ...We simply need more books like this one."
—*Bulletin of Monastic Interreligious Dialogue*

THE NEW SOCIAL FACE OF BUDDHISM:
A Call to Action
Ken Jones ~ Foreword by Kenneth Kraft
320 pages, ISBN 0-86171-365-6, $16.95

Jones presents an astute, well-informed, and balanced analysis of the philosophy, history, and future of socially relevant Buddhism. At a time when clear social action is needed more than ever, *The New Social Face of Buddhism* is vital reading for activists, scholars, and everyone seeking to transform their spiritual practice into a force for social, political, and global change. A groundbreaking book, Jones' work is a wellspring of inspiration that should not be missed.

"*The New Social Face of Buddhism* points the way to a revolution in contemporary spirituality." —Joan Halifax, Abbess, Upaya Zen Center, and co-founder of the Zen Peacemaker Order